Rita Richmond

COMPLETE HANDBOOK
OF
VOICE TRAINING

COMPLETE HANDBOOK
OF
VOICE TRAINING

RICHARD ALDERSON

PARKER PUBLISHING COMPANY, INC.

West Nyack, New York

Library of Congress Cataloging in Publication Data

Alderson, Richard.
  Complete handbook of voice training.

  Bibliography: p.
  Includes index.
  1. Singing--Instruction and study. 2. Voice.
I. Title.
MT820.A45   784.9'32   79-550
ISBN 0-13-161307-3

This book is dedicated to my wife, Ann,
without whose devotion and encouragement
it would not have been written.

COMPLETE HANDBOOK
OF
VOICE TRAINING

A WORD FROM THE AUTHOR ON THE
PRACTICAL VALUE OF THIS BOOK

This book is a practical approach to teaching vocal music to young singers. It contains a broad number of principles and procedures which have been developed from my experiences as a teacher of studio voice and as a choral director. Each chapter deals with the various elements of singing, explaining what good singing is, and how to develop a good voice.

For several years I have wanted to put all my ideas on paper concerning the relationship of modern vocal research with modern vocal training. The *Complete Handbook of Voice Training* is the result. It offers new ways to teach singing as well as showing why many of the old techniques are still valid. Thus it is a ready reference book for the professional teacher. This book will fill a void in the library of every vocal teacher who wants to find a new approach to an old problem or to discover some different ways to explain the basic principles of singing.

The materials found here will be most appropriate to the established teacher who has a grasp of the physiology of the voice and has found a teaching method of his own. However, the explanations and exercises will also be useful to the young teacher and the voice student who is studying vocal pedagogy.

The *Complete Handbook of Voice Training* takes a positive approach to teaching voice. It establishes principles of good posture, efficient breathing, rich tonal quality, and effective communication. Singing is exciting, and learning to sing well is of inestimable value!

Breathing is the foremost element of good singing. Thus the chapter on respiration is the longest in the book. In it is included a sample lesson on breathing to sing, explanations of the importance of proper posture, and the best techniques of teaching breathing. There are also physical development exercises which will increase the student's vital capacity and endurance. Every student is encouraged to participate in a body building program outside the studio.

A particularly important aspect of singing is the concept of the attack "on the rebound of the breath." Through this concept I relate the old concept of singing on the breath to new ideas which I have cultivated. A section of the chapter on making the proper sound explains how the student may achieve this technique, and legato-staccato vocalises are presented as aids in teaching this most useful concept.

Besides learning how it feels to sing, the student learns what it sounds like to sing well in the chapter on making the proper sound. In that chapter I describe the sustained ringing, humming sound which is most desirable in classical singing. To achieve this sound the student may think of a wave-like tone, or he may sing a vocalise based on long notes while thinking of a series of short notes. He may also practice sliding from one note to another, as in a portamento or glissando. He learns through these exercises that the tone travels mentally and is not static. Anyone who is learning to sing will find these ideas beneficial.

Some of my favorite vocalises are found in the chapter on resonance. I believe that the pharynx should be quite large during singing, no matter which vowel is sounded. So much of the material in that chapter is designed to teach the student how to lower his larynx by breathing properly, how to raise his velum without stiffening it, and how to expand his pharynx. The chapter relates breathing and phonation to resonance and shows the student that the elements of singing are interrelated.

There is an entire chapter on vowel sounds. Vowels are shown to be a function of vocal resonance, and they may be used extensively in teaching enhanced resonance. Mixtures of vowels are proposed as the means to encouraging both depth and brilliance in the voice. As the most difficult element of singing to teach, resonance requires the most varied approaches in order to communicate with the student. Thus I have devised a substantial number of exercises, vocalises, and analogies to teach a student how to enhance the resonance of his voice.

Several theories of registers are explored in order to establish a practical approach to changing registers smoothly. I think a concept of registers is a significant adjunct to teaching voice, so I have devoted an extensive part of the book to registration. One of the major ways of learning to change registers smoothly is through vowel modification exercises such as those I have included. Also, the important differences in dealing with male and female register changes are investigated thoroughly, and several vocalises are included for treating each.

Of course, the element of articulation is discussed at length because of the ultimate importance of communication in singing. Each major articulator is described, and exercises for strength and agility are devised for each one. The lazy tongue, flaccid lips, and tense jaw are trained to function properly through exercises and vocalises. There are also a number of suggestions concerning difficult consonant combinations in the high range, such as substitute consonants, independent mechanical articulation exercises, unified vowels, and so on.

Besides establishing ideal guidelines to teaching voice, this book helps the teacher solve specific vocal problems. In each chapter several areas of vocal technique are analyzed so the teacher and student may understand their causes. Then a broad range of solutions to each problem is given through exercises, vocalises, analogies, concepts of tone, and so on. The book is organized so that the reader may look for a general subject in the table of contents or a specific vocal problem in the index and find references to many useful techniques and solutions. I have included the most basic kinds of vocal exercises upon which the teacher may either develop other, alternative exercises or to which he may adapt his present teaching procedures. Some of the practices in this book, so far as I know, are unique to my teaching, and I have found them to be successful with students of all ages.

Here are a few specific problems and their solutions which may be found in *Complete Handbook of Voice Training*:

1. Improper breathing
   a. Rhythmic breathing exercises
   b. Chest stretching exercises

      c. Awareness procedures, such as partially sitting or hold-
         ing an object at arm's length
      d. Sample lesson on proper breathing
2. Breathy tonal quality—excess escape of air
      a. Bright vowel vocalises
      b. Humming vocalises
      c. Staccato exercises
3. Strident tonal quality
      a. Dark vowel vocalises
      b. Breathing exercises
      c. Loose jaw exercises
      d. Legato vocalises
4. Nasality
      a. Velar exercises
      b. Substitute consonants
      c. Omission of nasal consonants
      d. Substitute words

The principles and methods in this book may be used in teaching singers individually or in groups. One chapter is devoted to dealing with members of a voice class as individuals. Two other chapters relate the basic principles of studio voice training to choral groups.

Everything in this book is intended to develop strength, agility, and a ringing quality in the young voice, but the techniques are also worthwhile for students of all ages and at any level of development. Even the finest professional singer will find these vocalises and exercises beneficial in warming up before a rehearsal or performance.

Finally, the chief purpose of this book is to shed new light on the subjective art of training singers. I hope the teachers who use this book will find a suggestion or an idea which will be valuable in their studios, classes, or choruses. If they do, the book will have served its purpose.

Richard Alderson

TABLE OF CONTENTS

1

THE SEVEN KEY PRINCIPLES
OF VOICE TRAINING

Any book on vocal pedagogy, like any successful voice teacher, must concern itself first with the teacher as a person before examining what and how he teaches. It is only in understanding ourselves that we can come to grips with the way we teach students. Over the years I have developed a set of key principles which help me keep in mind why I teach the way I do.

These seven principles are:

1. The Student "Buys" the Ears of the Teacher
2. The Teacher Develops His Own Concept of Tone
3. Teaching Is Based on One's Aesthetics
4. Singing Is an Athletic Endeavor
5. The Student Learns from Sound as Well as Feeling
6. Teaching Begins with the Best Areas and Moves Outward
7. Choral Groups and Voice Classes Are Individual Students

The first three principles have to do with the teacher, his concepts, and his background. To paraphrase Descartes, "What we think makes us what we are as teachers."

The last four principles concern the student and how we teach him. Hardly any activity is so subjective as learning to sing. Our students come to us as complex sets of hopes, expectations, fears, and doubts. We share their dreams and frustrations and cope with their fears and doubts in order to teach them an art whose pleasure in accomplishment is unequalled.

The rest of this book presumes these seven key principles as underlying my suggested teaching methods. Now and then they will be referred to specifically and elaborated upon.

THE STUDENT "BUYS" THE EARS OF THE TEACHER

The foremost problem in teaching someone to sing is the student's imperfect hearing. He hears his voice from the inside through the bony structure of the head rather than outside through the eardrum. We singers are doomed to a life of hearing only a muffled distortion of our voices as we sing. Afterward, we may hear a recording of the performance, but then it is too late to adjust this vowel or that pitch, this nuance or that dynamic. The teacher's task, then, is to teach as if he were inside his student, compensating for the difference in what he hears and what the student can hear. For this reason, the teacher's ears are his most important asset.

A voice teacher listens analytically in order to help students sing better. Not only must he know what he likes to hear in a voice, but he must know why. The ability to determine what happens when a person sings is of primary significance to good teaching. This means he must understand vocal mechanics, the physical construction of the voice and what makes it work. Like a physician, a voice teacher knows a great amount of general information to deal with rather limited, specific problems. He knows how a singer breathes, phonates, resonates, and articulates, and he is able to hear the source and cause of a singer's trouble in order to solve it.

Knowing the voice and understanding its problems are not enough, however. The best teachers are those who can convey knowledge and understanding to students, those who can make themselves understood. The teacher translates what he hears into intelligible concepts that help a singer develop his voice. This does not always mean direct, spoken explanations of vocal mechanics, but may be symbolic, psychological terms. These days it may even mean "body language," such as the stern look or clenched fist of a conductor. A former teacher of mine used to say, "Communication ends when conversation begins." While his point may be over-stated, his meaning is clear. When someone asks what time it is, he does not need to be told how to make a watch.

THE TEACHER DEVELOPS HIS OWN CONCEPT OF TONE

It is not enough to understand the mechanics of the voice. One must also have in mind the way a voice should sound. Developing this concept of tone is necessary to organized, logical instruction because it establishes recognizable goals for the teacher. In my opinion, a student can learn to support an ugly sound as easily as a beautiful one unless the teacher has a solid concept of the vocal quality he would like to hear.

Teaching Based on Tonal Concepts

So as not to be misunderstood, I must emphasize that it is neither necessary nor desirable to teach from the standpoint of tonal quality alone. The student should not become so involved with how he sounds that he cannot accept his untrained voice. Such teaching only bogs down in frustration. Concepts of tonal quality should be the underlying basis for teaching voice, indicating to the teacher's ears how the student is progressing. Certainly, the stu-dent must work on physical techniques as well as sound quality. A good tone will be the result of a good technique.

Also, I must say that the concept of tone I am talking about serves each student as an individual. With the proper approach to teaching, each voice is enhanced, not subdued. In no way should the students be seen as products of a cookie cutter, their voices sounding as alike as possible. Each voice is different, but the prin-ciples of teaching are the same. Certainly, teachers accept each student's voice for what it is and expect less beautiful sounds from the developing singers.

Establishing a Concept of Choral Tone

Establishing a proper concept of tone is also necessary for choral conductors in order to cope with the inherent differences between voices and instruments. The human voice is the most versatile, interesting musical implement yet discovered, but it must be treated with suitable care. While the voice may produce myriad colors even in its youth, it should not be made to compete with large, powerful groups of instruments at an early age. Nor should it try to match the straight tones of a church organ.

Developing Natural Voice Quality

A voice should be unforced, natural, and flowing. It should be produced in an easy manner, so the singer sounds and looks comfortable, and the audience feels the same. Our students should realize that the painful contortions and expressions on the faces of many popular singers and opera stars are the products of acting lessons rather than the result of injurious singing. The drama and pathos of the performance do not disturb the mechanics of the voice. If one listens to the singer without watching him, his voice sounds free and clear. If it does not, he is not a good singer and should not be a model for the student.

Vibrato

A freely flowing voice has vibrato. Why voices vibrate is still a mystery, but they should and do when properly produced. For hundreds of years instrumentalists have worked to develop vibratos so they could sound like the human voice. Later in the book I will discuss excessive vibratos which are offensive. Suffice it to say that a vibrato is a desirable ingredient of a good vocal quality.

Developing the Ringing Tone

Most teachers in the Western world teach what is known as "forward placement." This means that there is a ringing quality in the voice which is the result of very high pitched resonances. This quality makes the voice seem to be "placed" in the front of the face, or "masque." This does not mean, of course, that the voice should not sound rich as well. In fact, a good balance between the ring and the depth, or richness, of the voice is a continuous struggle in teaching the young student. Definite exercises must be used to develop both aspects and to keep them balanced.

TEACHING IS BASED ON ONE'S AESTHETICS

We teach according to aesthetics which are learned from personal experience, teachers, and model singers whom we admire.

We were students once, and our teachers brought to us their likes and dislikes which we either accepted or rejected. This acceptance or rejection helped to form our aesthetics and our teaching goals. Our knowledge of styles and interpretation and our feeling for tempos and volume are part of our aesthetics. If we like subdued singing, we will teach our students to sing *mezza voce*. If we like the impact of loud sounds on our eardrums, we will teach our students the "big sound." If we like a clear, ringing sound, that is what we will expect from our students, and so on.

Other Aspects of Aesthetics

Other aspects of our learned aesthetics are pitch accuracy, rhythmic execution, and diction. Each is a learned response and may be taught either directly or indirectly. At a startlingly early age children learn that one of the best ways to hear themselves in a group is to sing just a shade out of tune. Standing among persons who are singing the same part, one can hardly hear himself. But if he sings just a bit flat, his voice stands out in bold relief.

Vowel Sounds

Since pitches vary with vowel sounds, another way to find one's voice in a chorus is to sing a slightly different vowel from that of the section. Many times improper tuning in a chorus is the result of such different vowel sounds. The problem is complicated by the inherent differences in vowel sounds in the various registers or areas of the voice.

Rhythmic Execution

Rhythmic execution is more subtle and much more difficult to teach since it involves the autonomic nervous system. Some students will never be as adept at executing rhythms as others, although their reflexes may be sharpened through practice. The aesthetic aspect of rhythm has to do with whether the teacher requires exact, mathematical precision or expressive approximation of written note values. For instance, a dotted quarter note followed by an eighth note may be performed in an exact 3:1 ratio, it may be a triplet with a 2:1 ratio, or it may be doubly dotted in a 7:1 ratio or any of an infinite variety in between. How these rhythms are executed often depends on the kind of rhythms the teacher likes.

Speech Habits and Diction

The most pervasive problem the teacher faces is that of diction. Speech is learned at such an early age that it is difficult to change one's pronunciation or articulation. Thus a vocal fault is more ingrained in singing English than the same fault in another language. Also, each teacher has his own ideas about how English should be sung. Whether it should sound like American speech or not, and if so, which region of America has the best speech, are possibly the most difficult matters the teacher has to resolve.

Further, we must recognize that our aesthetics are based on Western culture. The way we sing is completely unacceptable in the Orient, as may be seen in the Noh and Kabuki styles. "Good singing" is not a universal norm but rather a collection of likes and dislikes on which we base our teaching. Even the most erudite music critic must learn a set of values on which to judge a performance.

Even in the Western world there are differences when it comes to judging "good singing." Each country has its way of singing based on the idiosyncrasies of its language. Within each country there are ethnic groups which have their own views of "good singing." Therefore, each of the major cultures has produced ways to teach singing. In this country our vocal pedagogy is a combination of all these influences. Not too many years ago, teachers guarded their beliefs and methods as if they were atomic secrets. Nowadays, however, we can admit that there are several valid ways to solve the same vocal problem.

SINGING IS AN ATHLETIC ENDEAVOR

A few years ago, one of my students who was a championship athlete like to call me "coach." I interpreted that name as indicating the highest respect because of the esteem with which most athletic coaches are regarded. It was working with this student that first gave me the insight that singing is analogous to sports. As in athletics, good physical health is necessary to singing, and rhythmic and muscular coordination are vital. The singer who waits poised, ready to sing the proper word at the proper pitch has the same kind of mental and physical preparation as a batter waiting for the ball to enter the strike zone. The body is balanced, the breath controlled, and the mind alertly and silently measures the time and amount of force required to do the job.

Physical balance and movement are as much a part of good singing as they are of serving a tennis ball. A good bowler has a mental rhythm which guides his steps toward the line, and he uses his muscular tensions and coordination to set the ball on the proper spot with the requisite rotation to send it where it should go.

Although we think of some athletes as being "natural," just as we speak of a "natural" singer, both must learn artificially imposed uses of the body. The baseball pitcher's elbow and knees were not designed for the screwball, slider, and even more sophisticated pitches. He has to learn how much stress these can take without injury and must develop the surrounding muscle tissue to hold the joints in position. The Olympic weightlifter conditions his body to lift great weights, but he will not be able to run like a track star as a result of his specific training.

Developing the Muscles for Singing

Similarly, the muscles used in singing must be developed in special ways. Breathing is not the same for singing as for swimming or even for playing an instrument. The larynx was not originally designed for producing sounds, and the demands we singers make on the tiny muscles, cartilages, and ligaments go far beyond their primary purpose of protecting the trachea and lungs from foreign matter.

The Importance of Daily Practice

In learning a sport the muscles must be made to perform the same functions over and over so they will learn what they should do automatically. That is why athletes practice daily, and why singers must also. I tell my students that muscles may not have brains, but they have memories, and it is that muscle memory which we must affect. A student cannot expect to sing correctly after having been told once. Producing a tone beautifully in the studio does not insure that he will remember how the next day. He has to sing the same way over again to teach his muscles how to respond.

When a student has trouble learning a new technique, I often tell him that seeing a target and hitting it are two separate things.

I know that his ear is not bad when he sometimes misses a pitch or sings a poor vowel.

Developing the Conditioned Response

In singing, as in athletics, there seems to be a system of computer tapes in our brains which are programmed for a conditioned response. That is why we are able to walk and talk without thinking first. To alter such an ingrained muscular pattern we have to erase the tapes somehow and put in a new program.

Besides the excitement of violent collision, one of the most fascinating aspects of professional football is its absolutely precise teamwork. Each of the twenty-two players knows what he is to do when the ball is snapped. In the same manner, singing requires feeling and counting together, whether there are two or two hundred on the stage.

A final analogy with sports is that anyone may participate in singing, from the sandlot to the professional arena. Singing is a participatory endeavor as well as a spectator sport, and anyone's inherited talent may be developed. As with sports, great singers are born and not made, but even the slowest, scrawniest kid on the team can enjoy the game.

I have found in my studio that analogies with sports are useful teaching tools because relating singing to athletics builds a ready rapport. Our sports-oriented society makes these analogies understandable since almost everyone has participated in some sport through a physical education class or under civic sponsorship. Many of my students never considered how similar singing was to athletics, but a comparison of the two brought home a point which had theretofore been elusive. When I tell students that a vocal attack is like the backswing, stroke, and follow through of a golf club, they get the idea.

THE STUDENT LEARNS FROM SOUND AS WELL AS FEELING

"The Mental Ear"

Before a student takes his first voice lesson, he builds up preconceived notions about his voice. He evolves a sense of vocal quality in his "mental ear," first from hearing others speak, then as he learns to speak himself. Without realizing it, the student determines what he thinks are good vowel sounds, proper resonances, and clear articulation. Speech is built mainly on consonants and admits such a wide variety of vowel sounds that a student comes to the voice teacher with every conceivable notion as to vocal color and beauty.

Development of the Model Singer

If the student wants to be a singer, he probably has a hero—a parent, teacher, or professional singer—who establishes for him goals which he believes he must attain to be successful. The influence of the model singer and the student's speech habits produce the innate desire to hear himself sing with a particular vocal color and style which will often be extremely difficult for the teacher to change. Any change will subconsciously attack the family, ethnic group, or hero on which the student bases his value judgments. In these cases, patience and understanding on the part of the teacher are invaluable.

How It Feels to Sing

Besides the psychological and sociological elements above, another notion which the teacher finds in many students is that "singing" should be difficult and in some way feel strange to the student in order to be "good." It is often hard to convince a student that the freely flowing tone which produces hardly any kinesthetic response is the best he can achieve. I have a close friend who is an excellent professional singer but who has never accepted the idea that he will not or should not feel himself sing. He tells his students not to try to feel every tone, but he is not able to overcome this tendency in himself.

Uses of the Tape Recorder

The trouble with all these preconceived notions is that they are founded on qualities the student hears on the outside but cannot match since he hears himself on the inside. Students must be made aware from the beginning that they will never hear themselves as they sound to an audience. The difference is so great as to be shocking and sometimes devastating to the student when he first hears himself on a tape recording. For this reason, I use a tape recorder judiciously to help my students get used to their own voices. I have to explain that they should hear themselves perhaps fifty times before they can make objective value judgments. Then I confess how much I dislike my own speaking voice on a tape no matter how many times I am told that it is good.

Learning Through Sound and Feeling

For reasons of the student's imperfect hearing, some of the best teachers insist that their students not concern themselves with the way they sound, and I agree that undue concentration on one's sound gets in the way of one's early vocal progress. But a student cannot sing without hearing himself, so some attention should be paid to what he hears and how he hears it. Every alteration of the shape and size of the vocal instrument changes the way the student hears himself. The higher the soft palate, the more concentrated effect of pharyngeal resonance. Whether the tongue is up or down, forward or back, changes the student's perception of his voice. In other words, the difference between the student's voice inside and outside varies with each vowel, register, or combination of these. Further, colds and allergies which affect a student's hearing make his voice sound different on the inside. The tape recorder will prove to the student that his voice may sound the same from day to day whether or not his ears are stopped up. Most of the time the difference in his voice when he has a cold or allergy is the result of his own compensations for the change in his hearing. The many small noises caused by phlegm in the pharynx or sinuses are greatly amplified to the student because they occur so close to his ears. The audience may never be aware of such sounds.

Mistaking Feeling for Sound

Some students do not realize that they mistake feeling for sound and vice versa. When a student begins to sing with a new technique, he feels new tugs and pulls that make him think his throat is "tight" or "closed." Thinking his throat is tight makes the student believe the sound is poor. Indeed, a new technique may make the student's voice feel strange to him. This strangeness is then translated into "badness," and he rebels at the new sound.

Mistaking Sound for Feeling

Similarly, a new vocal approach may sound strange on the inside to the student, so he thinks it "feels bad." The student must understand that a new technique will feel and sound different at first. That very difference is the purpose of studying the new technique. He should not try to sing a new way but expect to hear and feel the old sensations. The teacher must persuade the student to try the new approach without predetermining the vocal quality it will generate. He must hit the ball and look for it afterward. Only with a great deal of practice will he be able to tell ahead of time where the ball is going or how the tone will sound.

The Paradox of Uniform Quality

The student must understand that minor changes in the outside quality may sound like major changes on the inside. The paradox of uniform quality is a most important concept: *In singing a scale from the top of the voice to the bottom and back again, a uniform quality of tonal color on the outside will sound as if there are major changes on the inside, and a uniform quality on the inside will sound like major changes on the outside.* Simply put, when the student hears a lot of change on the inside, the quality is apt to be more uniform on the outside, and vice versa. The student must trust his teacher to tell him what sounds good on the outside and learn what that quality is on the inside.

It occurred to me some time ago that in order to approach the problem of imperfect hearing I would have to teach as if I were inside the student. My technical explanations and psychological symbols must take into account the difference in the way a student sounds to himself and to an audience. I try to explain that the particular quality the new technique produces, strange though it may be, is the best the student can make at the time. After feeling the new sensations for awhile and hearing himself in the new way, the student will come to accept these feelings and sounds as the norm. Eventually, he will no longer be bothered by the varying timbres caused by changes in registration and vowels.

TEACHING BEGINS WITH THE BEST AREAS
AND MOVES OUTWARD

No matter how inept or unskilled the singer, there are bound to be some areas of his voice and some vowels which are better than others. When I hear a student for the first time, I try to find these better areas and vowels to establish them as points of departure. This gives me a place to begin and overcomes the student's apprehension that I am going to concentrate on the worst sounds he makes.

Finding the Best Area of the Voice

First, I find the best area of the voice, usually in the middle range. I start all exercises in this area so the student's voice works best at the outset. Then I begin to expand outward a few notes at a time to add to the good area. Usually these exercises are diatonic and chromatic scales, so the expansion of the good area is slow but sure. If the student's voice seems to work upward best, we will sing ascending scales from the middle range. If the voice wants to move downward, we sing descending scales.

Breathing

Since all students have learned to breathe in order to live, I try to find the good aspects of their breathing which are conducive to supported singing. From these good aspects of support we move to the less good or poor, so the student's confidence in himself is constantly reinforced. Some skillful teacher might begin by saying, "I am sorry, but you are doing absolutely nothing right, and we shall have to begin from the ground up," and yet not discourage the student. But I have found that I must discover some area of achievement which is promising for the student to respond positively.

Best Vowels

In the first lessons I establish which vowels are better in the student's voice and concentrate the initial exercises on them. Later, I devise exercises which move from the good vowels to the less good or poor, either on scales or on the same pitch.

Substituting Vowels

Another teaching technique is to substitute a good vowel for a less good in sample words or in the text of a song. This gives the student the idea of proper resonance and support at that point. The substitute vowel is then changed back to the proper one, and the student tries to keep the latter vowel in the same frequency of resonance or "placement" as the substitute.

Substituting Consonants

The technique of substitution is also used in teaching articulation. The most obvious changes are from voiced consonants to unvoiced, and vice versa. Other techniques change the consonants which use the same articulators, such as "d" instead of "r" and "b" instead of "m." Several exercises in this book are based on this concept.

CHORAL GROUPS AND VOICE CLASSES
ARE INDIVIDUAL STUDENTS

Training a chorus is the same as teaching many individuals at once. The chorus is a blend of several unique vocal sounds, and each chorister's voice makes the chorus what it is. When properly trained, individual voices will blend without reducing their qualities or damping their resonances, because the same basic vocal principles apply to groups as well as soloists. The director's task is to encourage the less proficient singers to equal the better ones.

A great deal of individualized teaching may be done in groups because students learn from one another. Classmates may often make the solution to a vocal problem clearer than the teacher if they are given the opportunity to speak out. I have found the voice class to be a excellent way of teaching singing. It gives the student a time to sing in front of his peers, to hear others sing, to gain confidence, to hear suggestions, and to make constructive criticisms. The subject of class voice will be explored more fully in a later chapter.

Now that we have looked at ourselves as teachers and at our students, it is time to examine more thoroughly what and how we teach them.

2

HOW TO DEVELOP BREATHING
AS THE FOUNDATION FOR SINGING

The greatest human need is air. There is no stronger drive in man for oxygen. Cut off his supply, and he immediately begins to struggle. Deny him air for more than a few minutes, and he dies. Every physical act depends on air and on the way we breathe. It is no wonder, then, that any study of singing should begin with this most vital element.

BREATHING AS AN ELEMENT OF SINGING

1. The Motor of the Vocal Process

Breath is the foundation on which singing is established, and good breathing is the basis for all good singing. It furnishes the energy for phonation, resonance, and articulation. Without respiration, none of the other elements of singing would function. Perhaps in this observation was the beginning of the concept of breath "supporting" singing.

2. Supported Singing

Breath may be said to support singing because it is the *sine qua non* of uttering sounds. The term "support" is common with almost every teaching method, but an exact understanding is often lacking, probably because "support" is a psychological term which describes a wide range of feeling.

Support is a sensation of released energy, especially in the upper abdominal area and around the ribcage. It is more than just a matter of breath pressure and breath flow in that it involves resistance in the larynx which balances the released energy in the thorax. An unsupported tone may have too little breath pressure, too much breath flow, too little resistance by the vocal bands, too little resistance by the muscles of the abdomen or ribcage, or an improper balance of any of these.

Support depends on muscular tensions which oppose one another. In singing the muscles of inhalation must resist those of exhalation, or the breath will rush out uncontrolled. Such resistance causes a feeling of tension or "support" around the ribs, in the abdomen, and in the lower back. Pressure is created in the thorax which pushes in every direction, much like the pressure in a tire. The stronger the muscular tensions, the stronger the support.

Coordination of the muscles of inhalation and exhalation controls the amount of breath released, its force and its flow. Breath pressure may be compared to voltage in electricity, that is, the amount of power being used. The flow may be slow or fast, steady or unsteady, legato or staccato, and many other varieties. The control of breath pressure and breath flow contributes to volume, timbre, and intensity of vocal tone, depending on its coordination with the vocal bands.

The product of voltage times amperage is wattage, or the amount of work done. Just as the electric power companies furnish and control proper voltage and amperage in house current to produce the proper wattage in light bulbs and appliances, we adjust breath pressure and breath flow to the resistance of the vocal bands for a myriad of vocal tones. Also, just as the power companies have determined that 220 volts at 15 amperes is better than 110 volts at 30 amperes to produce 3,300 watts in an air conditioner, we increase our breath pressure and reduce breath flow to achieve a better, stronger tone.

IMPORTANCE OF PROPER RESPIRATION

1. How to Prepare the Vocal Apparatus

I ask every student, "What is the importance of good breathing to the singer?" And they invariably respond, "To help him sing a long phrase?" To which I answer, "No." Proper breathing prepares the vocal mechanism for singing. Respiration opens the vocal bands, and deep breathing widens the throat, lowers the larynx, and lifts the soft palate. The ability to negotiate long phrases is the last, if not least, reason to practice good breathing.

The sound preferred by most Western audiences requires the largest possible space in the pharynx—the area above the vocal bands and behind the tongue. Most of the coloristic adjectives, such as "warm," "dark," "deep," "rich," and so forth, describe tones which come from an enlarged pharynx. Thus, our Western breathing exercises train the pharyngeal muscles to expand and hold the area as wide as possible. In describing the pharyngeal position to the student I say that the larynx should be low, the soft palate high, the throat wide, and the tongue forward to create the large space necessary for a rich tone.

The position of the larynx and the velum are in opposition to one another, and the two actions of lowering the larynx and lifting the soft palate occur together. Where one teacher stresses the low larynx, another emphasizes the high velum, and both are asking for the same result—a large pharynx.

2. How to Lower the Larynx

The larynx should be encouraged to lower through indirect means. It should not be thrust down by drawing the tongue back, as in swallowing, nor by forcing the chin onto the chest. The latter actions cause the so-called "depressed larynx" which is abhorred by most teachers, and rightly so.

Deep breathing is the proper method of lowering the larynx. When the sternum is raised forward and the ribcage expanded, the larynx is lowered without tongue, throat, or jaw tensions because of the sternothyroid muscles which are attached to the sternum and the bottom of the larynx. If the sternum stays out and the ribcage stays expanded, the larynx will stay low even when singing an ascending scale.

In opposition to the deep breathing muscles which pull the

larynx down are the swallowing muscles which pull it up. Because we breathe deeply only with a conscious effort, but we swallow many times a day, the muscles which lower the larynx are much weaker than those which raise it. The swallowing, or tongue, muscles move the larynx easily either up or down. The breathing muscles must be strengthened over a long period of time to hold the larynx down. Only after extended vocal study and practice can the student expect to hold the larynx in a good singing position indefinitely, but the result is worth the effort.

Lowering the larynx may be felt by the student if he places the tip of one finger lightly upon the point of his Adam's apple while his throat is at rest, then breathes in deeply. First, I have him feel my own larynx as I breathe. While the larynx is in a low position, I sing a vocalise so he can see that the larynx does not move upward with an ascending scale. Then I have him feel his own larynx position and sing the same vocalise. Thus, he becomes aware of one of the major tasks in learning to sing.

Occasionally, a student becomes so engrossed with the position of the larynx that I must take his mind off it. Such concentration is not conducive to good singing technique because the student cannot focus on other equally necessary techniques. When a student becomes overly conscious of any single aspect of learning to sing, he generally forgets other important parts.

A few years ago a fine singer who was studying with me had the habit of putting his hand to his larynx before every attack. I asked him why, and he said that he was checking to see if his larynx was down. He agreed that such a movement would be awkward in a public recital, but he had a terrible time breaking himself of the habit. Long afterward when he no longer had the mannerism, in times of stress I would see his hand move some three or four inches, almost like the reflexive knee-jerk when the patella is struck. Habits such as this die hard.

3. How to Raise the Soft Palate

The velum, or soft palate, may be seen at the back of the throat and may be identified by the uvula hanging from it. If the student is not aware of his own soft palate, I have him look in my mouth, and I consciously raise and lower the uvula. Then I show him the tone which occurs when the velum is too low. The resultant nasality may not be considered obnoxious by the student, but when I demonstrate the tone quality with the palate raised, he can hear the difference. I try to persuade the student that while the more nasal tone may sound as if it would project, there is more ring and "carry" to the less nasal tone because of the enriched high overtones.

Finding the Velum. At first it is difficult for the student to feel his soft palate. And if he has a nasal speaking voice, he is usually so accustomed to it that he cannot recognize its nasality. Some of the exercises which I use to deal with the low soft palate depend on good breathing habits and a low larynx. Others are specifically designed to raise the velum. However, I prefer not to call undue attention to the soft palate because it may lead to stiffness in that area which is not good.

Nose or Mouth Breathing. Since the palate lowers when they breathe through their noses, students often ask whether they should breathe exclusively through the mouth to keep the palate high. I tell students to breathe through the nose during long rests or while moving across the stage because the nose is particularly equipped to strain foreign matter from the air and to warm it. During short rests and between phrases, the student should breathe through the mouth because it is more efficient in drawing in a great deal of air in a short time, and it helps to prepare the vocal instrument. This preparation may occur almost instantly at the end of a long breath through the nose. The last few ounces of air may be drawn through the mouth. I caution the student about constantly breathing through the mouth, as it has a tendency to dry the velum and pharynx.

Even the finest voices have difficulty if the velum is dry. Once on a Saturday broadcast of the Metropolitan Opera, I heard the great tenor Richard Tucker sing Des Grieux in *Manon Lescaut.* When he began the aria in the first act, he sounded as if in vocal trouble, but his singing later in the broadcast was magnificent, as usual. Some months later we were talking about the performance, and he brought up the subject of the first act aria. Mr. Tucker said that just as he was set to walk onstage, some stagehands delivering scenery for the evening performance opened a large door to the street, and a gust of cold wind dried his throat and soft palate. Without having a chance to recover, he had to go out and sing that difficult scene. It was the only time he could remember not receiving applause at the end of an aria. After he restored some moisture to his throat, Mr. Tucker was able to sing as he should, and the ovations he received were a mixture of admiration for his voice and relief that his earlier difficulty was shortlived.

4. How to Widen the Throat

Deep breathing allows the throat to widen as the larynx lowers and the velum rises. This is an automatic reaction, as may be seen in a yawn or sigh. The singer's task is to keep the throat open while singing. The natural tendency is for the throat to close or relax during exhalation, so that open-throated singing is really an artificially imposed procedure.

In a way the throat may be the most important resonator, because it is the first opening through which the phonated sound must pass. If the throat is not open, there is nothing the mouth or nose can do to overcome the resultant shallowness of tone. Since the major muscles of the throat are constrictors used in swallowing, it is difficult to teach the expanding muscles how to hold the throat open. Thus, most of our early work as teachers is designed to counteract the inclination of the throat to close.

I have found that when the throat stays open the singer may at first have a sensation of "hootiness" or muffled quality. This new sound may be hard for him to accept, so I have to assure him again and again that it only sounds muffled on the inside. Often I use a tape recorder to show him the actual tone quality on the outside. The sensation of hootiness generally passes quickly as the student gets used to the new feeling of an expanded pharynx.

5. Tongue Forward

The position of the tongue is also related to respiration and is the final aspect of an open throat. Frequently, placement of the tongue is a matter of disagreement among voice teachers, but it seems the discussion centers around the location of the front of the tongue. Most teachers agree that the back of the tongue should be forward so the epiglottis will not intrude on the laryngopharynx.

Earlier I mentioned that a yawn suggested the feeling of an open pharynx. At the beginning of a yawn the tongue is flat in the mouth and relaxed. But as the yawn progresses, the tongue either humps or curls backward into the throat, and the walls of the pharynx stiffen. Thus, I do not use many yawning exercises in the lesson because the tongue is usually too far back, especially at the end of the yawn.

The sigh—either voiced or voiceless—seems to work better than the yawn. During a sigh the throat stays open and the tongue relaxed. And the voiced sigh is a good example of phonation with an open throat. Also, the psychology of a sigh is more conducive to wide-awake singing than a yawn. Sighing is the reaction of contentment and well-being and lends itself to a positive approach to teaching and singing.

The tongue is such an important part of singing that it will be discussed in later chapters on phonation, resonance, and articulation. Exercises for the tongue will be suggested at those times. For the purposes of breathing, suffice it to say that the tongue should remain quietly out of the throat.

DIFFERENT KINDS OF BREATHING

I like to teach breathing by separating its various physical aspects. Through an understanding of his physique, the student is better able to achieve the coordination necessary to proper respiration. However, describing the different kinds of breathing is somewhat like separating the aspects of walking. Speaking of "knee walking" or "ankle walking" does not preclude the use of both knee and ankle in the act of walking. Of course, it would be impossible to walk without using both the knee and ankle. It is the same with breathing. We cannot breathe without using the intercostal muscles, the diaphragm, and the abdomen together. On the other hand, it is helpful to separate the aspects of breathing to concentrate on a limited area of the body.

1. Thoracic Breathing

By definition, all breathing is thoracic since the air is taken into the lungs, which are totally contained in the thorax. However, the use of this term focuses the student's attention on the rib cage and sternum. I usually begin a new student's lessons by explaining that the breastbone should try to move as far as possible from the backbone. Since the sternum is set at an angle, the movement is felt mostly from the bottom where the ribs join at the solar plexus. In deep breathing the breastbone moves upward and forward, as shown in the diagram.

This movement is entirely mechanical and skeletal. That is, the sternum may move outward whether the singer is inhaling, exhaling, or holding his breath. Since it is not therefore necessary to respiration, such movement of the sternum may better be viewed as part of the proper posture for singing than for breathing.

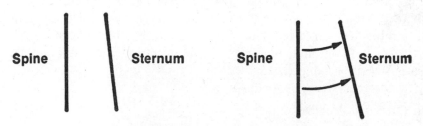

Spine   **Sternum**   **Spine**   **Sternum**

Illustration 2.1 Movement of the Sternum

The sternum may remain stationary once it has moved forward. Inward or downward movement is not necessary in exhaling, and most singers find that their respiratory muscles function better if the sternum does not move up and down with each breath. Holding the sternum as far as possible from the spine takes practice. But after awhile the student becomes accustomed to the posture and is no longer conscious of ribcage expansion.

2. Intercostal Breathing

The terms intercostal and thoracic breathing are often used interchangeably. The intercostal muscles are named for their attachment to the rib cage, so intercostal breathing might also be called "rib breathing."

The external intercostal muscles pull the rib cage out and hold it there, thus affording a larger area for the lungs to occupy when they fill with air. The ribs do not cause the lungs to expand, however, and the lungs may contract during exhalation without the ribs lowering. Thus, movement of the rib cage may also be considered mechanical and skeletal. If the intercostals hold the rib cage firm, the epigastrium may control the diaphragm better. Unless the ribs are held rigid, the abdominal muscles will draw them in, reducing the size of the thorax.

The internal intercostal muscles lower the rib cage to its normal place of rest. These muscles also resist the movement of the ribcage outward, thus holding it steady to furnish support. The sets of intercostal muscles antagonize one another and are best strengthened by exercises which expand the rib cage and hold it firmly, such as those described below.

The elaborate system of muscles which moves the sternum, rib cage, and upper chest is more complex than I care to deal with in a lesson. I explain that the intercostal muscles expand the rib cage and hold it except during long rests, at which time the ribs draw in to a more normal position. I believe the best breathing is accomplished when the ribs do not move in and out, but remain steady. A functional, empirical explanation such as this generally satisfies the student.

3. Clavicular Breathing

I present this aspect of respiration to the student at the same time as thoracic and intercostal breathing. As with them, the term "clavicular breathing" centers the student's attention on a part of the skeleton—the upper chest—which may move independently without regard for respiration. As another term for "high chest breathing," clavicular breathing has come under attack, and rightly so. The radical movement of the upper chest offers no help in singing and presents a great many problems, such as moving the larynx out of position, deterring proper support, forcing out the breath uncontrolled, and hindering pharyngeal resonance by shortening the neck.

In proper breathing there should be practically no feeling of movement in the clavicles. As the sternum moves away from the spine, the upper chest rises, and there is a tendency of the shoulders to move upward or outward. This involvement of the sternocleidomastoid muscles is not necessary and should be counteracted by keeping the neck and head relaxed. The shoulders should be encouraged to stay straight and equidistant from the sternum and the spine.

As the chest is lifted the shoulders should not feel stiff, nor should the chest be so high that breathing is labored. Usually, the student can see in a mirror that the proper posture for singing is also physically attractive. The shoulder points are back far enough to remove any hint of a slouch, but the scapulae do not meet or feel rigid.

The West Point "brace" is an extreme example of thoracic,

clavicular movement. It is not a good model for singers, though, because of the rigidity involved. In a military posture there is the tendency to suck in the abdomen, pull in the chin drastically, and bow the neck, none of which makes for good singing.

Teenage boys accept an expanded chest readily, because there is something manly about such posture. On the other hand, the girls do not adapt as quickly as a result of the additional weight of newly developed breasts. Girls are frequently reluctant about adopting a posture which seems to thrust their breasts forward. Here again, the mirror shows that the new posture does not look nearly as exaggerated as it feels. Quite a few of the girls have said, "My mother says that I should stand this way even when I am not singing." So I tell them, "All right, mind your mother and stand up straight like a lady."

4. Diaphragmatic Breathing

All breathing is diaphragmatic. There can be no movement of air into or out of the lungs without activity of the diaphragm. But for all its size and importance to singing, the diaphragm is very difficult to feel. It is virtually hidden by the rib cage and may only be found by pressing the fingers under the lower ribs. For such a large muscle, the diaphragm has relatively few sensors, which makes it hard to cultivate any awareness of its movement apart from the muscles of the abdomen. For this reason, some of the old masters spoke of diaphragmatic and abdominal breathing interchangeably. Thus, most of the breathing exercises which are suggested later are designed to strengthen the diaphragm along with the surrounding muscles.

I think it is important to explain to the student that the diaphragm flexes or tightens during inhalation and relaxes during exhalation. This flexion causes a partial vacuum in the lungs, and air rushes in to fill the void. There is quite a different sensation in the normal muscle energy of inhalation and that of the controlled exhalation necessary for singing.

The action of the diaphragm may be compared to the biceps as it flexes to raise the hand and forearm. Once having flexed, the biceps cannot then push the hand and forearm back down. There must be an antagonistic muscle—the triceps—which pulls the hand down as the biceps relaxes. The coordination of these muscles determines how slowly or rapidly the hand rises or falls. Also, outside forces, such as whether the hand is grasping a weight, help to decide the relative strengths necessary in each muscle to fulfill its assigned task.

In this same manner the diaphragm must be coordinated with its surrounding muscles for efficient respiration. Since the diaphragm relaxes in exhalation, it cannot by itself exert force on the escaping air. Control of the escaping breath comes from other sets of muscles. How this occurs is explained in the succeeding paragraphs.

5. Abdominal Breathing

The complex set of heavy muscles of the upper abdomen—the epigastrium—are connected in such a way as to exert a great deal of influence on the diaphragm, especially in allowing it to relax slowly and steadily. In proper respiration the epigastrium moves outward during inhalation and holds rather firmly during exhalation. These muscles may sink inward somewhat during exhalation, but should not be consciously pulled in. The old concept of pancostal breathing, that is, pushing or squeezing out the air, does not lend itself to the quality of singing generally taught these days, because of the tensions created in the vocal mechanism and the tendency to let the larynx rise.

To avoid the feeling of pulling in the epigastrium during exhalation, I try to use a slight outward pressure. While the epigastrium may not actually move outward as I sing, the idea helps overcome the inclination to sink rapidly or pull in. As the upper abdomen holds steady, the lower abdomen moves inward gradually, contributing to good control of the breath.

Abdominal breathing may be taught by the most straightforward means because the student may see and feel the muscles of the epigastrium as they move. He may control the epigastrium directly and learn to regulate it precisely. Further, the student relates well to new concepts of abdominal breathing because the results are quick and are directly proportionate to the changes he makes in his muscular behavior.

6. Back Breathing

An aspect of breathing which has become better known and more important in recent years is the use of the back muscles.

These heavy, plate-like muscles offer a large source of strength and support for deep breathing just as they do for lifting heavy objects. Just as lifting with the back properly straight and tense is more efficient than lifting with the abdominal muscles alone, breathing to sing may be improved by using the back muscles to take some of the strain off the epigastrium. The lower back muscles are especially suited for resisting the pull of exhalation. When they are properly tensed the back muscles allow the epigastrium to be more flexible and independent.

Learning to use the back muscles is not as easy as improving abdominal breathing. The back muscles are primarily designed to hold the skeleton upright and are not as readily flexed during respiration as the epigastrium. As muscles which generally function by contracting, they are also not as easily trained to expand and hold the rib cage as the intercostals.

In efficient respiration the back muscles expand along with the intercostals to help hold the rib cage out. In this way they are antagonistic to the pull of the epigastrium on the ribs and aid in the steady relaxation of the diaphragm. The muscles of the back must be balanced with those of the chest, ribs, and abdomen. A good practice is to feel expansion of the back muscles while keeping the sternum and rib cage out.

It is not necessary for the expansion of the back to push the shoulders forward in a stoop, because that would force the sternum and rib cage down. Neither should the scapulae protrude as the back expands. In correct singer's posture the scapulae lie flat but do not meet. The clavicles remain horizontal, and the shoulder points are equidistant from the sternum and spine.

Because of the difficulty in training the back muscles, the student needs specific exercises designed to promote the feeling of back expansion. Several of these are described later in the chapter where I discuss specific problems.

All the aspects of respiration—thoracic, intercostal, clavicular, diaphragmatic, abdominal, and back muscular—must be combined for effective breathing to sing. Just as the knee and ankle must cooperate in walking, the various parts of breathing must work together. When they do, balanced tension in all the muscles produces a symmetrical posture which is both efficient and attractive.

A SAMPLE LESSON IN BREATHING

After explaining the kinds of breathing and the various parts of the body involved, I watch the student breathe as he sings a simple exercise. In that first act of breathing I see how much he already understands about breathing—he may have had voice lessons before—and how many of the concepts I will have to teach him.

If he has not studied before and knows nothing of breathing to sing, I begin with the skeletal and posture aspects. Generally, I think of the first three kinds of breathing—thoracic, intercostal, and clavicular—as a unit. The sternum moves out, the chest moves up, and the rib cage expands all around. I show the student that this movement is mechanical by demonstrating that I can expand the ribs and chest while talking, thus they do not affect inhalation or exhalation.

Developing Posture

If he, or especially she, has difficulty lifting the thorax into its proper position, I have him or her stand against the wall while trying to touch it with head, shoulders, back, buttocks, legs, and heels. Obviously, this is an awkward position in which to sing, but it creates a feeling of posture which is better for singing than the normal, casual stance.

Once again I have him sing a scale or vocalise while standing against the wall. While he may not sing much better, he begins to develop the awareness necessary for further instruction.

After a few scales, I ask him to step away from the wall but maintain the posture. Most students slump a bit when away from the wall, but their posture is better than before. If possible, I have a mirror opposite the spot where they stand against the wall, so they may see their posture does not look as rigid as it may feel. Then when they step away from the wall, they can continue to see if their posture is the same or if they slump.

Feeling the Epigastrium

When the student begins to use the proper posture, I have him put one hand on his upper chest and the other on his epigastrium. As he sings a vocalise, I ask him if there is any movement. I want the student to feel the epigastrium move, but not the upper chest. If he feels no movement at all, I have him breathe deeply and exaggerate the movement of the abdomen. Most students have trouble moving the epigastrium outward, especially the athletes. Their muscles seem so rigid they will not stretch. Sometimes there is not a good understanding of abdominal movement, so I let the students place their hands on my chest and abdomen as I demonstrate what I am saying.

After a few breathing exercises, I continue with vocalises as the student places his hands again on his chest and abdomen. It is important to correlate the training of the breathing muscles to singing so the student keeps ultimate goals in mind. From the beginning he learns that breathing is an element of singing and is different from any other method of respiration he may learn.

Feeling the Back and Sides

When the singer's epigastrium begins to move to my satisfaction, I then ask him to put his hands on his sides with the thumbs in front, fingers in back. Again we sing vocalises and he finds out whether or not the side and back muscles are moving. Usually they are not, so I offer an exercise which will encourage those areas to expand.

As he feels his sides and lower back, I ask the student to stand tall with as much space as possible between the lowest rib and the hip bone. This avoids any tendency to squat while learning back breathing. I may even have him stand on tiptoe. We combine breathing exercises and vocalises until he begins to feel some expansion in the back. By that time at least a half-hour or more has gone by, and we are through with the first lesson.

A general idea I try to keep in the forefront of such a lesson is that breathing to sing presumes that muscles are in motion. All of the exercises are designed to make the respiratory muscles move from the normal, casual position. This idea is important because rigid muscles which do not move are inimical to good singing.

Using Rests for Breathing

Another important idea is that the scales and arpeggios the student sings are designed to develop his breathing as well as tone quality and facility. The rests within the vocalises are as significant as the notes, because they are intended to coordinate the end of one phrase with the beginning of another by breathing in rhythm in between. When the pianist plays chords with the vocalises, I ask him to keep a steady tempo during the rests so the singer will learn this coordination. Thus, breathing becomes an integral part of the vocal line and the singing experience.

I try to relate breathing to the particular sport which the student plays. If he plays baseball, he should imagine he is at bat. The muscular movement before he swings is quite like the feeling of lift in breathing to sing. He could not imagine his chest collapsing as he swings a bat, any more than he should feel it collapse while he holds a note.

The same analogies apply to serving a tennis ball, swimming, driving a golf ball, and most other sports. Gymnastics also requires this feeling of lift. The muscles are ready but not rigid, synchronizing with the breath to prepare the body for the task at hand.

In the following weeks the student and I will work on various breathing exercises to strengthen the respiratory muscles. I try to choose exercises which are best suited to the student's weaknesses. Besides breathing drills in the studio, I recommend a program of physical training which will help keep the student healthy. Physical fitness is important to good singing, and I advise all my students to maintain such a regimen.

SYMPTOMS OF IMPROPER BREATHING

1. Lifting the Shoulders

A common mistake among young singers is lifting their shoulders when they breathe. The cause of this was described earlier in the section on clavicular breathing. I ask the students to hold their arms out in front with palms down as they breathe. If their shoulders rise with each inhalation, their arms will feel a tug. Watching their arms and looking in a mirror are two ways the students become aware of this improper method of breathing. If the voice lessons are taught in a class, the members of the group may observe one another and even lay their hands on each others' shoulders to help relax the muscles of the neck and head.

2. Use of the Throat as a Valve

In the chapter on phonation we will see that the vocal bands may be thought of as a valve at the top of the trachea. But this concept is not useful in teaching singing. The conscious use of the throat as a valve to interrupt the flow of air from the lungs leads to many problems, the worst of which may cause damage to the vocal bands.

An audible symptom of such use of the throat is noisy inhalation, or gasping. When the throat is properly opened, there is absolutely no sound to inhaling either through the nose or mouth. I teach my students to breathe noiselessly because it is more efficient. More air may be drawn into the lungs in a shorter span of time. Also, a noiseless breath prepares the voice better and is less likely to dry the throat.

I prefer the students to breathe slowly except where the musical phrase requires a catch breath. Students who breathe in short jerks never seem to have their bodies settled in time to sing properly. Their vocal mechanisms are not prepared, their throats are not open, and so forth. Also, there is a psychological aspect of hurrying, fright, anxiety, and other nervous problems in the catch breath. The common antidote for fright and anxiety is slow, deep breathing. Therefore, I like for the students to practice a little preventive medicine in their performances. If I insist they breathe quietly in their lessons, they are more apt to breathe that way when they sing in public.

3. Rigid Breathing Muscles

Usually when a student breathes properly, some of his muscles can be seen moving. Breathing is an act of muscles in motion, and deep breathing should cause external abdominal and back muscles to move noticeably.

Some of the exercises which help make the epigastrium move in and out are (1) lying on the floor and breathing with a heavy book on the stomach, (2) standing against the piano and forcing the abdomen out in such a way that one is pushed away from the piano, (3) pulling the stomach in to look as thin as possible, then pushing it out to look as fat as possible, and (4) other variants of these which the teacher can invent to achieve the same purpose.

The overriding concept in these exercises is that constant pressure on the muscles will cause them to stretch beneficially. Any exercise that punishes the muscles by hitting them or otherwise applying quick, jerky tension is more apt to cause a knotting reaction and may even cause bruising or other injury. Such exercises would not stretch the muscles and, therefore, would not remedy the matter of rigidity.

4. Improper Release of Breath

Some students are unable to sustain a tone without wavering or sliding off pitch, even when they have good breath capacity. Such a problem may be caused by an improper concept of respiration. They simply do not understand what is involved in good breathing. After I have gone through an explanation and shown the student a few exercises, if he is still unable to sustain a note well, I look for other symptoms.

If the rib cage collapses during exhalation, there may be a weakness in the exterior intercostals and back muscles. Probably the rest of the student's physique is poorly developed as well, so I suggest a series of developmental exercises which he should practice for several weeks or longer.

Sometimes an improper release of breath is caused by the student's aggressively pulling in the epigastrium. Other times it may be caused by weak abdominal muscles, which would allow the breath to rush out. In coping with such problems I demonstrate that pulling in on the epigastrium is a perfect way of achieving the vocal production effected by Marlon Brando in "The Godfather." While that may be worth an Academy Award for acting, it is not the best kind of singing.

DEVELOPING AWARENESS OF THE
BREATHING MECHANISMS

One of the most fundamental problems I have found in students is the lack of awareness of where the breathing mechanisms are and how they feel. After I have explained to them the various aspects of respiration, I ask them to try the following:

1. Partially Sit

The student starts to sit but stops about three inches above the chair. In this position he should feel some stress in the muscles around the rib cage, the abdomen, and back. He can feel with his fingers for the areas of tension and perhaps feel inner tension in the diaphragm. If he stands and partially sits several times, he should become more and more aware of the external breathing muscles.

2. Hold a Heavy Object at Arm's Length

This exercise is designed to achieve much the same as partially sitting. Holding a chair at arm's length causes stress on the intercostals, epigastrium, and back muscles, but in different ratios from partially sitting. I first became aware of this exercise standing in the hot Texas sun holding a Garand M-1 rifle at arm's length. After a while, I became aware of every muscle in my body. Naturally, it is not necessary to carry the demonstration to that extreme.

3. Express Delighted Surprise

Inhaling and saying "Ah. . ." as if surprised and delighted is a good example of the breath and larynx coordinated through psychological means. The student imagines a time when he was happily surprised, and the response of the muscles is automatic. As with other instinctive features of singing, the teacher's task becomes one of helping the student sustain the response for a time so it becomes useful in singing. This exercise is related to singing on the rebound of the breath, which is discussed later.

4. Inhale Through a Pinhole

A current advertisement on television for a breath freshener asks us to test our breath by sipping through a small opening in the mouth. The result of this test is to show that the breath freshener is still working. Actually, the test shows a positive response even when a person has not used the product. The small opening causes the inhaled air to be cooler through a jet effect.

For our purposes the test is good for demonstrating the pull of the back muscles, which are usually difficult to sense. Drawing the breath through a small opening in the mouth makes the back muscles expand. Putting the hands on the sides and back and sitting in a slight crouch help induce the feeling of expansion. In this way the student learns a new aspect of intercostal and back breathing which is not shown in the previous exercises.

5. Pant Rapidly and Vigorously

On a hot day everyone has seen a dog lying on his side panting with the heat. The rib cage and abdomen were moving violently in and out. Imitating this action is excellent for increasing the awareness of the epigastrium and of developing stronger muscles. The student holds his rib cage steady, and the abdomen moves rapidly in and out with each panting breath.

6. Whimper

An exercise similar to panting is that of whimpering. The difference, of course, is that the student makes a vocal sound in whimpering, so the throat does not dry out as in panting. Actually, I prefer whimpering to panting because it involves phonation and the muscle response is not so violent as in panting. The problem with whimpering is the students' reluctance to make a sound which is associated with hurt or pain during childhood. Psychological embarrassment often causes the student to laugh when I demonstrate whimpering, but I understand the motivation and coax them gently to try it. If we can overcome the psychology, the student and I find that whimpering is a valid approach to coordinating breath and sound.

7. Staccato Vocalises

In the next chapter I have written some staccato vocalises which solve problems in phonation, but they may also be used to improve breathing. A good staccato which originates on the breath involves the epigastrium in much the same way as whimpering but is real singing, which is important to the student.

There should be a small amount of air immediately preceding the sound of the voice, and the student should feel as if the vocal bands were "riding on air." There should be no feeling of restriction or squeezing in the larynx while singing staccato. The vocalise is generated by the breathing muscles, especially the epigastrium, and is felt in the abdomen, around the sides, and in the back.

If the student has difficulty with staccato vocalises, I ask him to sing them very slowly, beginning each attack with an "h" and a bit of air before the vocal sound. As he improves, the amount of "h" and preceding air lessen, and the tempo quickens. Eventually, he should be able to sing rapid staccato exercises without an "h" and without tightening his throat.

DEVELOPING COORDINATED BREATHING

Besides the exercises above which concern awareness and development of the breathing mechanisms, there are several which I have found useful in further coordinating respiration.

1. Proper Posture

To maintain the expansion of the rib cage the student may hold his arms over his head, lifting his chest and ribs. Then he lowers his arms but leaves the thorax in the upraised position. The arms relax and hang to the sides.

With the chest and rib cage expanded and the arms hanging freely, the shoulders find a comfortable, natural position. This is usually back of their normal, slumped posture, but they should not be braced in the military manner. Expansion of the back will overcome a tendency to pull the shoulders too far back, and the high, extended chest should keep the shoulders from slumping. The shoulders should not feel rigid or tense.

The head should be erect without tension. There should be a feeling of "leading" with the forehead instead of the chin. The chin should hang free, neither thrust forward nor pulled into the V of the chest. The neck should be straight, but not elongated. The student may feel as if the muscles of the back of the neck are lengthened a bit to hold the head erect, but this is only a feeling.

The weight should be on the balls of the feet. This does not mean on tiptoe, but assuredly not on the heels. The position of readiness to hit a baseball or receive a tennis service or volley is good. An agile boxer, other than a heavyweight, assumes this position of readiness. His muscles are moving, his breath controlled, and his mind alert.

The legs should be free to move without the knees locked. The concert singer should feel as ready to walk or run as the opera singer who must move as well as sing. Locked knees have a tendency to cut off the circulation and can increase fatigue at a startling rate. Simply moving the knees or shifting the weight relieves these symptoms and revives vigor in the performer.

Finally, the student should stand tall and straight. He should resist the impulse to bend forward or backward to squeeze out the air. Bending forward may seem like an intimate, ingratiating pose to the singer, but it usually hampers the free movement of the epigastrium. I look for wrinkles in the midsection of the student's

shirt or blouse as an indication of settling down of the thorax. I ask
the student to keep the material wrinkle free by standing straight.
Also, a familar sight is the solo wind player in a dance band bending backward, instrument pointed toward the ceiling, going for the
high note. While that posture may force a little extra pressure for
an instrumentalist, it restricts the free flow of air necessary for
singing.

2. Controlled Exhalation

Breathing to sing is essentially controlled exhalation, and all
of my suggestions to this point have been to enhance such control.
There are two further concepts which I find meaningful: epigastrium independence and singing on the rebound of the breath.

I believe the epigastrium should act independent of the intercostal and back muscles. The intercostals hold the rib cage in position whether the singer inhales or exhales. The back muscles assist
in this as well as affording resistance to the abdominal muscles. So
the epigastrium may learn to move in and out and to tense and
relax without regard for the tension and relaxation of the other
muscles. When the epigastrium is independent, breathing can be
most efficient and most finely controlled. Small muscular adjustments which are imperceptible to the eye can be made instinctively
through the autonomic nervous system and the desire for various
subtle tonal shadings. Through this sort of muscular independence
a fine Lieder singer perfects the art of coloring his voice.

The old masters often spoke of the proper attack as "singing
on the breath." This meant starting to sing with the glottis open
and letting the breath cause the sound to begin. My idea of singing
on the rebound of the breath evolved as a way of feeling just that
sort of attack. I ask the student to think of the breath as a ball
which bounces up *in slow motion* after it is dropped, so the breath
is not locked in or held immobile between inhalation and exhalation. The breath is constantly moving in or out during singing.
Thus, the glottis stays open.

When we hold our breath, the natural defense mechanism of
the body makes the glottis close, the ventricular folds cover the
vocal bands, and the epiglottis lower over the ventricular folds.
This action keeps water out of the lungs while swimming, mucous
and food out of the trachea, and so forth. It takes extreme pressure
to open a tightly closed glottis, and such constant pressure could be

injurious to the vocal bands. The concept of singing on the rebound and the device of expressing delighted surprise help to avoid closing the glottis before exhaling.

Occasionally a student may appear to be breathing correctly, but the muscles are not accomplishing their purpose. One student of mine flexed the abdominal muscles almost to the point of belly dancing, but her tone was still erratic and strident. I discovered that she had misunderstood another teacher's instruction and was trying to move her epigastrium in time to her vibrato. After this erroneous concept was dispelled and proper breathing methods employed, her vibrato became regular, her tone quality became rich and mellow, and her ability to sing through a phrase improved immeasurably.

DEALING WITH WEAKNESS OF PHYSIQUE
OR SMALL VITAL CAPACITY

A singer may develop a larger chest cavity and vital capacity through strengthening the thoracic muscles. The interior dimension of the thorax may be increased by stretching and lengthening the intercostal and back muscles and ligaments. Such increased lung capacity provides a larger breath supply, and the greater strength furnishes additional breath pressure and flow. The following exercises may be beneficial to any singer no matter what his natural physique.

1. Rhythmic Breathing

The singer breathes in rhythm as deeply as possible and controls both inhalation and exhalation. At first I ask him to breathe as fully as he can to the count of four, then exhale as fully as possible to the count of four. He does several of these in a row, each time trying to inhale a few ounces more of air than the time before. There should be no feeling of squeezing or forcing out the exhalation. The student must learn to release the air at a predetermined rate by relaxing the abdomen.

Then I ask him to breathe in to the count of eight and out to the count of eight. The idea is that he is to inhale and exhale a greater volume of air over a longer period of time, thereby increasing his capacity and control at the same time. The longer the rhythmic period for breathing, the more the muscles will stretch.

As with earlier exercises, the stretching should be through constant pressure, not through short, sharp jerks.

This exercise may be extended to counts of twelve or sixteen each way. Or, it may be varied to different numbers for inhalation and exhalation, e.g., inhaling for two beats and exhaling eight, and so forth. Generally, at this point I have not asked the singer to hold his breath. Also, I watch closely for signs of hyperventilation. A student in poor physical condition could faint if he did not rest between periods of deep breathing.

2. Holding the Breath

This exercise may be combined with the one just above after the student has increased his vital capacity somewhat. The idea here is that holding a large lungful of air will keep the muscles taut and stretched. This is important because large muscles may be strengthened by clenching as well as flexing. Keeping these muscles stretched as much as a minute at a time will increase their resilience quickly. A minute is quite a long time to hold one's breath, however.

Sometimes I tie a piece of knitting yarn loosely around the student's chest and ask him to hold his chest expanded to keep the yarn from falling to the floor. If he relaxes his chest cavity, the yarn slips down. Such exercises prove to be good sport for the male students who enjoy the masculine pride of expanding the chest. They may also be useful with girls if the psychological aspects of holding out the breasts is not a problem.

Expanding the chest and increasing its size need not be confined to the voice studio. As young singers we used to practice our deep breathing while sitting in class or walking across the campus. In a short time this posture became normal for us.

Holding the breath may appear to be at odds with the concept of singing on the rebound. However, there are exercises which we might call "utilitarian" rather than "performance," that is, they serve a purpose in developing strength or technique but would not be used in a concert. Holding the breath helps to increase chest size and strength and is, therefore, useful even though we do not hold our breath during singing.

3. Singing with Expanded Chest

As soon as possible, I incorporate singing into the above exercises. I believe the student should relate all that is done in the studio to singing, so I ask him to sing rather than exhale silently to a count of four or eight. Usually he can sing to a longer count than when he only exhales.

The student may also sing vocalises and songs with the string tied loosely around his chest. He can learn to move around the studio while singing and still keep the chest expanded so the string will not fall. I have found that even the smallest, weakest singer can improve his vital capacity through these exercises.

EXTENDING THE LENGTH OF MUSICAL PHRASE

Good tonal quality is the primary purpose of good breathing, but extending the length of phrase which a student can sing is close behind. As a student practices his breathing exercises, he should find that he is able to sing longer phrases as a by-product. However, there are a few further suggestions which help him approach long phrases.

1. Begin at the End and Work Backward

As a student I was taught that while muscles may not have brains, they have memories. So it occurred to me that perhaps I could teach mine to remember how it feels to end a phrase with breath to spare. I learned to pace my breathing for a long phrase by singing the last few notes several times, then working backward adding a few notes at a time, I sang to the end of the phrase with plenty of breath. If the phrase was quite long, I might not be able to negotiate it in the first practice session because the muscles are not trained so quickly. Over a period of time, however, my muscles learn how to sing a particular phrase and acquire the strength to do it comfortably. I have found this approach useful in long roulades as well as slow, held notes.

2. Divide the Phrase into Fractions

After working on the long phrase from the back, I sing it through entirely several times to see at what point half my air is gone, two-thirds, three-fourths, and so on. Then I write small fractions into the score just a few notes beyond those points so I can try to reach a bit farther with one-half the breath, two-thirds, etc.

For the performance I have the fractions placed in such a way that when I reach the ½, I have half my breath left but am more than halfway through the phrase. As I pass the other fractions, I know where I am with the breath and in the phrase, and I can end with breath to spare. I never plan a phrase that takes the last ounce of breath. There is always some in reserve, because the throat closes as the last air escapes, and that does not make for good singing.

3. Break Up Long Baroque Phrases

I am convinced that some phrases in arias of the Baroque period were never meant to be sung on one breath. Either the aria was designed for a section of the choir, as in Bach's "Christ lag in Todesbanden," or the composer assumed that the singer would separate the phrase into meaningful groups. As with the ornaments of the Baroque, phrasing was left to the singer.

The examples illustrate Handel's phrasing in two famous arias. In Illustration 2.2 he wrote short rests between the sequences to indicate the style of performance. In the second the notes are tied together, but the sequences could be separated by short breaths if the performer wished. Tying all the notes together does not preclude breaking up the phrases. It is not necessary to

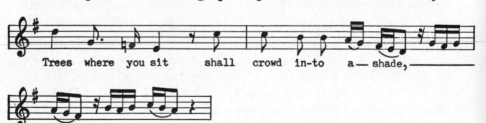

Example from "Where're You Walk"

Illustration 2.2

sing the phrase on one huge breath, nor must one complete the original word and insert short texts on each sequence in the manner of a Medieval trope. Baroque audiences were evidently used to hearing words broken in this way.

If a phrase is too long for the student, I look for breaths between the sequences. In Illustration 2.3 breaths may be taken in place of the eighth-notes which are tied to quarter-notes, or in place of the third beat of the dotted half-notes. Of course, I do not

Example from "O Sleep, Why Dost Thou Leave Me"

Illustration 2.3

suggest the student breathe at every possible place, but only those where necessary.

Breathing between sequences seems to be especially appropriate in Bach arias because the ends of his phrases are so often set to short syllables, and the next phrase begins without room for a breath. Otherwise, the tempo must be so fast that a breath is not needed, but the majesty and style of the piece would be lost. Surely, there may have been singers in Bach's day who could negotiate all his runs without breathing in the middle, but such a singer would be exceptional. Actually, in churches with a great deal of reverberation a breath between sequences cannot be heard, so what may sound awkward in the studio is not apparent in the performance.

HANDLING OTHER BREATHING PROBLEMS

1. Reluctance to Move the Body

Earlier I mentioned the timidity of girls at thrusting the breasts forward when expanding the chest. My female colleagues also have to deal with this reluctance and sometimes are no more successful in overcoming the student's embarrassment than are male teachers. I find that ignoring the shyness while insisting on proper posture is generally the best policy. A matter-of-fact attitude works best for me.

In some girls, or course, the problem is not only psychological but physical. Their new breasts are so large the muscles of the back have difficulty supporting the extra weight. In those cases an exercise program is mandatory. Even if the girls were not voice students, they would need to develop their skeletal muscles so their posture would be good. Here again a matter-of-fact attitude is the best way for me to help the student.

Besides the reluctance of the girls to expand their chests, the problem I encounter most in young singers is not wanting to move the abdomen outward while not inhaling. Thus, their rib cages collapse when they sing. The students think they will look fat or ungainly if they push out their stomachs, and these days our culture abhors fatness.

Three approaches to this problem seem to succeed for me: admitting that the epigastrium grows as a singer matures but such growth is necessary for a career, demonstrating that the outward thrust of the epigastrium feels more radical than it looks, and accepting a viable alternative method of breathing if the student cannot make the epigastrium move.

In the first instance I appeal to the student's career motivation. For most students developing a good voice is as important as maintaining a perfectly flat abdomen. Actually, unless the student is going to wear bathing suits or scanty costumes onstage, any bulge which appears in the epigastrium will be completely hidden by concert clothing or costumes. In no way does this approach imply that I promise a career to anyone who learns to breathe well. It simply puts into perspective a concern for physical looks to the student who is contemplating a career in singing.

Secondly, I demonstrate to the students by breathing deeply that the epigastrium does not appear to move as far as it feels to them. They can see this when I breathe as well as when they look in the mirror or observe other students in the class. This approach is especially appealing to the student who is not career motivated but is studying voice as an avocation.

In a few cases the students have not been able to make their epigastriums move for psychological or physical reasons, so we have had to devise alternative methods of breathing. Most of the time these are based on movement in the lower rib cage. I teach the students to expand the rib cage during inhalation, and if the epigastrium does not move, the bottom of the rib cage will slowly sink inward. Through coordination of the lower rib cage with the lower back muscles the student may learn to control the diaphragm.

The best test for any method of respiration is, of course, how it helps the student to sing. The voice is such a complex and wonderful instrument, no single method is perfect for all singers. Teachers and students modify the general principles of singing to fit the students' needs. If the voice sounds free and supported, then the method of respiration must be valid.

2. Overdeveloped Muscles in Teenage Athletes

Some teenagers, especially boys, have already begun exercise programs to improve their physiques. Weightlifting and home gymnastics equipment have become a large part of the sports market. While these exercises may be useful in developing a trim body, they often lead to conditions which are inimical to singing.

A problem which I find rather prevalent is the overdevelopment of the abdominal muscles. One student who was the place kicker for the football team could hardly relax his respiratory muscles, another was the captain of the women's track team and primarily a jumper. The nonaerobic exercises, such as isotonics and weightlifting, tend to tighten and shorten the abdominal muscles so they resist the stretching to deep breathing. This development coupled with a reluctance to push the abdomen outward makes it difficult for me to teach a student respiration.

In teaching choruses or voice classes I have the students check one another in these exercises. I find that peer group acceptance is often a much stronger force than parent-teacher suggestions. In groups, students compete in the best sense of the word for posture and physique which are good and beautiful.

ADDITIONAL BREATHING EXERCISES

Besides the drills and vocalises used in the studio and practice room, there are several exercises which I recommend to my students to increase breath capacity and endurance. They are based on the aerobic principle of deep breathing and increased flow of blood. Exercises which require deep breathing help improve body circulation, promote good health, and inspire general wellbeing.

1. Jogging or Running

The student should have his physician's approval before beginning a program of vigorous exercises. If the student is in poor physical health, he should not begin with jogging or running but should start with body conditioning until he is able to run. Walking rapidly enough to require deep breathing is a good first exercise. When the student is physically able, some time should be set aside each week for vigorous jogging and running. The benefits to health are valuable even to nonsingers. Increased circulation and deep breathing remove impurities from the system that would not be expelled otherwise.

For the singer the increased endurance and breath capacity are often dramatic. He learns to breathe deeply, not in gasps, and he finds that abdominal breathing will give him the energy to jog long distances. I first begin by jogging one hundred steps, then walking one hundred, then jogging one hundred, and so on. In that manner the breathing is deep but not exhausted. After running hard I may have to breathe clavicularly for a minute or so, but then I breathe abdominally.

2. Wind Sprints

Professional athletes vary their running exercises between jogging and short, rapid runs called wind sprints. The latter are designed to increase lung capacity for short bursts of energy. They cause the runner to breathe clavicularly, which in turn helps to develop the stretched muscles which expand the rib cage. Wind sprints are quite vigorous and should only be attempted by singers in good physical condition.

3. Swimming

For general physical exertion there is probably no exercise as thorough as swimming. All the muscles are coordinated with rhythmic breathing, and there is a sense of dynamism which is exciting. The major problem with swimming for singers is getting water in the ears, nose, and sinuses. Even if the water is clean and clear, it may cause irritation to the mucous membranes. And chlorine treated water can be downright harmful and painful. As much as I enjoy swimming and appreciate its good effects, I prefer other exercises which avoid the high risk of infection.

4. Tennis, Volleyball, Etc.

Team games are excellent for developing breath capacity and endurance if they require running and vigorous movement. Even running to hit a tennis ball against the side of a building is good for singers. Many times exercises are more enjoyable if they involve several persons, whether they are team games or not.

The student will have to choose how violent a sport serves his purpose. Such games as hockey and football may be more dangerous than necessary for simply building the body. While some voice students are championship athletes, most singers consider the chance of losing their teeth or scarring their faces as too great in those sports.

Some team or group sports are fun and engender good fellowship but are not useful for respiration, such as golf or bowling. These games do not require vigorous deep breathing. Only those exercises or games which are aerobic will develop breath capacity and endurance.

5. Aerobic Exercises

The Canadian Air Force has published a booklet of exercises designed for persons of all ages and physical conditions which I recommend highly to my students. These exercise programs are arranged in logical order of difficulty to be followed for a period of weeks. As the student grows stronger, the exercises become more difficult. They may be done any time of the day or night alone or in groups, and require no equipment. They are excellent for students or teachers who have peculiar work schedules and habits. The booklet may be purchased at most book stores.

6. Relax the Neck

While this exercise may not be related to increased lung capacity, it is important to free flowing singing. The student sits with back straight, head and neck relaxed, chin on chest. He clasps his hands behind his head and lets the weight of the arms pull gently downward. He should not consciously press down but just let the weight of the shoulders and arms exert their force on the neck muscles. The student should stay in this position for approximately a minute. After a few seconds there may be a burning sensation in the neck as the muscles resist the weight of the arms, but it is not unusual or harmful. The stinging disappears when the neck muscles relax and stretch. Then there is a feeling of release of nervous tension, relaxation in the neck and shoulders, and muscular freedom which will contribute to good singing.

HELPFUL SPORTS ANALOGIES

1. Coordinated Breathing

As in most aerobic sports and gymnastics, singing requires coordinated breathing. The breath must be in the rhythm and tempo of the activity. It should not be locked in. Singing with the breath uncoordinated or locked in would be like playing tennis or swimming without breathing at all.

2. Muscular Tensions Work Together

A truism in singing is that there should be "no tension." But what we really mean, of course, is that there should be no unnecessary tensions that do not help the singer. As in athletics, our muscles of singing oppose one another. No set of muscles works independently of the muscles around it.

Some muscles are meant to stay set. Others are tense but moving, like the mainspring of a watch, applying pressure as they relax or uncoil. Just before dashing away from the starting blocks, the track star's muscles are tense and ready. At the sound of the starter's gun, his muscles spring into action. So it is with the singer. He waits for the appointed time in the music, muscles ready to move. When the moment arrives, his muscles move into action, and he begins to sing.

3. Throwing or Swinging

There are three parts to throwing a ball or swinging a club successfully: preparation, attack, and follow-through. In respiration the inhalation is the backswing or preparation. The force and distance of this motion is requisite to the amount of energy necessary for the attack. Just as the backswing is different for driving, chipping, or putting a golf ball, so the preparation for singing a phrase depends on its length and volume level.

Exhalation is the attack—the throw or swing—in singing. This action requires control, coordination, and finesse and is the reason for studying. All the muscular strength, technical knowledge, and disciplined training are evidence here. This is the execution of the perfect bunt, the service ace, or the hole-in-one.

Just as important as the preparation and attack is what happens immediately afterward, that is, the follow-through. A common mistake in putting among student golfers is to stop the clubhead an inch or so past the point of impact. When this happens, the ball literally pops away from the club and goes flying across the green. The better way to putt is to follow through so the ball rolls smoothly.

In the same manner, stopping the tennis racket within a few inches after hitting the ball applies hardly any power to the stroke. The tennis player must continue the motion of the racket to insure a powerful, accurate shot.

As with these examples, a singer must follow through with the breath so there is an harmonious, accurate release of the tone. Stopping the breath within inches of the end of the sound causes the tone to lurch or wrench violently. Not only does this make for poor audience enjoyment, but it also places the singer in an awkward position to begin the next preparation. The matters of attacks and releases will be discussed more fully in the chapter on phonation.

4. Shouting or Leading Cheers

While I do not recommend shouting or leading cheers to my students, there are analogies here which apply to singing. First, the student cannot imagine shouting without using breath support and flow. Locked breath muscles would make shouting impossible. Also, the shout at a game is accompanied by a rapid, radical movement, such as pounding a neighbor on the back, waving the hands or fists in the air, and so forth. These muscles must be coordinated with and prepared by the breath just as in singing.

A perfect example of coordination of breath and phonation is in the cheer leaders. These exuberant, shouting gymnasts must prepare their materials as carefully and train their bodies as well as the team for which they are shouting. A cheer leader in poor health or with uncoordinated actions would inspire only sympathy for the team. Just so, a singer must appear healthy, ready, and energetic to invoke the most enthusiastic audience response.

OTHER USEFUL ANALOGIES

1. Violin Bow

Practically every student has seen a violinist play. Sometimes he draws the bow rapidly across the strings, sometimes slowly.

Sometimes several notes are played with one stroke of the bow. Or there might be only one note per stroke. The action of the bow fits the demands of the phrase.

The breath may be compared to the action of the violin bow. Sometimes the breath must flow rapidly, sometimes slowly. At times there are only a few notes, perhaps even one, in a breath span. Other times there are many notes. The fluidity with which the violinist draws the bow across the strings illustrates the smoothness with which a singer releases his breath. Whether the phrase is long or short, fast or slow, the pressure of the breath is smooth and the flow is steady.

Also, not every inch of the bow is used in each phrase. Sometimes only a small part of the bow is needed for a short motive or the upbeat into a longer phrase. Similarly, not every ounce of air or vital capacity is used on every phrase. At times only a small breath is needed, so the singer inhales just the requisite amount of air.

A common error among young singers, especially in choral groups, is to inhale a lungful of air and expend it as slowly as possible for as long as possible. They pause for breath at the most unlikely places, split polysyllabic words and prepositional phrases, and sing through grammatic and syntactic pauses, depending on each one's breath capacity. The analogy of the violinist's bow demonstrates the fallacy of such breathing.

2. Taffy Pull

I like to compare respiration to pulling taffy. There is resistance involved, but the action is smoothly and evenly expansive. There is no rebound in pulling taffy, just a slow relaxation of the materials when the pressure is released. In the same manner the respiratory muscles expand smoothly and evenly with a feeling of support, but the lungs do not snap like an inner tube, nor the epigastrium bounce like a rubber ball. Rather they relax slowly when the pressure of breath support is relieved.

There is no contradiction between the concept of singing on the rebound of the breath and the analogy of pulling taffy. In the former the idea is that the breath rebounds slowly, that is, at the same speed it went into the lungs. In the latter analogy the idea is that breath support is smooth, moving tension which does not snap back when released. The taffy pulling analogy illustrates breath support for long notes, slurs, crescendos, and decrescendos.

3. Balloon

Air may be released simply by opening the neck. There is no need to squeeze the balloon. In the same manner, air will flow from the lungs without pushing or squeezing. While the analogy is not all inclusive, because the lungs do not have the elasticity of a balloon, it has a limited use in explaining singing as the controlled release of air. Also, balloons have buoyancy and lightness, which is indicative of the proper feeling of breathing to sing.

Now that we have looked at the first element of singing, respiration, we will see how it relates to the next element, phonation or making a vocal sound.

3

HOW TO MAKE
THE PROPER SOUND:
Principles, Techniques and Exercises

As the vibrator of the vocal mechanism, the vocal bands serve several functions—making pitches, furnishing the rudimentary timbre, and possibly initiating the vibrato. Without the vocal bands there would be no sound with which to work. Considering that the original purpose of the vocal bands is to close the glottis to protect the lungs from foreign matter, it is nothing short of amazing that all the beauty and usefulness of the human voice depends on these two combinations of muscle and ligament a little more than a half-inch long.

MAKING PITCHES FOR SINGING

The vocal bands are not inert materials to be shaped or stretched, but are themselves sets of muscles and ligament which share in quite a complex action when pitches are sounded. As the breath flows from the trachea through the larynx, the vocal bands close and open in wave-like motions. Sometimes the opening and closing motions are like scissors; sometimes like clapping hands. However, the significance of these differences and their correlation to singing has not been established. Since the mechanism of the voice has been so well described in many books on vocal pedagogy, there is no need to go into great detail here. I shall confine myself to a few analogies which have been helpful in teaching the proper function of the vocal bands.

Rubber Band Analogy

The vocal bands can be compared to common rubber bands found in every office and home. The farther they are stretched, the thinner the bands become, and the higher the pitch they emit when plucked. When the tension is released, the bands return to their primary shape and size. Also, the larger rubber bands produce lower ranges of pitches, while the smaller bands produce higher pitches. Further, the texture of the rubber bands influences the quality of sound produced. (See Illustration 3.1.)

The vocal bands are not struck or plucked to produce sounds, but phonation involves their being stretched and shaped by various laryngeal muscles. The pitch of a vocal tone equals the cycles or

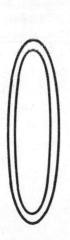

Rubber band	Same rubber band	Same rubber band, partial
Low tension	High tension	Medium tension
Thick	Thinner and longer	Thin and short
Low pitches	Higher pitches	Highest pitches

Illustration 3.1

fluctuations per second of the vocal bands, that is, to sound the A above middle C the bands must vibrate 440 times per second. The longer the vocal band is stretched, the thinner it becomes, and the higher the pitch produced in the larynx. The lowest part of the range is produced by short, thick bands. The middle voice is produced by stretching and thinning the bands. The high voice may be phonated either by a section of the bands which is short and broad or long and thin, depending on the timbre required. Men's vocal bands make lower pitches because they are larger than women's. Basses' vocal bands are larger than tenors', altos' larger than sopranos', and so on.

Also, the texture of the vocal bands influences the quality of the voice. Very supple bands which allow a great flow of breath through the glottis produce smooth, mellow sounds. Stiffer bands which resist the breath pressure allow less air in the sound and produce firm, ringing sounds. The combination of shape, size, and tension controls pitch and timbre. Because the vocal bands move in such complex ways there is an enormous number of shapes, sizes, and timbres possible within a single voice.

The Balloon Analogy

The vocal bands act much like the neck of a balloon when air is escaping. The loose edges of the neck flutter rapidly, and sound is produced by its alternate opening and closing action. The escaping air draws the folds of the balloon's neck together by alternately increased and decreased air pressure above and below the lips of the balloon, and the sound is caused by the interruption of the flow of air rather than the mechanical rubbing together of the lips.

The larger the opening of the balloon, the slower the fluctuations, and the lower the pitches emitted. Conversely, the smaller the opening, the faster the fluctuations, and the higher the pitches. Also, the pitches may be varied in the balloon by pulling the neck of the balloon into different shapes and sizes.

As with the balloon, the vocal bands are activated by the passage of air through the glottis. The flow of air pulls the bands together, and the alternate increase and decrease in pressure above and below the vocal bands opens and closes them rapidly. It is this interruption of the air flow which produces the sound, not the physical rubbing together of the bands or the friction of the air across them.

The Fire Siren Analogy

At first the analogy between a fire siren and the voice seems farfetched, but I have found it to be helpful in dispelling the idea that the vocal bands produce sounds in the manner of a violin string or other mechanical way. The fire siren operates strictly on the interruption of an airstream.

Two perforated rotating discs are connected in such a way that their holes coincide. As long as the discs are still (or move at the same speed), air will pass through the holes silently. But if one of the discs begins to move (or they move at different speeds), the air flow is interrupted, and a sound is heard. The faster the siren moves, the faster the interruption, and the higher the pitch emitted. Just as important, too, is that the stronger the flow of air, the louder the sound.

Certainly, the vocal bands are not rotating discs, but the analogy is still useful. As with the siren, the sound of the voice is the result of interrupted airflow. The faster the interruption, the higher the pitch. And the stronger the airflow which is interrupted, the louder the sound produced. Strong breath pressure resisted by strong vocal bands produces an intense sound. That is why a supported tone is more intense than an unsupported one, and why a good tone requires more breath pressure than a poor one.

The Brass Instrument Analogy

Of all the orchestral instruments, the best analogies are with the brasses. The lips may be compared directly with the vocal bands—sometimes called vocal lips—and breath support and performance ranges are comparable. A proper sound on a brass instrument comes from coordinating lips, breath, and resonators. A colleague tells me that his brass students play vocal exercises at first to learn proper tone, embouchure, and so forth.

However, the tonal quality of a brass instrument depends on hard surfaces of fixed dimensions, so the player is confined to a narrower range of timbres than the singer. If the trumpet could be stretched or squeezed into different shapes and sizes as it was being played, it might have more of the scope of tonal colors which are possible in the human voice.

The Reed Instrument Analogy

Reed instruments produce sounds by interruption of airflow, but only the double reeds are strictly analogous to the voice. The two reeds move in opposite directions just as the vocal bands. Reeds do not move three-dimensionally, however, and are confined to a fixed size and shape. Reed players must cut each reed to the proper thickness and suppleness for the desired timbre.

The String Instrument Analogy

Some of the old masters compared the voice to string instruments, but they were mainly referring to the remarkable capability for shadings of dynamics, flexibility, and nuances. A string instrument is perhaps the closest competitor of the voice in its versatility, and many good analogies may be drawn between them. However, there is hardly any analogy in the production of tone. The string instrument is played through friction, and that is not a useful concept in teaching singing.

FURNISHING THE RUDIMENTARY TIMBRE

Just exactly why and how we are able to make our vocal bands move is still a mystery. We only know that if we want to make a sound, we can. We teach a child to speak simply by encouraging him to imitate our sounds. He tries his best to please us, and the resultant sounds slowly become intelligible words. We reward the child so he continues to try to make the sounds we want to hear. He calls upon a hidden process which has become known over the years as "the will to phonate."

It is the same with teaching singing. In encouraging the student to make various qualities of sound, we must cope with the same hidden process. The student cannot feel his vocal bands as he does his rib cage, and if we call too much attention to the student's throat, he closes it reflexively. Thus, there are so few direct methods of approaching this element of singing we are compelled to teach through symbols, imitation, and reward.

Excite the Imagination

We teach a child to talk by exciting his imagination. Rather than going through a lengthy explanation of breath and muscles, we merely ask him to say "mama" or "daddy," and he responds the best he can.

The famous mimic Rich Little once explained that before he can imitate a celebrity he has to imagine what it would be like to speak in ways other than his own native voice. When he mimics John Wayne, he has to imagine first what it would be like for him to sound like John Wayne. Later he begins to make adjustments of the tongue and mouth to refine his act, but he begins by using his imagination.

Voice students proceed in much the same manner. They use their imaginations which have been excited to conceive what it would be like to sound differently. The result is not always what they expect, but the teacher is there to guide them in judging the worth of those results. We tell them the next step to take and begin to suggest adjustments in the vocal mechanism which will refine their singing. The most difficult students are those whose imaginations cannot be excited or who cannot accept the results of that excitement.

A few years ago I was teaching Beethoven's "In questa tomba oscura" to a young baritone named Bill, and try as he might he could not grasp what it would be like to sing with a full, rich sound. One day I asked him to show me how the song would sound if another student, a big bass named Woody, sang it. The result was astounding to both of us. Bill showed a voice he had never used before. So I asked him, "Bill, why don't you sing like that all the time?" To which he answered, "Because that's Woody's voice!" Sad to say, I could never convince him that the fuller, richer sound was really his voice because it came from his body.

How to Coordinate Phonation with Breath

Breath furnishes the impetus for the sound. After the student learns proper breathing, he must learn how the breath is used. The open throat, lowered larynx, and so forth mentioned in the previous chapter must now be related to the production of sound. The sound produced by the "will to phonate" is intensified through breath support, becomes richer because the larynx is lowered, and so on. As I said earlier, the breathing exercises which involve phonation, e.g., whimpering, sighing, and delighted surprise, are an excellent way to begin the coordination of breath and sound. Later in the chapter there will be specific exercises to deal with this more extensively.

Controlling Breath Flow and Pressure

Making the proper sound depends on controlling the breath as it escapes. The support muscles are directly related to the vocal bands as they provide pressure and control the airflow through the glottis. Breath pressure and flow influence timbre as well as intensity in the tone.

There seems to be a direct connection between the tension on the abdominal muscles and the consistency of the vocal bands. When a great deal of pressure is applied to the abdominal muscles, the bands become stiff and resist the resultant air pressure. The wave-like motion of the bands is quite vigorous, and the sound becomes harder and louder. On the other hand, when the abdominal muscles are relatively relaxed, the vocal bands also relax, and air flows out more rapidly. In this case the sound is mellow and soft. If the bands resist the air pressure too strenuously, the sound becomes strident and harsh. If the bands are too limpid and let too much air through, the sound is weak and breathy. Thus the student has to learn the coordination of breath pressure and flow.

Illustrations 3.2 and 3.3 show the effects of the consistency of the vocal bands coordinated with low and high rates of breath flow.

Cross Section of the Vocal Bands

Direction of airflow

LOW RANGE

Dramatic Sound	Mellow Sound
1. Consistency of vocal bands	1. Consistency of vocal bands
a. Thick	a. Thick
b. Stiff	b. Supple
2. Rate of breath flow	2. Rate of breath flow
a. Tense abdomen	a. Relaxed abdomen
b. Medium breath flow	b. Great breath flow
3. Quality of sound	3. Quality of sound
a. High intensity	a. Low intensity
b. Many overtones	b. Fewer overtones

Illustration 3.2

Cross Section of the Vocal Bands

Direction of airflow

HIGH RANGE

Dramatic Sound	Flute-like Sound
1. Consistency of vocal bands	1. Consistency of vocal bands
a. Thin	a. Thin
b. Stiff	b. Supple
2. Rate of breath flow	2. Rate of breath flow
a. Tense abdomen	a. Relaxed abdomen
b. Low breath flow	b. More breath flow
3. Quality of sound	3. Quality of sound
a. High intensity	a. Less intensity
b. Several overtones	b. Few overtones

Illustration 3.3

I find that students grasp changes in abdominal pressure as a concept and a physical fact. I ask for more support and abdominal tension without mentioning the concurrent stiffening of the vocal bands, which is below their level of consciousness. However, if I wish them to have more breath flow, I ask for the abdominal muscles to relax a bit and for them to feel a "cushion of air" between the vocal bands. The main thing in both cases is to see that the airflow is sufficient no matter how tense the abdominal muscles are.

Controlling Vibrato

Vibrato is the fluctuation of pitch, intensity, and timbre inherent in trained, mature voices. As the why and how of making a sound are mysteries, so is the origin of the vibrato. The control of the vibrato appears to lie in the breathing muscles, just as does the control of timbre. Therefore, remedying unruly vibratos must begin with mastery of good breathing.

Tremolo and wobble. The vibrato rate may vary from about

four to eight cycles per second and still be considered in good taste. The pitch variance should be evenly divided above and below a central pitch and encompass no more than a third of a tone. The overall effect of the vibrato should be of stability and evenness. When the vibrato is too fast and uneven, it is called a tremolo. When the vibrato is too slow and the pitch variance too great, it is called a wobble.

Tremolos and wobbles, as varieties of vibrato, are susceptible to the training and control of the abdominal muscles, as mentioned above. The better the abdominal muscles work together, the better the support, and the more acceptable the vibrato. I almost never mention a vibrato problem to a student, or he might become preoccupied with it. We work on breathing exercises, and the vibrato problem solves itself. While the trained professional singer can consciously control his vibrato rate with good effect, I believe the student should not try.

MAKING A GOOD SOUND

Making a good sound requires three actions: attack, sustain, and release. These are analogous to the backswing, stroke, and follow-through of a golf shot, tennis service, or any of a number of sports actions. Muscles must be in motion to make a good sound. While the three actions are coordinated into one smooth effort, they may be separated in order to be studied and improved.

Attack

Probably "attack" is too strong a word to describe the release of air through the glottis, but since it has become accepted I will use it here. Vowel attacks are the most difficult, so I shall begin with them. Consonants will be dealt with later.

On the Breath

In the preceding chapter I explained the attack on the breath or on the rebound of the breath. Until the latter part of the nineteenth century most teachers accepted this Italian approach to vowel attacks. After several years of controversy the attack on the breath is once again considered the best way to begin a vocal tone. The following vocalises are designed to teach a legato vowel attack on the breath.

How to Attack on the Breath

1. Begin by saying "mame-mame-mame-mame-mame."
Keep the sound of the vowel constant. Do not let the lips close so
tightly that pressure builds up in the mouth or throat. There
should be no cessation of sound. The humming feeling of the "m"
starts the vocal bands vibrating gently, then the mouth opens to
"ay." This vocalise should be said and sung as if there were one
long "ay" sound slightly interrupted by a series of "m's."

Continue by singing the vocalises in Illustration 3.4

Practice singing the "mame" attack until it begins to feel like
"ame-ame-ame-ame-ame," without stopping the vowel sound.
These latter attacks should be on the breath. By imagining the
initial hum or "m" the student prepares his vocal bands for the
correct pitch and vowel as he inhales.

Each of these vocalises includes a written rest which is important as the release of one series and the beginning of the next.

Illustration 3.4

2. Change the exercise to "bay-bay-bay-bay-bay." Be sure no
pressure builds up in the mouth or throat. The "b" should not
explode. Next, try "babe-babe-babe-babe-babe." There will be a
slight buildup of pressure, but only in the front of the mouth, and it
should not stop the sound completely. Try alternating "babe-babe"
with "bay-bay" to feel the real legato in the latter. (See Illustration
3.5.)

3. New vowels may be substituted in the vocalise according o
the student's needs. Female students may find "mom-mom-mom-

Bay, bay, bay, bay,   bay.
Babe, babe, babe, babe,   babe.
Abe, abe, abe, abe,   abe.

Illustration 3.5

mom-mom" and "bah-bah-bah-bah-bah" easier in the upper voice. The principles of the vocalises are the same.

4. Similar vocalises which may be substituted for variety are "nay-nay-nay-nay-nay" and "nah-nah-nah-nah-nah" for "may" and "mah," and "day-day" and "dah-dah" for "bay" and "bah."

5. Change to "zay-zay-zay-zay-zay" and "zah-zah-zah-zah-zah." The voiced "z" starts the vocal bands buzzing in a somewhat different way from "m" and "n." The "z" should be sung on the same pitch and at the same intensity as the "ay" and "ah."

Aspirated Attack

Sometimes it is preferable to begin a tone with a strong pulse of the diaphragm, that is, with an "h." Such staccato attacks teach coordination of the breath and phonation, because the student must begin the tone with breath. This sort of exercise is good for teaching girls the proper approach to the low register. Lots of breath before the tone assures one that the vocal bands will be free to function as they should.

In staccato exercises the student should feel a slight pulse in and out in the epigastrium. There should be more movement on the open vowels than the closed. It is sometimes necessary to think of a small inhalation between each syllable, but eventually this should disappear. Staccato vocalises are sung on only one breath, just as the legato.

Staccato Exercises

The first staccato exercise is usually "he-he-he-he-he," as shown in Illustration 3.6. "He" is easier to phonate than the other vowels, so I use it and gradually open the sound to "hay" without the long diphthong.

He   he   he   he   he____.
Hay   hay   hay   hay   hay____.

Illustration 3.6

Exercise 1. The vowel should be clear. The student should precede each attack with a slight bit of breath. Proceed slowly at first so the student has time to plan each attack. Place one hand on the epigastrium immediately below the sternum to feel the pulse of breath.

Exercise 2. Change the vocalise to "ha." Again the vowel should be clear. Speed of execution will come with facility. The student should not become impatient and hurry too fast.

Exercise 3. The best staccato vocalise is "hip-hip-hip-hip-hip" (Illustration 3.7). It is also the most difficult because of the back pressure from the "p." The vocalise should not become "pip-pip," which is much easier. The final note may be staccato or legato, as the teacher wishes.

Hip   hip   hip   hip   hip.
Ha   ha   ha   ha   ha____.

Illustration 3.7

Exercise 4. These vocalises may be sung on "haw" and "ho," following the same procedures as above. The "ho" should be executed without the long diphthong. The dark vowels are apt to be less effective in vocal training than the bright, especially "hoo," which I never use.

Perhaps the student could begin with the aspirated attack and move to the attack on the breath by constantly reducing the strength of the abdominal pulse. This would prevent the "h" be-

coming a crutch in his singing, which would disturb his concept of a
legato line. Under optimum conditions the "h" should be silent and
be used only for the initial attack.

Legato-Staccato Exercises

Exercise 1. Omit the "h" from the attack (Illustration 3.8).
There will still be a pulsation in the epigastrium, but it will be
lighter than before. There is still the feeling that air precedes the
vowel, but the vocalise is sung on one breath. Each tone is separate and distinct from the others. This vocalise is especially useful
for sopranos who sing ornamented coloratura pieces. The breath
should be broader and not so deep as in legato singing. Some
singers feel that the breath pressure is exerted in the thorax above
the diaphragm in light staccato and legato-staccato singing.

Illustration 3.8

Exercise 2. The sensation of this vocalise (Illustration 3.9) has
been described as a chuckle or light laugh. The best vowel is "ah"
for men and women alike. The notation may be as shown in the
preceding vocalise or as that below. The musical period and the
composer's style determine the kind of notation used to indicate
this effect.

Glottal Attack

In some instances it is necessary to separate vowels with a
light glottal plosive executed on the breath. Examples of such
instances are "he is," "you are," "I am," and so on. The practice of
inserting consonants between the syllables should be avoided, such

Illustration 3.9

as, "you war" and "I yam." Students should separate vowels like these in the manner of the legato-staccato vocalises above.

An extreme example of the glottal attack may be executed by closing the glottis tightly by pulling the vocal bands together as if swallowing or swimming under water, then forcing air through the bands with an audible click. This harsh approach to singing might justly be called an attack because of the vigorous use of the vocal bands. The widespread use of such an attack seems to have originated in a misunderstanding of Manuel Garcia's term *coup de glotte*. In French the word *coup* may mean a stroke of the hand or a blow of the fist, and the term was used for some fifty years before Garcia explained himself. It now appears he meant an attack on the breath, a "stroke of the glottis" rather than a "shock of the glottis." Only in rare instances is such a harsh attack necessary for dramatic purposes. Large groups of choristers as well as soloists may learn the more artistic attack on the breath.

Consonant Attacks

Most of the vocalises above begin with consonants which help the vocal bands phonate. In learning the various vowel attacks the student is also learning a limited number of consonant attacks. The other consonants and their exercises can be found in the chapter on articulation.

SUSTAINING THE TONE

The very heart of singing is the ability to sustain the tone, the art of *sostenuto*. A flowing, ringing sound is the reason the singer

studies. The best sustained tone is resonant, free, and is based on
the characteristics of humming. This is the so-called "buzz in the
masque." One of the best nonvocal examples of a sustained tone is
the bowing technique of violinist Jascha Heifetz. It is virtually
impossible to tell when this great artist changes from upbow to
downbow without looking.

Sustaining a tone is analogous to a pingpong ball suspended on
a vertical stream from a bubbling fountain. The lively ball dances
around effortlessly. The point of the analogy, of course, is that the
stream of water is not trying to push the pingpong ball in a particular direction or "to the back wall."

Wave-Like Motion

A sustained tone is like a small wave or the ripples on a pond.
There is free and effortless motion which has life and energy in
such a tone. A straight tone may be sustained, but it sounds driven
and lifeless. The ripples are analogous to the vibrato in an
energized sound. I find the vocalise in Illustration 3.10 effective in
teaching this concept.

The student thinks the upper set of notes while singing the
lower set. It may help to sing the upper notes once or twice to get a

Illustration 3.10

feeling of the internal motion of a sustained tone. The student begins in the best area of his voice and on the best vowel he can sing to learn the art of sostenuto. He raises and lowers the pitch of the vocalise by half-steps, maintaining his best vowel. After he has achieved a good sustained tone, he may change vowels, probably to his next best, and begin the process again.

HOW TO MOVE FROM NOTE TO NOTE SMOOTHLY

A companion concept to the sostenuto is the legato line. Notes must be connected so closely and changed so smoothly that there are no stops or spaces between them. A legato sostenuto may be compared to connecting dots by tracing lines between them to draw a picture. The spaces between the dots is filled completely. The end result is a comprehensible unit.

Series of Short Notes Tied Together

A line on a chalkboard may be seen as a series of dots so close together one cannot see the spaces between them. A long note is a series of components so close together there is no audible space between them. And a legato sostenuto line is a series of long (or short) notes with no spaces between them. Thus the concept of a sustained tone is extended to include slurs, portamentos, and glissandos.

Legato Sostenuto Exercises

The vocalise (Illustration 3.11) should be executed without breaks between the long notes or a feeling of a new attack as the notes move. The connection should be smooth.

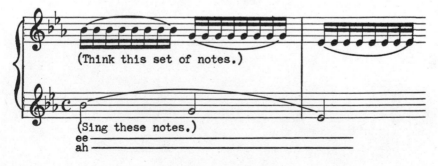

Illustration 3.11

Large intervals may be easier to negotiate slurred together than half-steps and whole-steps (Illustration 3.12). The vowels here have been successful in these vocalises, but the choice of vowels depends on the singer. Each of these exercises should begin with his best vowel. The suggested combinations have also been successful with my students.

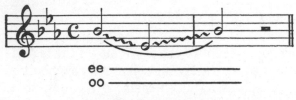

Illustration 3.12

The glissando marks may have to be overdone at first to give the student an idea how much slur or portamento is possible within the bounds of good taste. Most students think slurring is inartistic and therefore fail to connect the notes well. The modification of the "ee" to "ay" on the high note helps the student to open his mouth and to keep the throat open (Illustration 3.13). A more complete explanation of vowel modification may be found in the chapter on vowels.

Illustration 3.13

As the student improves his ability to connect widely spaced intervals, he begins to attempt narrower ones (Illustration 3.14).

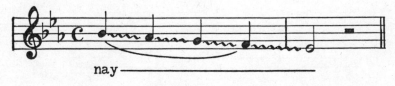

Illustration 3.14

Here again the execution of the glissando may have to be overdone to avoid the clicks and stops in some students' voices.

Gradually the note values may become shorter and faster as the student gains facility in legato phrasing. The execution of this vocalise (Illustration 3.15) is different from the legato-staccato above. Here there is no pulsation in the epigastrium, but rather a constant, slight pressure outward. The lower abdomen tucks in a bit during such a phrase.

oh ——————————————
ay ——————————————

Illustration 3.15

This vocalise (Illustration 3.16) combines the diatonic scale with intervals into a rather difficult exercise. There will be a tendency to click on the descending thirds because of the release of tension on the vocal bands. The successful execution of this vocalise should give the student a feeling of accomplishment.

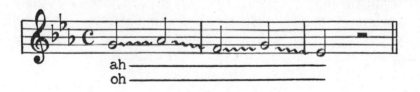

ah ——————————————
oh ——————————————

Illustration 3.16

The vocalise (Illustration 3.17) may present some difficulty because of beginning on a fairly low note and being based on an ascending chromatic scale. It is a bit easier to sing on a hum at first, then one of the dark vowels. The exercise not only helps develop a smooth line in the voice but is effective in teaching the chromatic scale.

Illustration 3.17

HOW TO RELEASE THE TONE

Just as important as a good attack and legato sostenuto is the release of the tone. A vowel release should be smooth and give the effect of the tone continuing, as if echoed. The best way to do this is to let the vocal bands open to release the tone. Air passes between the bands as they open and relax.

Inhale to Release

I prefer the bands to open on an inhalation because it prepares the throat for the next phrase. The breath which releases the end of one phrase is coordinated with the beginning of the next. Admittedly, this is not easy to do at first, but in the long run it is a most effective way to release a vowel.

Inhalation Release Procedure

1. Sing a long tone. At the end of the note diminish volume.
2. Quickly release pressure and inhale.
3. Avoid a pressurized crescendo while holding the tone. Sing a balanced, easy tone which is carried by resonance.
4. Indicate to student by holding hands together lightly in front and away from the body, thumbs up.
5. Release quickly, moving hands up and away while inhaling.

Applied to Choral Release

1. Hold last tone with conductor's hands steady and quiet.
2. At release describe a small arc with hands and release tension in forearms by relaxing hands; hands may rise or drop quietly after release.
3. May be executed with or without baton.
4. Ending a phrase by squeezing the fingers into a fist indicates a harsh glottal release. Closing the throat increases tension rather than releasing it.

Exhale to Release

It is sometimes as feasible to release the tone by letting the bands relax and the air continue to exhale silently through the glottis. This produces practically the same effect as inhaling to release and is a bit easier to learn. Exhaling to release works quite well at the end of a phrase before a rest. The drawback is that the air is moving in the wrong direction for the next phrase. The singer must stop exhaling and begin inhaling before he is ready to sing again. The exhaled release is preferable, however, to the glottal stop.

Glottal Stop

Some students imagine that their throats should close before the tone will stop. Thus they squeeze their vocal bands together at the end of the phrase. This produces several poor results, e.g., change of vocal color, change of vowel, lack of echo, and a potential for throat injury if practiced over a long period of time.

Incorporate Attack—Sustain—Release in Each Exercise

We may separate the three actions in order to study them, but a good vocalise includes them all. The student learns preparation, stroke, and follow-through every time he sings and integrates his breath into the process of making beautiful sounds.

As with the attack, these explanations have to do mainly with vowel releases. A discussion of consonant releases may be found in the chapter on articulation.

PROBLEMS AND SOLUTIONS

At the root of many problems of singing is the student's concept of singing. Depending upon his model, the student may shout or croon. He does not understand which muscles should work and which should relax. Helping a student develop a good concept of singing is often half the teacher's battle. Besides the inherent concept of singing, there are several conditions or problems centered in the area of the larynx for which the following remedies are suggested.

HOW TO DEAL WITH BREATHINESS

Breathiness is caused by the improper approximation of the vocal bands. As I said, the bands meet each other three-dimensionally, closing from back to front and from bottom to top, then opening from back to front and from bottom to top in a wave-like motion. As this complex action occurs, some adjacent portion of the bands may not arrive at the midpoint of the glottis at the same time, so they do not meet.

Inherent in Youth

An excess of air in the tone is inherent in many young voices because all their laryngeal muscles do not develop at the same rate. The muscles inside the larynx suddenly and dramatically outgrow those outside the larynx. Therefore, a young singer may not be able to coordinate the muscles which make his vocal bands close properly. Such improper approximation of the bands will disappear with further maturity in most cases.

Weakness in the Vocal Bands

Breathiness may also be caused by weakness in the vocalis muscles. The bands fail to resist the breath pressure and allow breath to escape without producing sound. When I taught in the South, I found quite a number of women who were reared to think that a quiet, breathy sound was more genteel. Thus the vocalis muscles had never developed to their potential. Of course, this phenomenon is not the product of only one region.

Improper Concept of Sound

This is different from an improper concept of singing. Here the student has a vowel or timbre in his mind's ear which does not match the others. It does not ring and is breathy, but he cannot hear it well. He has to learn how to hear the "line" in a series of equalized vowels which are based on a homogeneous approach.

Swollen Vocal Bands

If the vocal bands are swollen from irritation of some kind, e.g., infection, allergies, or misuse, they often will not approximate properly. I ask new students if they have been to a physician if their voices are breathy or sound irritated. If they have not, I recommend a visit to the doctor so the student and I will know whether or not his vocal bands are swollen. If they are, the throat specialist should treat the problem before the student begins to sing seriously.

Vocal Nodules

Swollen vocal bands may eventually develop callouses or corns at points of greatest friction or abuse. These nodules, or nodes, must be treated by a throat specialist. Complete vocal rest may be called for, perhaps along with medication, until the callouses have subsided. In the most severe cases surgery may be indicated to remove the offensive tissue, but this is generally a last resort.

If the vocal nodules have been caused by misuse, the student should work with a speech therapist to overcome the habits which led to the development of the nodules. The real cure is to keep the nodes from recurring. The speech therapist will help the student understand the use of his voice better through a set of exercises which most likely will include humming and bright vowels. A colleague and I have had success relieving vocal nodules in conjunction with a throat specialist who treats a good many singers. The vocal bands themselves actually remove the nodules through their interaction and approximation.

EXERCISES

In dealing with an excessively breathy voice the following vocalises have proved effective:

1. Breathing exercises from Chapter 2.
2. Humming on any of the scales and arpeggios already shown, executed in the best area of the student's voice.
3. "Ming-ming-ming-ming-ming" and "mang-mang-mang-mang-mang" on any of the scales and arpeggios shown.
4. Bright vowels combined with "m" and "n" at first, though not too high on the closed "ee."
5. Bright vowels by themselves and with other consonants, especially the attack and release on the breath.
6. Staccato attacks on bright vowels.
7. Staccato-legato attacks after the breathiness begins to clear up.

An interesting example of treating breathiness through these exercises is the case of a folk singer who came to me for help after virtually losing her voice for some weeks. The malady began with an upper respiratory infection which involved the larynx. While she was running a fever and suffering from congestion and a sore throat, she continued to sing a series of concerts until her voice suddenly disappeared. She consulted a physician who recommended complete vocal rest for six to eight weeks, at the end of which time her voice was breathy and she was told that one of her vocal bands was partially paralyzed. Then she came to me to see if there were anything to be done to recover her voice. I found that most of her problem was an improper approach to singing, poor breathing habits, and a related dysfunction in the larynx. I had her begin with simple breathing exercises, then incorporate gentle phonation such as sighing, moaning, and so on. Then she began humming vocalises of three, four, and five notes in the middle of the voice. After a few weeks of breathing and humming exercises, she started to sing bright vowels. Before long she was singing simple songs without the former breathiness and with no discomfort in the throat. The last time I saw her before she left on a new concert tour she was singing well and had added several upper notes to her voice which had not been in her former repertory.

HOW TO DEAL WITH HOARSENESS OR HUSKINESS

Just as breathiness, hoarseness or husky sound may also be caused by swollen vocal bands, polyps, or nodules. Continually hoarse students should consult a physician. Many pathological conditions may require surgery, X-ray treatment, and so on. After such treatment the speech therapist and singing teacher can work together to help the student regain the use of his voice.

Stiffness of Vocal Bands

Sometimes the vocal bands do not function easily enough and are not supple enough to phonate properly. Perhaps the vocalis muscles are too stong for the opposing laryngeal muscles. For whatever reason, the bands are like stiff oboe reeds which need softening and thinning.

Too Low Breath Pressure

If the abdomen is too loose, not enough breath will flow, and the vocal bands will stiffen from lack of breath pressure. The teacher can demonstrate this by exhaling every ounce of air possible and trying to talk. In this case the student should breathe deeper, support more, and let more air through the vocal bands.

Exercises

These vocalises have been useful in reducing hoarseness caused by improper breathing and phonation, with no pathological involvement:

1. Breathing exercises from Chapter 2.
2. Slides, slurs, portamentos, and glissandos shown previously, coordinated with good breathing.
3. Humming as mentioned before to thin and soften the vocal bands.
4. Bright vowels as mentioned before.

HARSHNESS OR STRIDENCY

A harsh or strident sound is usually the result of driving the voice. It may also sound as if the tone is "sitting on the vocal bands." The strident tone is not breathy or hoarse, but it lacks life and buoyancy.

Too Little Breath Flow

This is different from too low breath pressure. In this case the rib cage may be expanded, but the abdomen is too tense and does not let the breath escape. There is plenty of breath pressure, so the bands stay taut, but there is not enough breath flow to make the bands vibrate.

Vocal Ligament Too Hard

The student may stiffen the leading edge of the vocal band—the thyroarytenoid ligament—to the point of producing an edgy sound. Perhaps he is trying to sound too mature or trying to develop the vocal "ring" too soon and too rapidly.

Tightly Squeezed Throat

In order to harden the vocal ligament, the student may squeeze the walls of the laryngopharynx. The sound is thus produced much like forcing toothpaste from a tube, or squeezing the end of the garden hose to make a stronger stream of water.

Stiff Walls of the Throat

If the laryngopharynx is not squeezed tightly, it may be stiffened to produce the same effect. The stiffening holds the vocal mechanism in place, producing a feeling of control, but the resultant tone is harsh and cramped. Sometimes the teacher is able to see the student's veins bulge in his neck when he stiffens the walls of the throat.

Stiffly Raised Tongue

In conjunction with a stiff throat the student may have a stiff tongue. The tongue is in its normal position with the tip forward, but it is raised, drawn back in the mouth, and is stiff. The suprahyoid muscles between the larynx and the point of the chin bulge and are quite stiff. The student can place his thumb on these muscles while they are at rest, and he will notice a distinct tension if these muscles are involved improperly in phonation. Again, this stiffness of the tongue offers the illusion of control, but the results are a strident, harsh tone.

Raised Larynx

The stiffened suprahyoid muscles pull the larynx into a high position. The pharynx is thus noticeably smaller, and the sound lacks the low overtones or "depth."

Stiff Velum

When so many parts of the vocal mechanism are tense, it is not unusual for the velum to stiffen by reflex action. Generally it stiffens in a lowered position in opposition to the raised larynx, causing a high degree of nasality.

Irregular Vibrato

Many strident sounds have irregular vibratos as well. Depending on the way the breath is applied to the vocal mechanism, the vibrato may be rapid and shallow like a bleating sheep, or it may be almost nonexistent, that is, a straight tone.

EXERCISES

Yawn Through the Nose

With the mouth partially open the student draws air through the nose and mouth at the same time—a kind of yawn through the nose. This helps relax the muscles of the pharynx and tongue. This exercise may be coupled with the other breathing exercises suggested earlier to loosen the vocal mechanism before the student sings.

Dark Vowel Vocalises

The best sounding "oh" and "oo" vowels require a raised velum, so they are helpful in dealing with a harsh tone. Besides those in the paragraph on legato sostenuto, these vocalises in Illustration 3.18 may be beneficial.

These exercises may start as high as E-flat or F to be sure the student's velum is in the natural raised position of the high register. They should be executed with a soft sound, perhaps even a bit breathy to the student's ear. The result may not be a finished concert sound at first, but after a while the student will notice a nice change in his timbre and a feeling of ease in his vocal production.

Illustration 3.18

Loose Tongue Exercises

The student rolls his tongue forward with the tip down behind the lower teeth. The blade of the tongue protrudes from the mouth, but there is no pressure on the teeth. This is not the tongue's singing posture, but indicates its position and movement.

Next the student says "ah-ee" several times, feeling the movement of the tongue forward and back. The jaw and lips should not move. After saying "ah-ee," he may sing it to the vocalise in Illustration 3.19.

Illustration 3.19

The combination of vowels may be sung to any of the scales and arpeggios shown earlier.

The student then may change to "oh-ee," first saying and then singing to the arpeggio above. The lips are rounded and do not change shapes as the tongue moves forward and back. Thus the "ee" becomes a mixed vowel similar to the German umlaut "ü," or the French "u."

Mechanical Tongue Movement

If the student has trouble saying or singing these vocalises without moving his lips or jaw, he may say or sing "ah" or "oh" while moving his tongue forward and back mechanically. This will show him that the frontal vowels are made with the tongue, not with the lips or jaw. Only in the case of a lazy tongue are the lips and jaw required to form the frontal pure vowels.

Companion Exercises

Companion exercises to the previous ones require the tongue to move in the opposite manner. The student says "ay-ah" several times without moving his mouth. The tongue may be a bit more clumsy in the front to back motion than in the back to front of "ah-ee." After saying this he may sing the vocalise in Illustration 3.20.

Then the student may change to "ay-oh." Again the "ay" is a mixed vowel when the lips are rounded, much like the German umlaut "ö" or the French "eu." If the student has trouble execut-

Ay – ah – ay – ah – – ay.

Illustration 3.20

ing these vocalises, he may say or sing "ah" or "oh" and move his tongue from front to back mechanically.

Loose Jaw Exercises

The best jaw loosening exercises are based on "yah." The initial "y" is actually a very short "i" or "ee" preceding the open-mouthed vowel. Thus it relates to the previous tongue exercises. The difference is that the jaw is made to open dramatically from the closed vowel position to the wide "ah."

The student places his fingertips on the chewing muscles which cover the jaw bone—the masseters—and says "yah-yah-yah-yah-yah" several times. Then he should close his teeth and squeeze the masseters as if chewing. Notice how much more the muscles bulge and how much stronger they are in chewing than in opening. Opening stretches the muscles. In order to open the mouth wide enough vertically for good singing, the student has to stretch the masseters beyond their usual length. For Europeans whose language requires an active jaw this is no problem, but for Americans who speak with closed jaws and clenched teeth there is some corrective work to be done.

After saying the "yah" exercise, the student may sing the vocalise in Illustration 3.21. There should be no breath between the syllables. Each attack is firm.

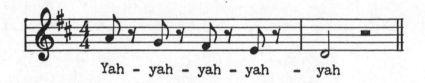

Yah - yah - yah - yah - yah

Illustration 3.21

Staccato-like exercises make the jaw open more quickly than legato. There is not the space between the notes of a true staccato, just the feeling.

The student may then sing:

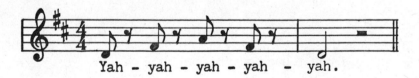

Yah - yah - yah - yah - yah.

This staccato may be alternated with the legato:

Yah-yah-yah-yah - yah.

A more vigorous jaw exercise is:

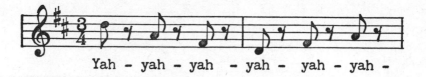

Yah - yah - yah - yah - yah - yah -

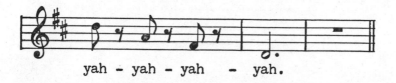

yah - yah - yah   - yah.

This may be alternated with the legato:

Yah-yah-yah - yah-yah - yah -
Yah —————— yah —————

yah-yah - yah - yah.
yah ——————— yah.

The vocalise above may combine the jaw exercise with a legato sostenuto vocalise which keeps the jaw open longer. Other examples of this sort of combination are in Illustrations 3.22 and 3.23. The latter may be sung two ways.

Yah — yah — yah — yah — yah

Illustration 3.22

Illustration 3.23

HOW TO CORRECT A MUFFLED OR SWALLOWED TONE

A muffled tone may aptly be called swallowed because the swallowing muscles have interfered with those of singing. Often this quality sounds better to the singer than an open tone because he hears the trapped sound better. The tone is also richer since it has fewer high overtones than a bright sound which is escaping. I speak to my students of singing the vowel in front of the tongue rather than behind it.

Tongue Forced Back and Down

In swallowing the tongue is pushed backward into the pharynx as three sets of constrictor muscles squeeze the pharynx. With the tongue forced back and down the epiglottis intrudes on the pharynx and becomes a muffling agent. Since we use them many times a day, the swallowing muscles are quite strong and may easily overcome the action of the inhaling muscles which lower the larynx but leave the tongue in a forward position.

This is somewhat different from the tongue position which causes a strident tone. In the swallowed tone the tongue is down in back and not so stiff.

Depressed Larynx

Usually the larynx rises during swallowing, but in this sort of phonation the tongue may also force the larynx into too low a position and block the passage of sound with the epiglottis. Also, the hyoid bone is often tipped awkwardly and held inflexible. In this unusual attitude the larynx is said to be depressed.

Velum High and Stiff

In swallowing the velum rises to prevent food entering the nasal cavity. Thus the velum may rise too high and become rigid when a tone is swallowed. It blocks too much of the nasopharynx and causes the tone to be stuffy or muffled.

Throat Too Small and Limp

With the tongue back and down the pharynx is difficult to expand. The walls of the laryngopharynx are left limp and flaccid, and the chamber is too small to be an optimum resonator.

Tongue Turned Up

A common fault in young baritones and basses is curling the tip of the tongue up to produce a darker sound. This position does not include all the associated problems of depressed larynx, high velum, and so on, so the tone may feel and sound free. Curling the tongue actually may widen the throat, thus producing a richer quality, but the upturned tongue blocks the passage to the outside.

EXERCISES

Flexible Tongue

Often the singer must look in a mirror to see whether the tongue is up or not, because he is used to feeling it in that position. To put the tongue in its proper place the singer may have to resort to a kind of overcompensation for a while. He may vocalize with the tongue lying relaxed on the lower lip. Sometimes he may have to hold his tongue by the tip to overcome poor habits.

The loose tongue exercises suggested earlier will help keep the tongue forward and out of the throat. The student may also sing a series based on "l," such as "lee-lee-lee-lee-lee," "lay-lay-lay-lay-lay," and "lah-lah-lah-lah-lah," to rapid scales and arpeggios. The tip of the tongue should move freely without backing up between each syllable. The effect is one long note on one vowel which is slightly interrupted by the up and down movement of the tongue just back of the incisors.

Dropped Jaw

The jaw exercises already mentioned will help the student who sings with a muffled or swallowed tone. The jaw may not be as much of a problem here as in the harsh sound. The student works for independence of jaw and tongue.

Velum Exercises

In order to articulate the nasal consonant "ng" the velum lowers to touch the upraised back of the tongue lightly. Thus vocalises which are based on "ng" and broad vowels should help lower the velum to a more normal position. The late Bert Lahr's comic exclamation "ng-ah, ng-ah, ng-ah" is a prime example of such a vocalise.

The student begins by saying the word "hang" or "hung" and elongates the final "ng." He feels the velum touch the back of the tongue. Then he says "hang-ah" or "hung-ah" and elongates the "ng" before opening the "ah" vowel. This shows him the up and down motion of the velum. Then he may sing the vocalise in Illustration 3.24.

The vocalise should not be executed too high because the velum rises naturally in the upper register, making the "ng" difficult to produce without laryngeal tension.

Other Exercises

1. Bright vowels as shown earlier, especially those combined with nasal consonants.
2. Humming vocalises, which help place the velum in its best position.

Illustration 3.24

HOW TO DEAL WITH A HOLLOW OR HOOTY QUALITY

The best analogy I have found to describe the hooty quality is that of a smoke ring. The tone has quality around the edges, but has no center or core. It also may be compared to the hoot of an owl or the moo of a cow. Therefore, vocalises based on fire sirens, owl hoots, and so forth, would be counterproductive here.

Lack of Vibrato

More than likely the student will sing without vibrato if he has a hollow quality. The vocal mechanism is not coordinated with the breath, so the tone is held straight. As I have said, when the other factors work right, the vibrato will cure itself.

Breath Pushed Out

If the student's concept of breathing is to push or squeeze the breath through the glottis, the bands may bow, and the result will be a hooty quality which will lack vibrato. In these cases the student will begin with proper breathing exercises. Then he will learn to coordinate the breath with phonation.

Lack of Ring

When the vocal bands are bowed, the tone produced lacks ring. Even with a well lowered larynx, the so-called singer's formant may be lacking. Perhaps the larynx is held in an unusual attitude by the inordinate air pressure and flow. In any event, all of the above aspects seem to go together.

EXERCISES

The following exercises may be helpful in remedying a hollow or hooty voice:

1. Breathing exercises, concentrating on relaxing the abdominal muscles during exhalation, sighing, etc.
2. Attack on the breath exercises, executed lightly and without strong thrust.
3. Humming lightly but clearly on scales and arpeggios.
4. Staccato exercises, maintaining clear vowels.

A graduate student came to me as a mezzo-soprano who was having difficulty finding a way to sing high notes, negotiate register changes, and sing consistently throughout her voice. Her tone was quite hooty, lacking ring and projection. Although she was in her fifth year of voice study, we began with fundamental breathing exercises, learning the attack on the breath, and trying to sing with a free, clear tone. Before long her voice became brighter with each new-found freedom, and her range began to extend upward. One day in a lesson everything seemed to be going well, so I decided to see just how high she might vocalize. We were both shocked and delighted to hear her vocalize to the E above high C, whereas the F-sharp at the top of the treble clef had been a struggle only a few weeks before. By the end of the school term my "mezzo" had become a real coloratura soprano and was singing somewhere every week.

OTHER PROBLEMS AND ANALOGIES

Overcautious Attack

Some students seem to be reluctant at the beginning of a phrase, either out of shyness or overcaution. Perhaps they do not wish to make a mistake. With these students I encourage a spontaneous reaction to the meaning of the text, such as stepping forward and throwing their arms out as they sing a phrase. In this way the attack is not overplanned, and the result is a pleasant surprise.

Hit the Ball, Then Look for It

A common problem for a golfer is not keeping his head down. He wants to look up to control the flight of the ball, and his body moves out of position as the clubhead meets the ball. If he keeps his head down until after the clubhead has struck the ball, he may not see the flight of the ball as well, but the chances are better that he will like the shot.

Flaccid Approach to Singing

Earlier I spoke of the concept of singing which was lackluster and croony. In encouraging students to sing with more energy and vitality, I always ask if they play a sport. With one student I was having a particularly difficult time getting the point across, so I asked what was his favorite sport. "Swimming," he answered. To which I replied, somewhat frustratedly, "I'll bet you float a lot!" Some years later I found he had told that story to several of his own students to make the same point.

Watch the Ball into Your Hands

For the student who fails to support throughout the phrase, I offer the analogy with the baseball player at shortstop who takes his eye off the ball before it gets to him. That player will probably miss the ball and muff the throw to first base. The end of a phrase is just as important as the beginning, and we reach the end successfully by continuously supporting the phrase.

Push the Door, Don't Hit It

For the student who finds it difficult to conceive of a coordinated release of breath through the glottis, I suggest this analogy. Hitting a door which is ajar will not close it. The door merely stands and trembles. Pushing the door closes it effectively with a minimum of effort. The force is applied evenly, smoothly, and directly, and the door closes. Likewise, the singer should move evenly, smoothly, and directly toward the end of the phrase. His body functions easily, the muscles respond evenly, and he sings smoothly.

In this chapter we have examined the element of phonation as a separate function, but in practice we cannot isolate phonation from resonance. Therefore, the next chapter should be seen as inseparable from this one in understanding the development of the singing voice.

4

DEVELOPING A RICH VOICE:
The Symbols and Psychology
of Resonance

The sound which emanates from the larynx is weak and consists mainly of a strong fundamental pitch and successively weaker overtones. It is resonance which enhances, strengthens, and beautifies the tone. As such, resonance is in many ways the most important element of singing. Unfortunately, it is the most difficult to teach.

We have no direct access to tuning the resonators. The changes we may make by direct control in the vocal tract are crude and practically valueless in adjusting a harmonic overtone series a few microtones up or down. Our ears are the only clue to resonance and timbre. Persons born deaf speak without a concept of the quality of the human voice.

Borrowed Symbols

The dilemma of teaching resonance gave rise to most of the symbolic and psychological pedagogy through which most of us were taught. Symbols were borrowed from the other senses, such as the "focussed" tone. As we could understand drawing the feathery edges of a spotlight into focus on a wall, we could comprehend the difference in a diffuse or breathy tone and one which was "focussed." Borrowing terms from our tactile sense gave us tones which were "warm or cold," "dark or bright," "heavy or light," and others.

Placement

Another even more vague concept is that of "placement." Since sounds are merely disturbances of air molecules, there is really nothing to place. But because the singer could feel secondary vibrations in various parts of his body while singing, his reliance on such feelings caused the notion of placing the tone in the chest and head. This led to a theory of "registers" which has become untenable in the light of modern research. I sometimes find "placement" to be a useful concept in teaching to explain the sympathetic vibrations in the masque. At the same time, I try to make sure the student understands the symbolic nature of the concept.

In the course of this chapter I shall try to relate some of the older pedagogical concepts of resonance to modern scientific research.

THE RESONATING SYSTEM

Before investigating ways to produce more and better resonance, perhaps it would be good to mention how the voice resonates. Most scholars are now agreed that vocal resonance is produced by vibrating air within chambers. There appears to be little significant vocal resonance produced by solid materials, e.g., bone, teeth, cartilage, palate, and so forth. These air chambers are able, within limits, to change shapes, sizes, and relationships with each other. There has been a great deal written about the acoustics of linked resonators of various shapes and sizes, so it is not necessary to discuss the subject at length here. Suffice it to say that the fundamental pitch phonated in the larynx is amplified, and various harmonic overtones are greatly strengthened, by the resonance chambers of the vocal tract. Vocal timbre is determined by the relative strengths and weaknesses of the reinforced overtones.

Natural Resonance

Resonators are set in motion by a primary vibrator. If they vibrate in tune with the fundamental pitch and overtones of their chamber, such vibration is called natural resonance. A good example is found in blowing across the top of an empty bottle. The resultant sound is the natural resonance based on the tuning of the bottle. The shape and size of the bottle control the pitch and timbre of the tone.

Forced Resonance

Resonators may also be induced to vibrate the pitch and overtones of a strong primary vibrator, no matter what the natural tuning. Such vibration is called forced resonance when the vibrator and resonator are not in tune. A tuning fork placed on the same open bottle mentioned above will force the bottle to vibrate at the fork's pitch. The bottle's resonation will amplify the sound of the fork. The sound will not last as long as if the fork were allowed to vibrate freely in the air, but it will be louder. If the tuning fork were either the same pitch or an overtone of the bottle, the sound would be even louder because the resonance would not be forced.

In the case of induced resonance the size and shape of the bottle will influence the timbre of the tone produced. A tuning fork or a tin whistle tuned to the same pitch will vibrate the bottle at the same frequency, but the timbres would be different. Timbre is the product of the vibrator and the resonator.

Vocal Resonance—Natural and Forced

The vocal sound is amplified and enhanced by both natural and forced resonances. The natural resonances of the vocal tract produce the various vowel sounds by assuming different shapes, sizes, and relationships (or ratios). They are vibrated into life by the action of the vocal bands. The musical pitches phonated by the vocal bands, however, seem to depend on a combination of natural and induced resonances in the vocal tract for their amplification. Tuning these two unrelated systems of resonance into beautiful singing is one of the major problems facing the singer and his teacher. The better in tune the laryngeal frequency and the resonators, the less the vocal resonance is forced and the freer the vocal tone.

The Pharynx

There are three main resonating chambers in the voice, the pharynx, oral cavity, and nasal cavity. The pharynx is divided into three parts, the laryngopharynx (the cavity just between the larynx and the hyoid bone), the oropharynx (the cavity above the hyoid bone and behind the faucial pillars), and the nasopharynx (the cavity behind the velum and below the nasal ports). The pharynx generally controls the lower frequencies of resonance, that is, the "warmth" or "depth" of the voice.

A smaller cavity within the vestibule of the larynx which may or may not influence the sound of the voice is the ventricle of Morgagni. The function of this cavity, between the vocal bands and the ventricular folds (the so-called false vocal bands), is still being debated by researchers.

The Oral Cavity

For purposes of studying vocal resonance the oral cavity is defined as that area of the mouth in front of the faucial pillars. There may be no division between the oral cavity and the oropharynx if the tongue is lying flat or is concave. The oral cavity generally controls the higher overtones of vowel resonance and musical pitches, that is, the "brilliance" of the voice (not to be confused with the "ring").

The oral cavity does not make tones but merely shapes and enhances them. Singers who have a concept of originating the tone in the mouth often defeat their own purposes. A better concept is that the mouth is a conduit through which the sound passes, being transformed into intelligible words along the way. This latter function will be covered in the chapter on articulation.

The Nasal Cavity

Of the three major resonators, the nasal cavity is the least important to good singing, but it may pose some of the knottiest problems for the teacher. There is even some doubt whether or not the nasal cavity is involved in singing. What we call nasal resonance may be controlled by the nasopharynx.

Nasal resonance, whatever its source, is controlled by the action of the velum. The lower the velum, the larger the nasopharynx, and the more nasality in the vocal sound. Conversely, the higher the velum, the smaller the nasopharynx, and the less nasality in the sound.

Most teachers agree there should be some nasal resonance in every singing tone, not just the nasal consonants. The concept of "hum in every tone" is based on that opinion. Although the velum is raised, it should not close the nasal ports or obliterate the nasopharynx. Such a velar position causes a stuffy or muffled sound. Rather, it should be high and forward to leave a small opening from the nasopharynx into the nasal chamber. The amount of nasal resonance in each sound is a matter for the teacher to determine.

Other Air Chambers

It is now fairly well accepted that the other air chambers of the chest and head are useless in the production of resonance. The maxillary and frontal sinuses or the ethmoid and sphenoid cells may vibrate in sympathy with the oral and nasal cavities, but their openings into the nasal cavity are too small to enhance the phonated sound. Feeling the sinuses vibrate may certainly be an indication to the singer of a properly resonated sound, but the small cranial cavities probably do not add to the sound which the audience hears.

The chest cavity, lungs, and bronchial tubes may also vibrate in sympathy with the laryngeal cartilages, but there is no source of egress for such vibrations. The trachea might offer some resonance to the phonated sound, but it is problematic. If it does, such resonance would be rather fixed because we cannot readily adjust the size and shape of the trachea. Thus, it would be a "given" which the teacher and singer would take for granted, rather than a malleable tool with which to work. Pragmatically, then, we can approach the teaching of resonance as if the trachea were not involved.

DESCRIPTION OF RESONANT SINGING

Recently a colleague of mine, a musicologist working on a description of oboe sounds, asked me about the terms used in vocal pedagogy to describe good singing. I explained that most of the terms were borrowed from our senses of sight and feeling, but he persisted until we reached some agreement as to understandable definitions based on the sense of hearing. As a result of his challenge, I have attempted here to describe a resonant sound and define it in aural terms.

Depth of Tone

We often speak of a resonant tone as having "depth." Synonymous with this are "full," "rich," "warm," and "dark." These terms have to do with the low harmonic overtones resonated in the pharynx. The larger the pharynx, the lower the overtones, and the more "depth" in the tone. We teach our students to sing with enlarged pharynges in order to achieve the quality of "depth."

Some vowel sounds are said to be "deeper" than others; "oh" has more depth than "ah," "oo" more than "oh," and so on. This aspect of depth is related to the overtone frequencies (or formants) which distinguish one vowel from another. The discussion of vowel formants in a later chapter will go further into this matter.

Sometimes we hear tones described as being "heavy" or having more or less "weight." Such terms can be confused with "depth," but weight in a tone has more to do with phonation than resonance. The size, shape, and consistency of the vocal bands control the amount of "weight," while the size and shape of the pharynx controls "depth." A good sound may have "depth" without being "weighty."

Brilliance or Brightness

When a voice contains a greatly reinforced series of high pitched overtones, it is said to be "brilliant," and is analogous to a bright light. In a "bright" voice the high pitched frequencies are paramount. Because high frequencies have more impact on our ears than low, they excite our emotions. The sounds of fear, panic, pain, and alarm are high pitched, so high frequencies in a voice stimulate us, and we describe their effects in terms of painful sight rather than comfortable feelings. Low frequencies in the voice lull us unless they are quite intense.

Projection

A complex system of high frequency overtones produces "brilliance" or "projection" in the voice. First, the overtones of the musical pitch are reinforced in a highly trained voice. Both the pharynx and oral cavity lend support to the weak high overtones of the fundamental pitch. Second, the frontal vowels resonate at very high frequencies, and the clearer or purer the vowel, the sharper the impact of these high formants. When the trained singer tunes the high frequencies of the vowel to those of the musical pitch, the sound "projects" extremely well.

There is a third high frequency in every good voice called the "ring" of the voice. This resonance occurs between 2800 and 3200 Hz, regardless of the sung pitch or vowel. In a sense this is an extra "singer's formant." The source of this "ring" is still debatable, but it seems to occur most in persons who sing with a lowered larynx, a high velum, and a great deal of power.

Spin

The metaphor of spinning may be related either to a child's top or a spinning wheel. The top spins freely, and by gyroscopic action stands alone without a visible source of power. A tone which "spins" is thus free, unencumbered, and unforced.

A spinning wheel produces a continuous string of thread, and it spins freely without jerks or halts in its action. A voice may also spin *un fil di voce*, a thread of voice, that is finely crafted and artfully used. Such a sound is free, unforced, and continuous.

"Spin" is also related to the vibrato, which is partially a function of the resonance system. I discussed the vibrato briefly in the previous chapter on phonation as it was related to the vocal bands. The vibrato further includes action by the laryngo pharynx in changing the vowel formant and timbre. "Spin" in the voice is the result of a vibrato evenly fluctuating above and below a central pitch and in and out of a central intensity and timbre. This aspect of "spin" gives the tone life and buoyancy.

As I have said earlier, vibrato is a combination of the functions of breathing, phonation, and resonance. But problems of vibrato are mainly solved through breathing exercises.

Definition of a Resonant Sound

We can define a vocal tone which has "depth," "brilliance," "projection," and "spin" in the light of the more scientific explanations above. A proper singing tone is one which combines strongly reinforced low and high harmonic overtones with comparably tuned vowel formants, which possesses a constant high frequency around 2800 Hz, and which is continuous, unencumbered by extraneous tensions or stops, and which is apparently self-generating.

RELATING BREATH—PHONATION—RESONANCE

I find it helpful to explain the relationships of breath, phonation, and resonance to my students through analogies or metaphors. As with any analogy they can only be taken so far.

Analogous Relationships

Breath, phonation, and resonance may be seen as members of a three-way partnership. Each is responsible for his own part of the sound produced, and each is dependent on the others to do their jobs well. As partners they are equally important in the production of a tone.

Another way of seeing these three might be with breathing as a powerful master over phonation and resonance, which are slaves chained together forever. The breath may function silently without phonation and resonance, but they are powerless without breath.

Perhaps a better metaphor concerning phonation and resonance would be that they are married and are thus independent but inseparable. Their individual roles in producing vocal sound are inextricably involved. There are times when their actions conflict and one or the other dominates, but the best results are when they work together harmoniously.

Breath controls the power and length of the sound. Phonation controls the variable pitches required by a musical phrase. Resonance controls the variable vowels and overtones required for beauty and power. The tone produced is a combination of the three elements.

Breath Flow and Pressure

In the chapter on breathing, breath pressure and flow were discussed as the voltage and amperage of vocal sound. This analogy should now be combined with our concepts of phonation and resonance. It is possible to phonate and resonate a given musical pitch in different ways by changing the relationship with the breath. The demands on the vocal bands and resonators thus change and the resultant timbres are different. Even if the vocal bands are swollen, they will attempt to phonate the desired pitch. They will have trouble in the upper range, however, because of their increased size and mass.

Under a given breath pressure, the stiffer the vocal bands, the longer they remain closed, and the more intense the sound produced. When the bands are more supple, the glottis remains open longer, and there is a loss of energy with consequently fewer and weaker overtones. It is thus more tiring to sing loudly with supple vocal bands because such phonation-resonance requires more energy from the breath. The breathing muscles tire faster, then the throat may assume more responsibilty in phonation and the vocal bands grow tired faster.

Some vowel sounds are associated with low intensity and low frequencies, especially "oo," and are thus more tiring to sing than the higher frequency, frontal vowels. The vocal bands seem to change configuration to phonate the different vowels, and the set for the dark back vowels seems to be thicker than for the bright front vowels. This will be discussed in more detail in the chapter on vowels.

Forte and Piano

Loudness is a subjective result of the disturbance of the eardrums by air molecules, both in amount of intensity (sound pressure) and frequency of pitch and overtones. To the human ear high frequencies sound louder than low frequencies at the same intensity. (Intensity, sound pressure, and amplitude are synonymous terms.) The concept of *forte* in the voice is the combination of high intensity and reinforced high harmonic overtone frequencies, especially the "ring" of the voice. The concept of *piano* is generally a reduction of both these factors, rather than just one. Good soft singing maintains many of the high frequencies of loud singing, although they will be weaker because the vocal bands are more supple and breath flow is greater.

Crescendo and Diminuendo

A musical pitch may grow louder by increasing the intensity and/or reinforcing the high frequencies. It is possible to "think" a *crescendo* or *diminuendo* by reinforcing the high overtones through the "will to phonate." It is better, however, to change volume levels through increases and decreases in both factors so the demands on the vocal bands by the breath and resonators are kept in balance. Conversely, it is possible to increase the breath pressure of a sound but not the overtones. Such a sound seems forced and becomes more a shout then a singing tone.

Messa di Voce

The supreme test of the old Italian singers was their ability to negotiate the *messa di voce*. The gradual *crescendo* from *piano* to *forte* and gradual *diminuendo* to *piano* is controlled by the gradual increase and decrease in intensity and high frequencies, especially the "ring" or "singer's formant."

In the *messa di voce* there may be the concept of starting the tone in the pharynx and bringing it forward into the masque, keeping the mouth open at all times. A different concept is starting the tone in the masque and increasing the shape and size of the tone vertically by opening the mouth. I prefer not to think in terms of moving the tone in the throat or mouth, although the latter concept has merit in a *crescendo*. I would rather think of a qualitative change from "soft" to "hard" to "soft," keeping a constant breath support. "Soft" sounds may be as large as "hard" sounds, and fill the auditorium, but they have a mellower, less dramatic impact than "hard" sounds. This concept avoids the trap of *piano* being equated with "small." Throughout this exercise the consistency of the vocal bands must be coordinated with breath pressure, flow, and reinforced resonance as seen in the equations below.

Coordinating Breath—Phonation—Resonance

The following equations show how breath, phonation, and resonance may be coordinated to produce a variety of timbres:

1. High breath pressure + great breath flow + supple vocal bands + large pharynx = mellow sound, low intensity, and reinforced low frequencies (flute sound).

2. High breath pressure + less breath flow + stiff vocal bands + small pharynx = harsh sound, high intensity, and reinforced high frequencies (reed sound).

3. High breath pressure + great antagonistic support + less breath flow + stiff vocal bands + large pharynx = fully resonant, ringing sound, high intensity, and reinforced frequencies at both ends of the aural spectrum (brass sound).

The difference between numbers two and three is in keeping the rib cage expanded and the diaphragm lowered so the pharynx stays large.

Head Voice and Falsetto

A good example of two different qualities which may be produced on the same pitch is to contrast head voice and falsetto.

Head voice is the phonation of the high range with a short longitudinal section of the vocal bands under moderately high pressure. The intensity and high overtones are the result of the shape and mass of the vocal bands, the length of the time the glottis is closed, and the complete closure of the glottis.

A falsetto tone is phonation of the high range with the full length of the vocal bands but with only the leading edge (the vocal ligament) vibrating under low pressure. The glottis appears not to close. The breathy quality and lack of intensity and overtones in falsetto are the result of the small mass of the bands, the low breath pressure, and the incomplete closure of the glottis and extremely short closure time.

DEVELOPING A RICH VOICE

The first thing in developing a rich voice is to learn to keep the pharynx large on all vowels and in all parts of the range. The larynx should be lowered, the velum raised forward, the tongue forward and loose, and the oropharynx widened. I have already offered several reasons why the vocal mechanism should be trained to assume these attitudes. Now I shall suggest some exercises to cultivate them.

Lowered Larynx

As I said in Chapter 2, the best method for lowering the larynx is proper breathing. Relax the tongue muscles which pull the larynx up, extend the sternum up and out to help the sternothyroid muscles pull downward on the larynx. In learning to keep the larynx down, the student must practice keeping the sternum extended and the upper chest high all the time. While the chest is high, the jaw and chin are loose. The natural tendency is for the larynx to rise as the notes move into the upper third of the range, but with patience and practice, the vocal bands will discover new ways to phonate the higher pitches with a low larynx.

"Drink in the Air"

A useful simile in learning to sing with a lowered larynx is to make the tone as if drinking in the air. As the German masters said, "Trinken die Luft." This is admittedly an impossibility, but the feeling is quite valid. By trying to drink in the air the student avoids pushing in with the abdomen, which in turn avoids pushing up the larynx. The effect can be dramatic in the change of timbre. Properly practiced, this concept helps keep the vocal mechanism in its optimum position.

Beginning of a Yawn

At the very beginning of a yawn the vocal mechanism is open and free. The student is just beginning to inhale. If at this point he reverses the process and allows the breath to flow out gently, he will probably maintain the lowered larynx, high velum, and so forth. This exercise must be practiced with only the beginning of the yawn. As the yawn progresses, the vocal instrument becomes tense, the jaw opens too wide, and the tongue is much too far back and stiff. Earlier, I suggested the exercise of yawning through the nose, which is also useful in learning to lower the larynx.

Pursed Lips

In Chapter 2 I suggested inhaling through a pinhole (pursed lips) to make the student aware of the breathing mechanisms. This is also an excellent exercise for learning to prepare and maintain the vocal instrument. The student purses his lips and draws in a somewhat labored breath. Then, without letting the chest move or throat change positions, he begins to sing.

This exercise may be coupled effectively with the concept of drinking in the air. The pursed lips exercise prepares the voice through inhalation, and the drinking air exercise maintains the voice during phonation and resonance.

Accept New Sound

In learning a new method of singing, the student sometimes tries to apply the new technique cosmetically to his old sound. If he can accept a new way of singing without worrying about the quality of sound for a while, he will soon see development in his voice. Preoccupation with the sound of his voice can be a deterrent to his progress, so he may have to be reminded to "hit the ball and look for it later."

Depressed Larynx

The larynx may be pushed down by the back of the tongue, or it may be depressed by downward pressure of the chin and jaw.

Both these actions disturb the proper adjustment of the vocal bands as well as the relationships of the resonators. Most offenders are basses and baritones striving for manly tone. Tongue and jaw exercises are offered later to control these problems.

Raised Velum

Many of the same exercises which are effective in teaching the lowered larynx are also productive in maintaining the raised velum, since the two actions are simultaneous and related. For instance, the beginning of a yawn makes the velum rise gently, and the student becomes aware of that area as he feels the space at the back of the throat enlarge.

Cool the Soft Palate

I often ask my students to inhale in such a way as to draw the air across the soft palate. The velum thus becomes a bit cooler, and the student becomes aware of the area. This exercise serves a limited purpose in that it is not a good way to breathe in a performance. Cooling the soft palate also dries it, and that will hinder one's singing.

Vertical Feeling

When the larynx is low and the velum is high, the pharynx is somewhat longer vertically than horizontally. I draw the student's attention to this vertical feeling and ask for a "more vertical sound" when the sound becomes shallow or loses resonance.

Once I heard Marilyn Horne explain that the vertical feeling had a great deal to do with her own singing. She said that she sings as if a pencil were standing in her throat with the eraser on her larynx and a sharp lead pointed toward her soft palate. "If that doesn't keep the palate high, nothing will!" she said emphatically.

Hung-ah, Hang-ah Vocalises

The vocalises in Illustration 4.1 are based on the movement of the velum during the production of the nasal consonant "ng." While the "ng" is held, the velum is lowered and touches the back of the tongue. This relaxes the constrictor muscles of swallowing. When the "ng" is changed quickly to the vowel "ah," the velum moves up sharply, almost snapping into position. The student is thus made aware of the movement of the velum, and the exercise may be repeated to increase the ability to move the velum independently and at will.

Hung – – – – ah – – – – –
Hang – – – – ah – – – –

hung – – – – – ah.
hang – – – – – ah.

Illustration 4.1

Non-Nasal Pharyngeal Vocalises

The non-nasal vocalises (Illustration 4.2) based on dark vowels are also good for establishing a vertical feeling in the pharynx.

They row.———————
Tee   roo ————————

illustration 4.2

Then the student may progress to brighter vowels, maintaining the vertical feeling on such vocalises as those in Illustration 4.3.

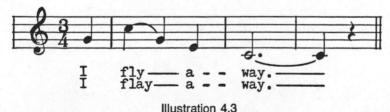

I   fly——— a – – way.———
I   flay——— a – – way.———

Illustration 4.3

Tongue Relaxed. Forward

The base of the tongue should be out of the pharynx as much as possible to create a large resonating chamber and should lie as quietly relaxed as possible. The tip of the tongue is left to find the positions necessary to articulate vowels and consonants in the mouth. The best position for the base of the tongue is in front of the third molars. The tongue may or may not be grooved when it lies flat. There seems to be no real evidence that trying to groove the tongue improves the tone, and probably such attempts hinder good articulation.

Loose Tongue Exercises

An excellent example of the importance of loose tongue exercises is the case of a baritone who had an excellent voice but who had trouble singing consistently. He had developed a rich, resonant tone and had one of the strongest voices I have heard. But he let his tongue hump far in the back of the mouth, distorting much of the beauty and clarity of the voice. I began by having him feel the difference in the muscles between the chin and larynx when the tongue was relaxed or stiffened. He found that the lax vowels do not stiffen the tongue, while the tense ones do. Through a series of loose tongue exercises he was able to free his tongue, which gave him a more ringing sound, clearer words, and several extra notes in the high range.

These exercises may be found in the previous chapter on phonation in the section pertaining to harsh or strident sounds. Others will be found in the chapter on articulation.

Open Throat

The oropharynx consists mainly of constrictor muscles which swallow food and drink. In order to enlarge this cavity into good singing position, the student first relaxes these muscles with the breathing exercises mentioned earlier. No amount of exertion will open the throat properly until the swallowing muscles are relaxed.

Feel Throat Stretch Open

After the swallowing constrictors are relaxed, the student feels the oropharynx stretch open from the inside. Sometimes this may be confused with feeling the throat close, but the sound is quite different. There is no pressure on the larynx, and the sound is not squeezed or forced.

More Size in the Sound

There is a real physical sense in which there is more size in the sound if the throat is expanded. The student feels that the sound is bigger on the inside, that it is expanding inside the throat, and there are more sympathetic vibrations in the chest.

More Body Around the Sound

This is related to getting more size in the sound. The student feels that he is expanding his body from the inside so it will encompass a larger sound. Largeness of course, is not synonymous with loudness. Just as a large person may be relaxed and gentle, so may a large sound.

More "oo" or "oh" in the Sound

This relates to the shape of the pharynx in producing "oo" and "oh." There must be a larger vertical space to resonate the dark vowels than the bright ones. This is especially effective in dealing with the overly bright or strident voice. The intent is to blend depth with brilliance. Also, the tone is more diffuse and less focussed on the inside, which may make the new sound hard for the student to accept.

Fire Siren

The student imitates a siren as it ascends and descends without regard for discreet pitches. To demonstrate this exercise I use a reinforced head voice, not a small breathy falsetto. Many times the girls will repeat the vocalise in my octave, but I insist on their raising the level close to an octave. Generally, the upper note is around high A-flat to B-flat. The exercise must be sung with a free, soaring sound which is easy on the throat.

After singing a few fire sirens up and down, the student holds the highest note "as if the fire engine were going down the street." This illustrates the feeling of the sustained tone with an open throat. At this point I have the student hold a long fire siren while I play the note on the piano, demonstrating that the vocalise was indeed a singing tone.

This exercise serves several purposes. First, it removes the production of high notes from the multifaceted frame of reference called "singing." The student makes pleasant, rewarding sounds without trying so hard to "sing." This is especially useful with female students who are reluctant to sing in the upper range.

Second, it demonstrates an unforced quality of sound in which the breath, phonation, and resonance are balanced. The energy is exerted from the abdomen instinctively, and the phonation-resonance system is left to its own devices, in the best sense of the phrase.

Third, it demonstrates the remarkable attributes of the vocal bands for legato pitch changes. No other instrument can produce every one of its sounds from top to bottom without pushing a valve or shifting a key or some other mechanical action.

Fourth, this exercise shows the student the various areas of sympathetic resonance. The glissando up and down simulates some sort of mental arc within the student's psyche. The teacher then can relate to the feelings which the student describes afterward.

Loss of Control

The student may experience a temporary loss of control of the timbre of his voice while learning to sing with an open throat. He may even have some brief trouble with pitch. This loss of control is the result of changing muscular responses, like changing the grip on a bowling ball or golf club. I explain that holding all these factors in balance is like holding a small bird. If you squeeze too tightly, you can injure the fragile creature. But if you hold it too loosely, it may fly away. It takes practice to know exactly how to hold a small bird without hurting it or losing it.

Expect a New Sound

The student is not equipped to judge whether or not a tone is properly resonant. Every sound is so diffuse and muffled on the inside, compared with what it sounds like outside, he cannot judge the effect of a new technique. Further, he cannot imagine what the new sound will be like when it is correct. Learning to sing with better resonance is largely a matter of the teacher's identifying the best sound as it is produced, and the student's remembering what it felt like, how it sounded, and how he produced it.

Loose Jaw

The jaw should be comfortably open and quiet. Our American speech patterns foster the habit of speaking with our mouths closed. Even the best television commentators hardly open their mouths to talk. Understandability is not based on opening the mouth, but good singing is.

The jaw should hang by its own weight and not be forced open against the strong chewing muscles. Such forcing actually closes the throat by sphincter action.

Jaw Exercises

To loosen a tight jaw the chewing muscles must be stretched. The student opens his mouth as wide as is comfortable without hindering the larynx. While the mouth is open, he massages the large masseter muscles which cover the jawbones until they relax and lengthen. He may also relax the jaw and pull the chin down gently to loosen and stretch these muscles.

The pharynx will enlarge by dropping the hinge of the jaw from the inside. Many Germanic teachers concentrate on this aspect of opening the throat as well as loosening the jaw. The idea is that the open mouth taught by the old masters meant opening at the back rather than the front. This relates to the idea that most of the resonance is made in the pharynx, not the oral cavity.

Loose jaw vocalises and exercises may be found in the chapters on phonation and articulation.

Loose Lips

The lips should be free to assume their normal shape when the jaw is relaxed and open. The lips should not thin out from tension, as such strain works its way into the pharynx and larynx. I prefer the student's mouth be shaped in a vertical oval to reinforce the lower harmonic overtones better. The so-called "spread" tone is caused by spreading the lips horizontally, thereby reinforcing too many inharmonic high overtones. A "spread" tone is more a shout than it is singing.

On the other hand, the lips should not be pulled in like a drawstring. Trumpeted lips produce a muffled or mushy pronunciation which greatly hinders understanding. The use and misuse of the mouth in forming words will be discussed further in the chapter on articulation.

AN APPROACH TO DEVELOPING RESONANCE

The following suggested steps have proved helpful for both beginning and advanced students as an approach to developing further resonance. The practice of these exercises presupposes the use of good breathing, open throat, low larynx, and so forth. It cannot be stressed too much that there must be a good sound for the resonators to enhance.

Find the Best Area of Tone Quality

Usually the best area of the beginning voice is in the middle to lower part of the treble clef, transposed down an octave for the men, of course. The suggested vocalises (Illustration 4.4) begin on E-flat or D major triads, although some students may need to start higher and some lower.

Nay ——— Nay ——— Nay.
Nee ——— Nee ——— Nee.
Neh ——— Neh ——— Neh.

Illustration 4.4

Each vocalise begins on the fifth degree of the scale and is a descending scale since that is much easier than ascending. The student begins near the top of the best area of his voice and descends through that area. "Nay" is usually easiest for a cold voice.

Move the Triads by Half-Steps

With the lighter male and female voices the succession is upward by half-steps, as the best area of these voices is apt to extend into the upper half of the treble clef. The heavier voices' scales descend by half-steps since the best area may be below the treble clef.

Find the Best Vowel Sound or Sounds

This process is in conjunction with finding the best area of the voice. The first vocalise begins with "nay," as the nasal consonant helps the vocal bands phonate and gives the singer an immediate sense of resonance and placement. It may be that "ee" or "eh" would be better as a first vowel, depending on the student, but one of the bright vowels is chosen because it helps the vocal bands approximate properly.

The "ah" vowel takes more energy to phonate well than any of the others, especially for the male students, so the voice should be warmed up before singing vocalises on "ah." Young voices have more trouble with "oh" and "oo," with the exception of sopranos in their upper voices, because of the tendency to be breathy.

Vocalize to Warm Up the Mind as Well as the Voice

The first series of exercises is intended to remind the students how to coordinate their breath, phonation, and resonance—to wake up their minds as well as their voices. By moving through the best area of the voice on the best vowel, the student's first singing of the day is rewarding and encouraging.

Move from Best Area Outward

After determining the best area and best vowel, the student continues vocalizing on the best vowel while extending the best area outward. The object is to relate the outer, more difficult areas of the voice to the more secure, best area. By using the best vowel, the student avoids confusing a poor vocal sound with a poor vowel sound. He finds a vowel which is in tune with the musical pitches of the vocalises, and by maintaining a constant vowel he learns to tune the areas of the voice which are not as good.

Work for Uniformity in the Voice

As the student continues to vocalize, he tries to sing all the notes uniformly. As long as he does not extend the range too high, a single vowel sound will be sufficient. Men need not be concerned with modifying the vowel below the e-flat above middle c. To that point the pure vowel will work well, especially "ay" or "eh." The women find that "ah" works better in the upper part of their voices, depending on how high the vocalises are practiced. More will be said about extreme range development and transcending the "lifts" or problem points of the voice in the chapter on registers.

Move from Best Vowel to Others

As the student begins to develop uniformity of quality and tuning on his best vowel, he may begin to change to other vowels which are nearly as good but which need tuning. The first such exercise (Illustration 4.5) may include only one musical pitch in the best area of the voice. Then he may sing scales such as that in Illustration 4.6.

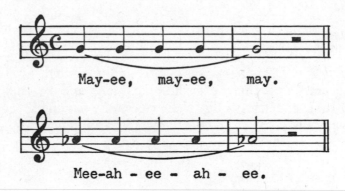

May-ee,   may-ee,   may.

Mee-ah - ee - ah - ee.

Illustration 4.5

May- ee, may-ee,   may.
Mah- ee- ah- ee-   ah.

Illustration 4.6

EXCESS NASALITY

In the beginning of this chapter I pointed out that the nasal chambers might not be important to good resonance, but could be the source of grave problems for the singer and teacher. I have saved the discussion of excess nasality for last because a positive approach to developing resonance is more important to every student's vocal growth.

More Than Aesthetics

Extreme amounts of excess nasality are really more than problems of aesthetics and personal tastes. Excess nasality requires the vocal folds to vibrate in unusual and asymmetrical configurations. Such sounds lack the "ring" of the voice and many upper frequencies of the vowels. Constant phonation of an excessively nasal resonance system can lead to laryngeal damage.

Pathological Problems

Several physical defects may cause excess nasality which the vocal teacher is not equipped to remedy. A cleft palate which cannot be completely closed by surgery or prosthesis leaves a constant opening between the nasal chamber and the oral or oropharyngeal cavities which defies vocal therapy. Children who have had tonsillectomies often have a larger space between the hard palate and the pharyngeal wall than the velum can cover. The latter condition may also be congenital. Sometimes accidental damage to the head may result in nerve loss which leaves the velum impaired. In these cases the student should consult a speech pathologist with whom the voice teacher can cooperate.

Correctable Problems

The soft palate may hang in too low a position as a result of faulty speech patterns. In some areas of the United States the speech sounds contain a high percentage of nasality, that is, a "twang," and the children in those areas learn to speak with a low velum at an early age. Remedying the excess nasality in a student from such a background will be based first on the student's recognizing the problem and being willing to correct it. The best example I can use for my student's is my own origin in East Texas.

To be sure, students from all parts of the country may have an area of the voice or some particular sounds which consist of a high degree of nasality. These are apt to be caused by problems in articulation which go unnoticed because the student does not hear himself accurately. If nasality is caused by an untrained or lazy velum, it can be corrected by the vocal teacher.

EXERCISES FOR EXCESS NASALITY

Usually a student who has a problem of nasality of the nature discussed here will need further exercises than those suggested above in the section on raising the velum. Some more radical program of exercises may need to be designed.

Hold the Nose

If some of the sounds of the voice are too nasal, the objectionable quality will show up if the singer holds his nose while singing. He may say or sing a phrase such as "I seek to sing." There should be an obvious nasal "twang" in the word "sing" which is not in the word "seek." The singer can hear if these words sound alike. He should try to speak and sing so there is no "twang" except on the nasal consonants. Sometimes this is all that is required as a remedy. The student hears the problem and automatically learns to change his phonation-resonance through the will to phonate.

Lazy Velum Exercises

The consonant "k" requires the velum to flex vigorously, to the point of popping the ears through the Eustachian tubes. The vowels "uh," "oo," and "oh" are the least nasal in their pure forms because the velum must be high in order to resonate them. Therefore, I find the best exercises to deal with the low velum combine "k" and the dark vowels.

Exercise 1. The student says "kuck-kuck-kuck" several times. This should not sound like "kunk-kunk-kunk." In the most extreme cases the student may imagine he is removing peanut butter from the soft palate with the back of his tongue. After saying this, the student may sing scales and arpeggios. These exercises should begin staccato because a quick action of the velum is important to correcting the problem. The student may progress to legato exercises when he is able to hold the pure vowel sound without lowering the velum. The range and pitch of the vocalises depends on the area of the voice affected by nasality.

Exercise 2. Change to "keek-keek-keek," and follow the above directions. This should not sound like "kink-kink-kink."

Exercise 3. Change to a long note on the word "sowed." This should not sound like "sown." Also, "soak" should not sound like "sonk." "Mood" should not sound like "moon." And so forth.

Substitute Initial Consonants

I sometimes change the nasal consonants in a musical phrase to consonants which are articulated in the same way except for the lowered velum. These substitutions demonstrate the necessity for a pure vowel no matter what consonant begins the syllable. Such phrases as "not now" and "my mother" become "dot dow" and "by bother." "Tomorrow morning" becomes "to borrow borning," and so forth.

Just recently I have had two baritones, Dennis and Ken, who sang with an excess of nasality. In each case we worked on the lazy velum exercises to cure the problem. At first neither man was able to isolate the excess nasality factor, so neither was able to tell when he was singing nasally. I recorded several sessions with each to show the difference in nasal and non-nasal singing. In a short while both Ken and Dennis were able to sing with a clear, ringing, non-nasal tone. The tape recorder reoriented their ears to the proper sound, and the lazy velum vocalises taught their vocal tracts how to form that sound.

Substitute Final Consonants

Some phoneticists hear a quality of sound in American English similar to the French nasal vowels in such words as "sing," "sand," and "punk." Their opinion is that the final nasal consonant impinges on the preceding vowel and colors it with nasality. Perhaps this is true in speech, but I think the extended vowels in singing should not be nasalized. I substitute "sabe" for "same" and "sat" for "sand," if the vowel is excessively nasal. I teach my students that the audience should not know until the final consonant whether the word is "bag" or "bang." A more complete explanation of substitute consonants and a chart based on their articulators will be found in the chapter on articulation.

Upper Register and Head Voice

Because the resonance of the upper register, either head voice or falsetto, requires the velum to be high, a student may find that a vowel which is nasal in the middle or lower part of the voice is not in the upper range. He may sing descending slurs or glissandos as shown earlier on the offensive sound and try to keep the vowel pure.

Pure "oh" and "oo" Exercises

The student will find that practicing vocalises on "oh" and "oo" will help train the velum to stay high. The exercises suggested earlier to achieve a vertical feeling in the pharynx are appropriate. Then he may move from "oh" or "oo" to another vowel on a scale or arpeggio, following the principle of moving from a best vowel to one less good.

Other Exercises Based on "oo" and "oh"

Earlier I mentioned the "fire siren" vocalise as a way of opening the throat. It may also be used to encourage the velum to rise and stay in a high position. The sweep into the upper range causes the velum to ascend auomatically, and the sound of the fire siren is obviously nasal when the velum is down. Also, the exercise is extremely difficult to achieve if the soft palate does not rise.

Some vocalises similar to the "fire siren" are the "train whistle," "hoot owl," and "steam boat." One of my colleagues, upon hearing a series of these vocalises, characterized it as the "wounded buffalo," but I have not found that concept to be productive.

Some Analogies and Metaphors

Sometimes merely asking the student to "put more air in the tone" helps rid the voice of excess nasality. "More air" implies more breath flow and a lessening of tension in the larynx. A concurrent lessening of tension in the pharynx which might be holding the velum in a low position would lead to a less nasal sound.

An old analogy for opening the throat, and therefore for lifting the velum, is that of the "hot potatoes." The singer is asked to imagine he has a mouthful of hot potatoes. The consequent broadening of the pharynx helps lift the velum. The analogy has to include a deep breath through the mouth in order to be effective.

What is perhaps the most famous analogy to good singing seems appropriate here, the "pear-shaped tone." A teacher of mine once said the stem should be sticking out of the singer's mouth. Such an idea is not too bizarre if it helps a student sing better.

The next two chapters on vowels and registers might have been included in the discussion of resonance. It seemed better, however, to separate them for ease of handling the materials.

5

HOW TO FORM THE
BEST VOWEL SOUND

Vowels are the natural resonance of the human vocal tract. In the previous chapter the example of blowing across the neck of an empty bottle is analogous to making a vowel sound. Actually, a better example would be snapping one's fingers or clapping one's hands over the bottle. In speech the vocal bands produce a sound which has many fundamentals and overtones at the same time, and the resonators select those which match their natural tunings for amplification. Each combination of the resonators has its natural tuning. The tuning, actually several clusters of overtones, may be changed by altering either the shape of one or more resonators, or by altering the connecting orifices between them, or both.

Because of our early orientation to speech rather than music, we are taught as infants to recognize these various harmonic overtone clusters as sounds of communication. That is, we interpret them to mean ideas rather than musical tones. Later, we are taught written symbols for these overtone clusters so they become words, further removing them from a musical frame of reference.

INSTRUMENTAL CHARACTERISTICS OF VOWELS

The difference between a tone from a flute or a clarinet is in the strength of the various harmonic overtones. Without overtones it would be impossible to tell a flute from a clarinet, violin, tuning fork, or any other pitch source. The overtones make the difference, as shown in the chart.

CHARACTERISTICS OF VOWELS

	Clarinet	Vowel "ee"	Flute	Vowel "oo"
13th overtone	—		—	
12th overtone	—		—	
11th overtone	——		—	
10th overtone	——		—	
9th overtone	———	———	—	
8th overtone	———	——	—	
7th overtone	———	———	—	
6th overtone	—		—	
5th overtone	—		—	
4th overtone	——		—	
3rd overtone	—		—	
2nd overtone	——		——	——
1st overtone	—	———	————	——
Fundamental	——	———	——	———

The sounds of the clarinet and flute have been compared on the chart with the vowels "ee" and "oo." Their overtone patterns are surprisingly similar. The clarinet's characteristic sound comes from the very strong high partials, and the vowel "ee" shows these same characteristics. The flute depends largely on its strong first overtone and very weak upper partials, quite like the vowel "oo."

If we had not been taught communication and words, we might have learned the sounds of the voice as a musical spectrum from high pitched "clarinet" to low pitched "flute" rather than from "ee" to "oo." If we had learned vowels in this manner, it would be much easier to understand how they fit into the complex scheme of singing.

THE FIXED FORMANT THEORY OF VOWELS

The dissimilarity between instruments and vowels is that instrumental overtones move up and down and remain the same relative distance from the fundamental pitch. Vowels are clusters of consistent areas of high frequency energy which appear to be fixed in the vocal tract no matter what musical pitches may be sung. Even in low men's voices almost the same areas of energy appear as in women's voices. These areas, or formants, are different with each vowel and are the basis for vowel identification. There are thought to be from five to thirty formants for each vowel, but the ear only needs to determine two to distinguish one vowel from the other.

The low vowel formant is produced in the pharynx as the largest, lowest pitched resonator. The high vowel formant is formed in the oral cavity, the smaller, higher pitched resonator. Since most vocal tracts—male and female—are about the same size, the various formants are close to the same frequency.

Formant Chart with Phonetic Symbols

This chart (Illustration 5.1) represents approximate areas of frequency energy.

The bright frontal vowels are identified by the widespread position of the high and low formants, while the dark back vowels are identified by the closeness of the formants. The low formants of "beet" and "boot" are almost identical, as are those of "bit" and "full." It is the much higher formant that makes the difference to the ear. One might almost say that "ee" is really "oo" and "ay" is "oh" with higher second formants. The importance of this idea will be made clear later.

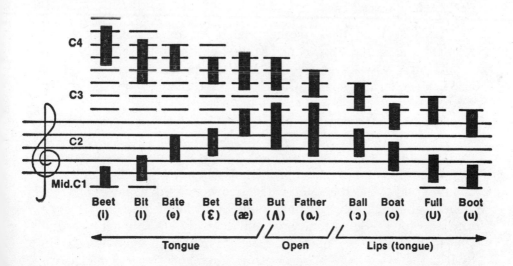

Illustration 5.1 Vowel Formant Chart

Tuning the Formants

The formants are not tuned to just one pitch. The different sizes of vocal tracts and the different colors which our ears may accept as a single vowel are the reasons for an often wide band of formant area. Thus a musical pitch may find a harmonic overtone within a formant area to which to tune. For instance, the word "beet" sung on the F above middle C will find either C4 or the F above C4 as an overtone, but the word "bit" on the same pitch may find C4, the A below, or the F below C4 as an overtone. That is why the tense "ee" and the lax "ih" may sound almost alike in some voices and be an octave apart in others. That is also why one voice on the wrong vowel can make a large chorus sound out of tune. The musical pitches may be right, but the vowel overtones are not.

Formants in Female Voices

Another problem which may be explained by the formant chart is the female's difficulty in pronouncing pure vowels above C2. There are fewer low formants above that pitch than below it. By the time the women reach the F2 at the top of the treble clef, there are only the low formants of "but," "father," and "bat" remaining. Thus, every vowel sounds like one of these, most likely "father."

Formants in Male Voices

Because most male pitches are below even the first vowel formants, men may sing vowel sounds which are reasonably close to the pure vowel frequencies. In the heavier voices, however, there is generally some adjustment of the vowel in the upper ranges.

The formant chart may give a clue to why there is often such a difference in a tenor's high B-flat and B. The musical pitch is above most of the first formants, so most vowels sound like some sort of "ah." There is an acoustical problem with producing the vowels at the far ends of the spectrum which shows itself in changes of vocal color in the high range. Above high B-flat all of the colors merge into one vowel. Some tenors who are closely kin to baritones find that high A is the last open note, others may push the openness up to B-flat, but all have to resort to a new phonation-resonance approach from B natural up. Even in the so-called countertenors who sing far above high C there is an acoustical shift above B-flat which may be the result of the structure of vowel formants.

PRODUCING A VOWEL SOUND

There are two major articulators which fashion the resonators into their vowel shapes—the tongue and the lips. Those vowels on the left hand side of "but" on the chart are essentially shaped by raising the tongue toward the roof of the mouth. Those on the right hand side of "father" are made by rounding the lips. There is some concurrent raising of the tongue toward the velum in forming the dark vowels. It happens reflexively, however, and should not be dwelled on as being primary to vowel production as this tends to tighten the tongue and force it into the throat.

I demonstrate to my students that raising the tongue toward the hard palate will change the vowel (ɑ) to (æ), (ɛ), (e), (ɪ), and (i) without moving the lips or jaw. The tongue moves slightly forward as it rises.

For the student who is unaware of the tongue's role in forming the frontal vowels, I use the tongue awareness exercises described in the preceding chapter. The tongue may have to be rolled out mechanically in order to keep the jaw and lips quiet. With a bit of practice the student will find the position in the mouth which best forms these "tongue" vowels. It will surprise him how much space there can be between his teeth and still form an understandable "ee."

I show the students that (ɑ) may become (ɔ), (o), (U), and (u) by moving the tongue back toward the velum without moving the lips or jaw. These vowels sound swallowed because of the action of the tongue and constrictors on the pharynx. I then illustrate that the dark vowels are freer and better in tune when they are shaped by rounding the lips, letting the tongue find a comfortable place somewhere in the mouth.

For the student who is unaccustomed to moving his lips while maintaining an open jaw, I sometimes resort to having him sing "ah" and push his lips into a rounded position, while keeping his teeth apart. The smaller the opening in the lips, the nearer to "oo" the sound becomes. After a while he is able to make the lip adjustment without his hands.

Muscle Memory

In a real sense our muscles have memories even if they do not have brains. As children we taught our vocal muscles a set of responses necessary to form the vowel sounds we wished to hear. As we begin to study singing, we may be asked to change those muscle responses to make a different vowel color. When we ask our bodies to learn the new responses, they often rebel from brainless muscle memory. Thus we have to manipulate them mechanically to teach them the new actions.

Computer Tapes

Our muscles react in much the same way as a computer program. Once the commands have been established in the computer's memory banks, the operator only pushes a button and the computer reacts as programmed. We must work hard to erase a muscle's memory tape and reprogram it to a new response. Because there are no eraser heads in our cerebral computer, we must continue to enter the new program until it completely covers up the old one.

Methods of Vowel Production

The two major resonators—the oral cavity and the pharynx—may be made to react to each other in two quite different methods. The first method is one in which the pharynx is held in the same shape and size no matter what the vowel sound. The mouth is virtually the sole source of vowel differentiation. The resonators are said to be "tied." While this method may produce more depth or low formant in all the vowels, it also may lead to serious constrictions in the articulators, causing a strained production in the upper voice and in the frontal vowels.

The second method leaves the resonators "free" rather than "tied," and the pharynx may adjust itself within certain parameters for better vowel identification and differentiation. These parameters are based on the physique of the singer and the nature of his voice. The mouth thus becomes more a conduit for the vocal sound rather than a major factor in its production, and the vowel formed between the mouth and the pharynx has a better chance to find a harmonic overtone which tunes with the musical pitch. The free method of vowel production depends more on finding natural resonances which fit both the musical pitch and the vowel, rather than forcing the musical pitch into a preset combination of resonators or depending on only one resonator to make all the adjustments.

Vowel Unification and Equalization

The principles presented in this book stem from and lead to the concept of unified vowel sounds. The best singing voice produces vowels which sound as if they were made by the same instrument, that is, they all have about the same ratio of high and low frequencies, about the same amount of "singer's formant," and are blended until the voice has no "breaks" or "seams." There is a "line" in the voice. It is this property of unified and equalized vowels which separates the skilled singer from the amateur.

Vowel unification and equalization require a homogeneous approach to breathing-phonation-resonance. The tone for each vowel must be generated by a consistent method of breathing. It must be phonated in a consistent manner, e.g., free of extraneous tensions, by adequate breath pressure and flow, and so on. And the size, shape, and coupling of the resonators must be consistent, e.g., the larynx low, velum high, tongue loose and forward, and so on.

All this means that the vowels in one area of the voice on a single pitch or in an integrated musical-textual line will sound related. It does not mean that a particular vowel will sound the same no matter what the musical pitch. No instrument sounds the same from one end of its range to the other, but there is a unifying quality of resonance and timbre when it is skillfully played. It is the same with voices. The low voice will be round and mellow, and the high voice will be brilliant, but there will be some of each of these components through the entire range.

VOWEL UNIFICATION VOCALISES—ALL VOICES

Vocalises for Single Pitch, Frontal and Open Vowels

Vocalise 1. The singer keeps the jaw and lips quiet in this vocalise (Illustration 5.2). Only the tongue moves up toward the palate. He may think "mom-mame-mom" to keep the resonance position constant. Unify the vowels.

Illustration 5.2

Vocalise 2. If the "ee" is better than "ay," this vocalise (Illustration 5.3) may be used to unify "ay." The tongue moves
slightly backward. The "ring" of the vowels remains constant. The
"ay" is much closer to "ee" than most students think. The tendency
is to sing "mee-meh." Avoid tongue tension by singing sounds
rather than feeling tongue positions. An alternate exercise is
"mee-mih," keeping the lax vowel very close to the tense one. The
three vowels in "meet," "mitt," and "mate" are extremely close in
the mouth and must be tuned by the teacher's ears.

Illustration 5.3

Vocalise 3. In this vocalise (Illustration 5.4) attack on the
breath and move only the tip of the tongue. The tongue is arched
into the closed vowel position and should hardly move. Avoid the
retroflex "l" which withdraws into the back of the mouth before
articulating the consonant like a whiplash. Alternate vocalises are
"lay-lih" and "lih-lee." As in No. 2, these are all quite close, and the
unifying resonance should not be disturbed by "l."

Illustration 5.4

Vocalise 4. The vowel movement is farther, skipping the intermediate positions (see Illustration 5.5). Only the tongue moves. First, the tip articulates "n," then the blade rises to form "ee." This should be practiced slowly at first to feel the complex movements of the tongue. Later these should become automatic. Throughout the vocalise the vowels maintain their resonance so there is no interruption of the flow or ring.

Nah- ee- nah- ee- - nah.

Illustration 5.5

Vocalise 5. This vocalise (Illustration 5.6) is the same as No. 4 except for the initial "n." The attack is on the breath without the aid of a nasal consonant. Form the "ah" while inhaling. Hear a bit of breath escape before the tone begins. Change to "ee" without interrupting the flow or ring of the tone. Only the blade of the tongue moves.

Ah- ee- ah- ee - - ah.

Illustration 5.6

Vocalise 6. Several actions are combined here (Illustration 5.7). Close the lips during inhalation. Feel a bit of breath escape

Mine-ee, mine-ee, mine.

Illustration 5.7

through the nose before the "m" begins. Open to "ah," then glide smoothly to "ih." With the blade of the tongue high, articulate the "n" with the tip. As the tip lowers, shift from "ih" to "ee." Usually easier done than said. The final syllable may be sung on an extended "ah" or "n," depending on the student's needs.

Vocalise 7. With this vocalise (Illustration 5.8) move through the frontal vowels in order to the open "ah." Keep the "line" flowing and the vowels unified. Let the mouth and articulators move freely without tension. Tune the vowels by ear. An alternate is to move from open "ah" through the frontal vowels: Mah-met-mate-mitt-meet. The tongue finds its new positions while the lips are closed on each "m."

Meet,mitt,mate,met,   mah.

Illustration 5.8

Vocalise 8. Other combinations of vowels may be used, depending on the needs of the student. The idea is to move from the best vowels to the next best, to third best, and so on.

Vocalises for Single Pitch, Back and Open Vowels

Vocalise 1. In this vocalise (Illustration 5.9) the singer keeps the jaw as quiet as he can. There will be some movement of the chin to relieve lip tension. The lips should be rounded but relaxed. The tongue should be relaxed and find a comfortable position. The singer may think "mom-mome" to keep the resonant hum constant. Unify and equalize the vowels.

Mah- moh- mah- moh - - mah.

Illustration 5.9

Vocalise 2. This vocalise (Illustration 5.10) is the opposite of No. 1. The lips open only slightly for the first vowel, then open farther for the second. The first vowel may be either the closed "boot" or open "full" vowel. The "moh" should be the same here as in No. 1. That is, there should be no difference in the vowel whether approached from the back or the front. The tongue should be relaxed and comfortable. It is necessary for the tongue to intrude on the pharynx to form "oh" and "oo," but it need not be stiff or uncomfortable. Certainly the tongue should not be stiffened to keep it out of the throat. The vocalise may have to be sung *piano* to find a good "oo." Driving the vowel will make it hard to manage.

Moo–moh– moo– moh – – moo.

Illustration 5.10

Vocalise 3. The initial vowel is sometimes problematic. The intention is to sing the vowel in "lord" without the "r." In some areas of the country words such as "law" and "cloth" rhyme with "lot" and "clock." In others there is an additional "r," as in "lawr." While in others these words are said with a diphthong, as in "la-ow" and "cla-oth." The best singing pronunciation is with one syllable formed by singing "ah" and slightly rounding the lips or singing "oh" and slightly opening the lips. Practice this vocalise (Illustration 5.11) with a frontal "l" rather than retroflex, so the vowel unification is undisturbed. An alternate is "law-loh" with no diphthong or glide on either vowel. Keep the jaw and chin quiet and move only the lips and tongue.

Law– lah– law– lah – – law.

Illustration 5.11

Vocalise 4. This vocalise (Illustration 5.12) is more vigorous than simply singing the diphthong "now." The tone begins with the tongue tip raised and the mouth in an "ah." The tongue lowers to reveal the "ah," then the lips round firmly to shift to "oo," as in "boot." The jaw may move slightly to relieve lip tension, but the vowel centers should be unified.

Illustration 5.12

Vocalise 5. This vocalise (Illustration 5.13) is similar to No. 4 without the "n," except the second sound is the open vowel in "full." The result is similar to "wow-wow," but the lips are not drawn up quite as tightly as in a "w." There should definitely be no glottal plosive between "oo" and "ah."

Illustration 5.13

Vocalise 6. This vocalise (Illustration 5.14) begins with the mouth closed, the upper teeth touching the lower lip. The vocal bands phonate the initial pitch with the articulators in this position. Then the mouth opens to "ah." The tip of the tongue moves up and down to articulate "l," and the lips round to "oh." Sounds somewhat like the word "follow," but the first consonant has a definite pitch.

Illustration 5.14

Vocalise 7. Move through the back vowels to the open "ah" (Illustration 5.15). Keep the "line" flowing and the vowels unified. Let the lips and tongue move freely without tension. Tune the vowels by ear, not in the mouth by feel. When the resonance is good, there is no feeling of the vowel in the mouth, and the articulators are free and supple. An alternate vocalise is to move from open "ah" through the back vowels: Mah-maw-moh-mŏŏ-mōō. The lips open slightly less each time, and the tongue finds its place without help from the singer.

Illustration 5.15

Vocalise 8. Other combinations of vowels may be used, depending on the needs of the student. Here again the student moves from the best vowels to the next best, and so on.

Vocalises for Scales and Arpeggios

Vocalise 1. In this vocalise (Illustration 5.16) the tongue moves down slightly in the shift from "ee" to "ay." If the jaw opens on the ascending fourth, the tongue may have to maintain its position or even move up slightly so the vowel will not open too far. An alternate vocalise is "zee-ih," which is much closer to "zee-ay" than is the open "zee-eh." The tongue and jaw should remain loose and the throat free. As the "ay" descends, there is a shift of energy, but the ring and flow of the vowel should be constant.

Vocalise 2. In this vocalise (Illustration 5.16) the lips round and the tongue lowers and relaxes between "ee" and "oh." The jaw

Illustration 5.16

may open on the ascending fourth to release tension in the pharynx, in which case the lips should round so the second sound is not "uh." On high notes the second sound may be the vowel in "full" to ease tension. On the descending arpeggio the jaw may relax slightly to aid in articulating the closed "oh."

Vocalise 3. This vocalise (Illustration 5.17) teaches unification between distant vowels over the span of a ninth. Try to keep the forward "buzz" of the "ay" in the "oh," not letting the upper tones slip backward. The velum and tongue change positions, but the concentration of energy should be in the masque. The vocalise should not be sung too high or too loudly, or the back vowel will migrate to "aw" or "uh." The "r" should be flipped on the tongue. If this is difficult, alternates are "they loh" and "they doh."

3. They row. ————————————————————
4. Tee   roo ————————————————————

Illustration 5.17

Vocalise 4. This vocalise (Illustration 5.17) is related to No. 3, but shifts the vowels as far as possible. The lips move from open to closed as the tongue flips the "r." Again, the concentration of energy should be in the masque, not on the velum or behind the tongue. The vocalise should not be sung too high or too loudly, or the second sound will shift to the open vowel in "full." The lips are closed firmly, but the articulators inside are free and loose with no feeling of constriction. Alternates are "tee-loo" and "tee-doo."

Vocalise 5. This vocalise (Illustration 5.18) begins with the pitches close together and gradually widens the musical intervals while maintaining the integrity of both vowels. The student may feel a slight broadening of the "ay" as it descends lower and lower, but the sound should not open to "eh" as a substitute. Of course, the exercise may be altered to "mee-eh," but this should be by design and not default. Another alternate is "mee-ih."

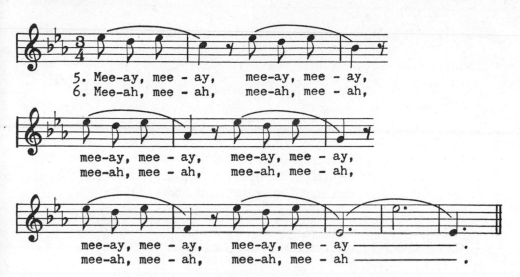

Illustration 5.18

Vocalise 6. This is an extension of No. 5. The vowel shift is farther and more difficult. The "ah" should not move backward as the tongue lowers, but should retain a ring or buzz near the "ee" position. Tune the "ah" by ear so the articulators may feel free and unrestricted.

Vocalise 7. This scale stays within the compass of a third while moving up an octave (Illustration 5.19). Thus the "ah" and "ee" are different at the top from those at the bottom of the range, but each "ah" is unified with each "ee" throughout the vocalise. Only the tongue moves within each pattern. The jaw may open as

Illustration 5.19

the level of each pattern ascends, but it should be quiet within each pattern. Tune the vowels by ear so the articulators are free and the shifts from "ah" to "ee" are smooth.

Vocalise 8. This vocalise (Illustration 5.20) includes several complex movements which must be smoothly coordinated. The initial "z" is phonated on the first pitch of the arpeggio, then the mouth opens with the tongue in the "ay" position. As the pitch lowers, so does the tongue, and the vowel shifts to "ah." Then the tongue tip rises to form "l" without the retroflex movement. As the tongue tip lowers, the blade shifts upward to "eh." Then the mouth closes to begin the complex actions described earlier in the "mine-ee" exercises. On the last note either the final "ah" or "n" may be extended, according to the needs of the student.

8. Zay-ah-leh - -mine———,   zeh-ah-leh - mine.

Illustration 5.20

How to Make Vocalises from Songs

A good way to teach unified vowels is to have the student sing his songs on one vowel or a combination of vowels. The exercise may concentrate on a problem vowel sound, or it may incorporate all the sounds in a particular musical phrase. In this way the student relates a vocal principle or concept to vocal literature and singing.

VOWEL MIGRATION

If the larynx is maintained in a low position into the upper range of the voice, the vocal bands must find new, different ways to phonate the upper notes. Also, the resonators must make minute shifts to help the vocal bands achieve their new adjustments. As these shifts and adjustments occur, there is a perceptible change in the color of the vowel sound from that made with the larynx in a high position. The formant frequencies and spacings are different, and this difference is a continuum of migrating formants which may be logically plotted and anticipated.

Such vowel migration is necessary for control of the voice and to maintain the beauty of "depth" in the voice. It happens automatically in all voices whose larynges stay low in the pharynx. Vowel migration may or may not be planned in performance, as it needs only the proper relationships of breath-phonation-resonance to occur.

VOWEL MODIFICATION

Not every singer can find the way to keep the larynx in a good low position in the upper range. The natural tendency of the larynx to rise as the musical pitch ascends and the inclination to keep the vowel color the same in all ranges of the voice are too strong for the student to overcome. He is unable to let the vowel migrate where it wishes—indeed, where it must. This student must learn the proper migration of vowels and plan them as carefully as he does changes of pitch and syllables. He uses a pedagogical tool based on migration called vowel modification. Knowing the proper sound helps his articulators and resonators function well.

Modifying vowels is as old as the *bel canto* style of voice train ing, although it was not practiced in quite the same ways as today. The reason for having to modify vowels was stated in the first chapter as the paradox of uniform quality: *In singing a scale from the top of the voice to the bottom and back again, a uniform quality of tonal color on the outside will sound as if there are major changes on the inside, and a uniform quality on the inside will sound like major changes on the outside.* Uniform color and beauty require a migration or modification of the vowel in the high range.

For a number of years I have used vowel modification charts based on ideas taught me by two memorable choral directors, one trained on the East Coast and the other on the West Coast. Their ideas combine as naturally as if they came from the same school. As I came to understand vowel formants in later years, I could see even better the reasons these charts are successful.

Female Vowel Modification Chart

This chart is obviously related to the formant chart shown earlier. As the voice moves upward, the vowels progress in the

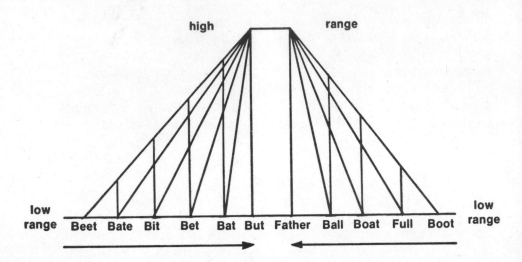

Female Vowel Modification Chart

Illustration 5.21

direction of the arrows. For instance, the vowel in "beet" should be shaped like "bate," "bit," "bet," and "bat" as the scale rises, constantly opening the jaw and lowering the tongue. The highest pitches are sung with the mouth and throat in an "ah" position.

On this chart "ah" and "uh" are equal since they are so close in formants, and because there is hardly any distinction between them in the upper voice. Most sopranos prefer modifying toward "ah," while most mezzo-sopranos find "uh" more comfortable. As long as the upper tones have a clear ring, I leave the decision to the student.

The modification of dark vowels moves toward "ah" by gradually opening the lips and lowering the tongue. The jaw may also be opened for better tonal quality on the upper notes. As the scale ascends the vowel in "boot" is produced in a progressively larger opening of the vocal tract in the shapes of "full," "boat," and "ball." By adjusting the articulators and resonators in this manner, the student may keep a semblance of the original vowel.

Two vowel sounds not included on either modification chart are the intermediate (a) of the British "bask," usually found between (æ) and (ɑ), and the American (ɝ) found in "bird." In the case of (a), I have combined its formants with (æ) on the formant chart and describe it as a broad version of that vowel in the vocalises. The students never sing the flat speech sound associated with "bat" in some areas of the country. Likewise, they never sing the hard "er" of many speech patterns. In accented syllables, such as bird, earth, or further, I prefer the sound be made with a lowered jaw and rounded mouth, in the manner of a German umlaut "ö." In unaccented syllables, such as further, or better, or leisure, I prefer the neutral vowel in above, sofa, and so on—the phonetic schwa (ə).

Female Vowel Modification Vocalises

Most vowels migrate in female voices as the pitch rises past the middle line of the treble clef, reaching "uh" or "ah" at about the last space or line. Above the treble clef most vowels sound alike in the female voice, so I teach the women to find "their vowel" which will be the basis for all other sounds in that range.

Often it is difficult to relate vocalises to songs. So a few well-known musical examples have been chosen to illustrate vowel modifications. The examples are in English, although the principles of modification are the same in all Western languages.

Vocalise 1. In this example (Illustration 5.22) the high E's and G's are above the first formant of "eh," so the migration is toward a bright (a) as in the British word "bask." A pure "ah" might be used, depending on the voice. A soprano should open the mouth as if to sing "ah" but keep a forward feeling as if singing "dal." A mezzo-soprano might wish to blend "eh" and the lax "oo" into an umlaut vowel. The umlaut is on the inside, however, as the lips are not rounded. Care should be taken that the blended vowel not tense the articulators in the velum and pharynx.

"The Lass with the Delicate Air" by Thomas Arne

Illustration 5.22

Vocalise 2. In this example (Illustration 5.23) the persistent "ee" in "believe me" is uniformly above the low formant of the vowel. If the singer thinks of opening the vocal tract wider as she sings higher, the vowel will automatically migrate to "ih" or a broad "ay." The words will thus retain enough of their pure characteristics to be identified. The singer may practice the passage first on the vowel "ah" to find the proper shape and size of the vocal tract. Then within that configuration she may sing "bih-lih-ayve mih" or "bih-lih-ave mih." The wide "ay" or bright (**a**) should occur within a smooth portamento. The "ay" will require more support than (**a**), but it will sound closer to the original vowel.

O — yes, be-lieve — me, —

"Love Has Eyes" by Sir Henry Bishop

Illustration 5.23

Vocalise 3. There are two major problems in this passage (Illustration 5.24)—the vowels and the consonants. "M" and "b" are both closed consonants, and "m" is nasal besides. The first suggestion to the singer is not to nasalize the "m." Simply closing the lips gives sufficient "m" in that high range; the velum need not lower. In closing the lips it is better here to let the lower lip move up, leaving the upper lip at or above the teeth. This will pull less on the velum and leave the inner articulators free to deal with the high vowels. If the singer is a soprano, she may modify the first high G to "mam" (rhymes with Sam), or change the whole syllable to "bab." If the "b" has no pressure behind it, it will sound like a non-nasal "m." The "er" should be modified to "uh" or "ah." Finally, the "me" is doubly bad because of the "m" and a pitch much too high for "ee." The syllable shifts to "mih" or "bih." After practicing the phrase on "ah" to find the proper room in the vocal tract, the singer executes the passage as "rih-mam-bah mih" or "rih-bab-bah bih," or some compromise between them. In the case of a mezzo-soprano, the phrase becomes "rih-mah-bah mah" with whatever small vestige of the original vowels she can muster. In any case the tone should flow as if the three high G's were one long

fate;   Re-mem-ber   me,

"When I Am Laid in Earth" by Henry Purcell

Illustration 5.24

note, not three separate attacks. This passage requires that vocal health and beauty take precedence over purity of vowel sounds.

Vocalise 4. This example (Illustration 5.25) is chosen because it is not so high, yet represents a peculiar problem in English. The word "and" contains a difficult vowel to sing beautifully combined with a nasal consonant "n" and a "d" which may pull the vocal instrument out of shape. If the vowel is modified to "ah" or "uh," the result sounds stilted to most American audiences. A better choice is to sing the original sound but lower the jaw and open the pharynx toward the (a) in the British "bask." Care should be taken that the "n" not intrude on the vowel by lowering the velum too soon. In some voices the "n" may be omitted, making the word "add." The ear does not insist on hearing nasal sounds in the upper range. Finally, the "d" may be executed by merely flicking the tongue tip up to the teeth or gums, coordinating the movement with the pulse of breath in the following "h." This should prevent the "d" from interrupting the flow of tone. If she can, the mezzo-soprano should articulate the "n" in conjunction with the "d." The two consonants require practically the same tongue movement, so the velum may be lowered slightly at the very end of the vowel sound. In an optimum execution the phrase might be visualized as "a—ndH-ih shall. . . ." The "ee" may have to be modified in a heavy voice.

and   He shall   give — thee thy heart's de-

"O Rest in the Lord" from *Elijah* by Mendelssohn

Illustration 5.25

Male Vowel Modification Chart

In male voices a vowel shift occurs between the top line of the bass clef and middle C. Thus the examples here concentrate above there. There is another shift in the male voice between D and F above middle C which will be explored in greater detail in the next chapter, "How to Change Registers Smoothly."

The male vowel modification chart is somewhat more complex than the female chart because here migration is less a function of vowel formants and more a function of adapting to low laryngeal phonation-resonance. Here again "ah" and "uh" are equal for much the same reasons as above. "Uh" seems to be preferred by basses and bass-baritones and "ah" by the tenors and high baritones.

The outer vowel sounds do not migrate to "ah" but to a closer neighbor. Some may migrate in either of two directions, depending on the voice, the word, the dynamic marking, and so on. For instance, a word such as "get" may sound better migrating toward "git" or "gate" than to "gat." On the other hand, a word such as "amen" will be more dramatic migrating toward "a-man" with an open throat and broad tongue. In a quiet passage "a-mane" will sound serene and restful. For the same reasons a phrase such as "Fall on your knees" might migrate toward the vowel "ah" on a high note, but "Lord God of Abraham" might be better modified to "oh" since it is marked *piano*. In all of these modifications there should be a feeling of vertical space in the pharynx.

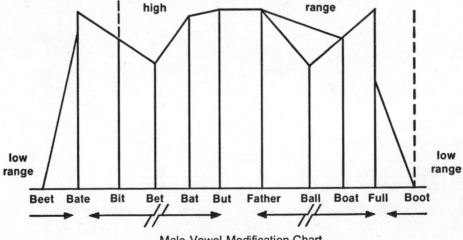

Male Vowel Modification Chart

Illustration 5.26

The dotted lines indicate vowels which may not have to migrate. The vowel in "bit" can be used to the top of the male range if there is a sufficiently high formant. Individual differences in vocal tracts and vowel perceptions make some singers produce a high frequency "ih" which is very close to "ee" but relaxed enough not to cause vocal tension in the upper range. Others' "ih" vowels are so low they are closer kin to "eh," as in the substitution of "melk" for "milk," "Ellenois" for "Illinois," and so forth. In the case of "oo" the dotted line continues straight up because in the light adjustment of head voice the vowel is not only possible but is the basis for all other sounds.

In both male and female voices the lighter range must have additional space in the resonating chambers. Thus the lips open (but not spread), the jaw drops, and the tongue lowers to release the pressure on the larynx. By continuing to think the pure vowel sound, the student may modify vowels without losing understandability. There seems to be only a small fraction of the pure vowel necessary in the modified sound to be correctly identified.

Modified Vowels = Same Vowels

The ultimate purpose for letting vowels migrate or causing them to modify is to make them understandable and beautiful at the same time. Understandability should not be completely sacrificed for beauty, but beauty should never be sacrificed for purity of vowels. Modification offers a compromise between the two, as I discovered early in my own vocal training.

Once when I had been studying voice only a short time, I was working on Max Reger's "The Virgin's Slumber Song." The phrase which begins "Ah, baby . . ." was particularly hard because it was near the top of my range. My teacher tried diligently to teach me how to sing a soft, round, high "ah," but I just could not manage it. Then in a practice session I was experimenting with various approaches and found that if I sang "Oh, baby . . ." I could control the sound. It was even more controllable if I sang "Oo, baby . . .", but I knew my teacher would never go for that. So the next time I had a lesson I tried out the "Oh, baby" approach, standing behind my teacher as she played the song. It was successful, and she was highly complimentary. Some time later after I had memorized the piece and was standing where she could see me, when we came to that part she said, "Don't sing 'oh, baby.' " So I opened my mouth and found that what sounded like "Uh, baby" to me came out "Ah, baby" to her. After that, a large part of my lessons was spent finding out the difference in the modified sound on the inside and on the outside.

The Ubiquitous "uh"

Both of the directors I mentioned earlier used the vowel "uh" to encourage a richer sound in their choruses. One often spoke of "putting a lot of 'uh' in every sound," and the other had a concept of vowel formation which he called "the ubiquitous 'uh'." It was his idea that vowels were produced like house paint: five gallons of "uh" plus a quart of "ee" equaled a rich, understandable vocal sound. He considered "uh" to be the basic laryngeal sound which was colored from some area in the left frontal lobe of the cerebrum. With that as his major premise, it was a natural second step to modifying vowels toward "uh" in the upper ranges. With "uh" as the basis for sounds he could easily explain to various sections of the choir just how to adjust a particular sound. Choral blend was based on vowels and listening to one another, rather than on trying to match vibratos, intensities, or other factors. The end result was excellent choral singing and healthy voices.

The Progressive Umlaut

Another concept of vowel modification in men's voices is "the progressive umlaut." The idea is that as the scale ascends, vowels from the opposite sides of the vowel chart are blended for sonority and ease of production. For instance, to keep "beet" from becoming a tense, screeching sound the singer rounds his lips somewhat as in "boot." The throat becomes less tense as the vowel migrates toward the German umlaut "ü." "Bate" may migrate toward the shape of "boat," thus assuming some of the characteristics of the German "ö."

Blending vowels from either side of the chart is a good way of assuring the singer that there will be sufficient space in the pharynx on the frontal vowels and sufficient high overtones in the back vowels. In all the blends care must be taken to keep all the principles of good breath-phonation-resonance foremost. Concepts of vowel modification and migration are designed to augment good vocal training, not to supplant it. As with the other principles, modified and blended vowels depend on the teacher's ears for final judgment and approval.

Male Vowel Modification Vocalises

Vocalise 1. This phrase (Illustration 5.27) is treacherously exposed, and the tenor must be very careful in modifying the vowel in "with" so the line will not be drawn out of shape. In most tenor voices the "ih" will remain pure in the high range, and only needs to drop the jaw to have sufficient space in the vocal tract for ease of production. The vowel should be encouraged toward a high "ee" formant while maintaining the lax vowel position. In some voices, however, the "ih" may have to shift toward "ay" for formant development. It should not be allowed to drift toward "eh," or the tone will become strident. Also, the word "with" is not important enough to stand that much dramatic tension. A tenor who can mix a bit of head voice into the upper range and not sing too loudly may blend the "ih" with the "o͝o" which is inherent in the "w." The lips should not be pulled in on the vowel. Rather, the umlaut is on the inside.

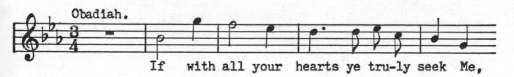

"If with All Your Hearts" from *Elijah* by Mendelssohn

Illustration 5.27

Vocalise 2. There are two ways these examples (Illustration 5.28) may be treated. Example a. If the tenor can sing a bright "ah" on the high A, he may give the word "dash" quite a bit of space and modify toward the diphtong in "die." The end of the diphthong disappears in the movement to "sh." Rather than have to darken the vowel to "dahsh" or "dush" if "die" is too constricted, the tenor may modify toward "daysh." This should be sung with the same energy and space in the mouth and throat as "die." The "ay" is not as dramatic as "die," but neither is it quite as difficult.

In example b., if the final word is sung on the alternate high A, the vowel migrates toward "vass" becoming almost the same vowel as in "die." Or, it may migrate toward "vay" with plenty of space in the mouth and throat. The idea is that both these vowels may be approached in the same way, with the same open throat and vowel position, and each will maintain enough of its original integrity to be understood.

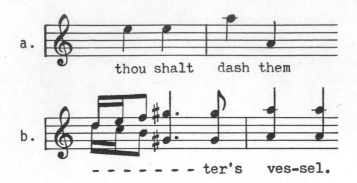

thou shalt   dash them

- - - - - - - ter's   ves-sel.

"Thou Shalt Dash Them" from *Messiah* by Handel

Illustration 5.28

Vocalise 3. Probably in Handel's day the upper notes were not the problem they are now because the pitch was so much lower then. Today's oratorio bass must contend with quite a few modifications which would not be necessary if the aria were a tone lower. Example a. (Illustration 5.29) "so" must modify to the lax vowel in "full" in order to have the space necessary for good production.

na - tions so   furious- ly rage   to - ge - ther,

why   do   the   peo-ple

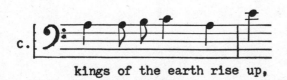

kings of the earth rise up,

"Why Do the Nations" from *Messiah* by Handel

Illustration 5.29

In example b., the word "do" may be sung by some baritones without migrating, but basses and bass-baritones should shift the vowel toward the same lax "oo." The feeling in both these modifications is as if the vowel were "uh" with the lips slightly rounded.

Example c. points out a word which is almost a modification in itself. There is such a tendency to sing the word as if it were "ahp," that the correct vowel becomes its own vowel shift. There is not as much internal pressure in "up" as in "ahp," and it feels so easy the bass may not trust the neutral vowel to carry. But it may have as much ring as "ah" and be much easier on the vocal mechanism.

Vocalise 4. This is the example (Illustration 5.30) mentioned in the anecdote. A bass or baritone may practice modifying to "oh," then opening the lips to the "ah" position. There should not be too much pressure or intensity, or the vowel will become too dramatic for the piece. The proper result is the neutral "uh" which rings like "ah" but requires less internal pressure.

"The Virgin's Slumber Song" by Max Reger

Illustration 5.30

Vocalise 5. Baritones often think they will perish before learning to sing this phrase well (Illustration 5.31). Actually, the "ih" may be sung in an unmodified form if it has strong enough high formants. A great deal of support is required, however. And there is a tendency to open the vowel to "resh," which makes the task doubly hard. To counteract such a tendency the singer may modify toward "raysh," which has a slightly higher formant.

The singer might also try blending the vowel a bit with the lax "o͝o," somewhat in the manner of a German "ü." The umlaut sound will not stand quite as much internal pressure as "ih," but it may be a safe compromise which will release vocal tension.

There was a question in the organization of this book whether or not the chapter on vowel modification should include a discussion of registers. The volume of material on each subject was so

frail-ty   that I   must   per-ish,

"Lord, Make Me to Know" from *A German Requiem* by Brahms

Illustration 5.31

great it was decided that two separate chapters were needed. If it
were possible, the two chapters should be read simultaneously. It
will become evident early in the next chapter how inseparable they
really are.

6

HOW TO TRAIN SINGERS TO
CHANGE REGISTERS SMOOTHLY

Devising a usable concept of registers or registration frequently creates a pedagogical dilemma between what seems to be and what ought to be. The dilemma is compounded by incomplete research, equivocal language, and differing aesthetics. For many teachers what seems to be—that every voice evidences changes of vocal quality at certain points—is questioned severely by teachers who hold firmly to what ought to be—that the voice should be unified and equalized so there are no breaks.

WHAT REGISTRATION IS

Ideas about registration in the voice are at least as old as the sixteenth century. Teachers could hear their students having difficulty singing through the entire range without the voice breaking or encountering places where the quality changed. Such a place was called a *passaggio*—a passage from one area to another. The best students were those who negotiated the *passaggio* effortlessly.

The areas on each side of the *passaggio* sounded almost as

different as the various sets of pipes in an organ. These clusters of pipes were called registers, why not use the same term in speaking of voices? Thus registers became the mental construct which was fashioned to give answers to questions for which there was no other explanation.

Registers as a Function of Phonation

The situation became more confusing after about 1835 when professional singers discovered a new way of singing. Until that time performers sang with a clear, "white" tone in which the larynx rose on each ascending pitch. The extreme upper range became either a controlled scream—what might be termed *bel grido*—or a falsetto head voice. When singers learned to sing with the larynx consistently low, the voice sounded darker, the upper voice was mellower and richer than the upper scream, and it was richer and stronger than head voice.

Registers as a Function of Resonance

A further confusion in the search for registers was the apparent change in tonal "placement" which occurred with a register shift. This concurrent shift fomented a combined theory of tone placement and registration which has persisted to the present in the symbolic names given to registers: chest, middle, and head.

There is also a lot of confusion of terms between registers and resonance areas, such as, chest voice and and chest register, head voice and head register, falsetto and head register, and so on. Most theorists speak of the male quality which is produced with the full vocal band and reinforced high overtones, either covered or open, as being chest voice. The soft, breathy tone with weak overtones and minimal mass of vocal band may either be head voice or falsetto, depending on the theorist. Within the male chest voice there may be three registers—low or chest, middle, and high, upper, or head.

Female voices have different resonance areas of chest and head voice which are similar to those in men's voices. Generally, the registers in female voices coincide with the resonance areas, except for the middle register which is sometimes considered a mixed voice rather than part of head voice. To avoid confusion I will use the terms low, middle, and high (or upper) registers to distinguish them from chest, middle, and head (or falsetto) voices.

HOW MANY REGISTERS

One Register, No Registers, and Pan-Tonic Registers

Various theories have been proposed which number the registers from none (registers do not exist) to pan-tonic (a register on every note). From a practical standpoint the theories of one register and no registers end with the same conclusion that breaks in the voice are the result of poor vocalism. Whether there is a single register into which the entire voice fits or there are no such things as registers is a moot argument. Similarly, a voice with a register on every note would require the same training as a voice with one register. Seemingly, these teachers viewed the voice from the standpoint of what ought to be and attacked the problem of register breaks in the same way they would any other vocal flaw, concentrating on good breathing, free phonation, and increased resonance.

Two, Three, Four, and Five Registers

For those teachers who heard what seemed to be register changes as an integral part of the voice, there were different problems: determining the number of registers, locating the parameters of each register, and devising transition techniques for each. There were theories of two registers (chest and falsetto) and three registers (chest, middle, and falsetto) almost simultaneously. Some teachers called falsetto "head voice" or "head register," which also caused some confusion.

Theories of four and five registers are later refinements of the three register theory, such as an extra low register below the bass clef and a "whistle" register above the soprano high C. Other teachers have heard register changes in the middle of all voices, while still others hear registers within the head voice.

In a system of two registers there is the question of a rather large area of the voice above the chest register which does not seem to vibrate in the head. The three register theory offers a solution by calling that area the middle register, mixed voice, or some such name.

One Voice or Two

Some theorists hear the human voice as a unity which begins with the low bass and ends with the high soprano, with the voices overlapping in the middle. These theorists hear register changes as acoustical phenomena which occur according to musical ranges regardless of the voice type. For instance, the register change around the E above middle C is the same shift whether at the top of the man's voice or at the bottom of a woman's. Thus, training the voice to negotiate that particular *passaggio* is the same procedure in men and women. This idea is related to Garcia's somewhat misleading concept that all notes below E were in chest voice and all notes above E were in falsetto.

Other theorists hear men's and women's voices as two similar instruments separated by an octave like wind instruments. They hear the register changes around the middle and top of the treble clef in a woman's voice as the same phenomena as the register changes above the bass clef in a man's voice. This is known as the octave phenomenon.

Light and Heavy Mechanism

In recent years teachers have begun to talk of registers in terms of light and heavy adjustments of the vocal bands. This concept removes the idea of registers from the concepts of placement and fixed ranges in the voice. Heavy and light mechanism are qualitative measurements. However, this concept focusses almost exclusively on phonation as a factor in registration. And the use of the terms light and heavy mechanism fails to explain the large middle register of the voice.

CAUSES OF REGISTRATION

Current research is beginning to shed quite a bit of light on the causes of registration. There are no firm conclusions yet, however, from which to devise new methods of teaching. Registration is evidently affected by the enormously complex changes in phonation and resonance already mentioned in earlier chapters. Because of the close relationship of phonation and resonance, it is impossible to determine which element is dominant in causing a register change.

Depth and Brilliance

Since registration is a combination of phonation-resonance, it may best be taught through many of the same approaches as resonance. I believe a useful concept of teaching registers includes blending depth and brilliance throughout the voice. Where a concept of blending heavy mechanism in the upper voice might lead to a weighty production, a concept of blending depth in the upper voice would not. Every note may be a mixture of depth and brilliance.

Water and Earth Analogy

A good analogy of blending sounds in a voice is that of water and earth. These elements may be combined into an infinite variety of muds, some thin and soupy, others thick and gravelly, depending on the ratios of the ingredients. In the same way sounds may be an infinite number of blends of depth and brilliance, depending on the ratios of the components. Any given note may be sung in many acceptable ways, and every note of the voice contains both earth and water.

TEACHING REGISTER CHANGES

I have found that an efficient way to teach register changes is to view them as extensions of teaching resonance and vowel sounds. They thus become qualitative changes which are not fixed to particular areas of the voice. A concept of registration is an adjunct to teaching good principles of breath-phonation-resonance, not a substitute. Registers are not predetermined problems, but are a handy term for explaining vocal techniques. This is not a denial of the physiological, acoustical factors which may cause registration in the voice. It is an acknowledgement that, like phonation, there are no direct methods of dealing with the immensely complex realities of registers.

Registration as a Teaching Tool

The place of registration as a teaching tool is analogous to an atom in a complex molecule whose elements are so intertwined they are inseparable except in theory. Registration is joined to phonation through the structural adjustments in the larynx necessary to singing several octaves of homogeneous sound. It is joined to resonance through the changes in the resonators on musical pitches, vowel migration and modification, and vowel equalization and unification. Laryngeal adjustments necessitate pharyngeal changes which cause sounds to migrate, especially above the shifts

of energy called register changes. Vowel modification is inextrica-
ble from teaching register changes. Thus the concepts of breath-
phonation-resonance +. vowels +. registers are combined as
thoroughly as a chemical compound.

Register Change = Vowel and Placement Change

Register changes may be effected through vowel modification.
A major difference in the sound of one register from another is in
the distribution of harmonic overtones. The lower the register, the
more strong high frequency overtones. The higher the register,
the stronger the fundamental pitch and the weaker the high overtones. In order to make the sounds of two registers match—that is,
to equalize the registers—the vowel in the higher register must
have higher formant frequencies to offset the loss of high harmonic
overtones. Equalizing registers is closely related to equalizing
vowels. For instance, an ascending scale on the lax vowel "eh" may
shift to the tense "ay" to facilitate a register change and equalize
the two registers. The end result will be a scale which sounds alike
below and above the register change.

Each vowel shifts into the high register according to its formants, with "ah" shifting on the highest pitch of all. "Ah" may be
sung in the middle register on higher pitches than the other vowels. "Ee" and "oo" shift into the high register on lower pitches than
other vowels. Therefore, the female vowel formant chart may be
useful in coordinating vowel modification with register changes.
Just as with vowel modification, vocal tension may be eased
through changing registers.

The register changes in male voices also follow the formant
chart. The high peaks on the male formant chart indicate vowels
which change into the upper register on high pitches. "Ay" shifts
higher than "ee" and "eh." "Ōo" shifts higher than "oh" and "ōo,"
and so on. "Ah" and "uh" shift on the same note, but "uh" is easier
to sing in the high register and gives the impression of a mellow or
"covered" "ah."

Register Change = Quality Change Inside

In passing from the low or middle register to high register
there is often a sudden change in the sound on the inside from
bright, clear, and ringing to dark, diffuse, and muffled, almost as if

something had stopped up the singer's ears. Often I have to record a student to prove that the sound is as bright and full above the register change as below it. I often tell my students that changing registers is like putting their fingers in their ears while listening to the stereo. Nothing happened to the stereo; they are simply hearing it differently. Likewise, nothing drastic happens to the voice in changing registers, but there is a great difference in the way the singer hears the upper register inside.

Register Change = Covered Tone

Many pedagogical concepts, such as the covered tone, have developed more as a result of the singer's inner sensations than from the sound outside. In my early years I learned to negotiate the *passaggio* into the upper register through "covering" the tone. The technique of covering was quite similar to the vowel change I described in the anecdote about "The Virgin's Slumber Song." The sound was more covered on the inside than on the outside. By using the covered tone I could sing higher, freer, and easier than with the strident sound I had before. Until I learned covering, the judges at contests and auditions always complimented my high *pianissimo* but deplored my tendency to shout on a high *forte*. After learning to cover the high register, I no longer received such disapproving criticisms.

The term "cover" comes from the French *voix couverte* (covered voice) or *voix sombre* (dark voice), terms coined to describe the new sound discovered about 1835 in Paris. Covered voice contrasted with the *voix ouverte* (open voice) or *voix blanche* (white voice). In open voice the larynx rose with the musical pitch. In covered voice the singer kept the larynx low throughout his range.

Open sounds have a higher proportion of brilliance than covered sounds because the rising larynx shortens the pharynx, shifting the low vowel formant upward. Thus covered voice was a new technique of phonation and vowel production. In open voice the velum lowers with the rising pitch, and there is a concurrent strain on the vocal bands. In covered voice the velum stays high, and the vocal bands adjust themselves to stay loose and flexible.

Over the years the term "cover" has taken on new meanings and has become almost a five letter expletive for some teachers. It is now used to describe the undesirable sound of a depressed larynx made by forcing the tongue into the pharynx, that is, swallowing or muffling the tone. It would be better to call such a sound "smothered" and reaffirm "cover" as a legitimate auxiliary vocal technique.

Finding the Registers

The following procedure is useful in determining where the registers change in beginning voices:

1. Sing an ascending G major scale from G to D; listen for changes in quality and intensity around B.
2. Then sing an ascending F major scale from F to C; listen for the same changes.
3. There should be a shift in quality and intensity between A and B-flat or between B-flat and C; occasionally a high voice will change between C and D in the G major scale.
4. This change of quality is where vowels begin to migrate, and is called the first "lift."
5. There should be another shift in quality a perfect fourth above the first lift, called the second lift; this phenomenon occurs in all voices.
6. There should also be a register change a perfect fifth below the first lift in women's voices; this change is not usually referred to as a lift, but it acts like one.

Lifts

The term "lift" is used to describe the action of the breath at register changes. As the singer approaches the point of change, he lightens the quality of sound rather than forcing the voice until it breaks. The breath seems to lift the voice over the register change. The pitches between the first and second lifts are considered a transitional area between the low and high registers in men and within the middle register in women.

CHANGING REGISTERS SMOOTHLY: MALES

High Male Register

The same procedures may be used to teach all male voices how to lift into the upper register. The only difference in teaching tenors, baritones, and basses is determining the notes where the registers change. The average transitional areas, or middle registers, between the lifts are given in Illustration 6.1

Bass   Baritone   Tenor

Illustration 6.1

Below the bottom notes (the first lift) all sounds are in the low register, and all vowels have their pure quality. Between the notes is the transitional area of a perfect fourth. There is some overlapping between voice types because some baritones are almost basses while others are virtually tenors. In the transition area, or middle register, vowels begin to migrate, as described in the previous chapter. Above the highest notes (the second lift) is the high register. The same technique which helps a bass sing above D will help a baritone above E-flat or E and a tenor above F or F-sharp.

Turning Over or Hooking the Voice

An internal phenomenon in changing from the middle to upper registers, that is, lifting into the upper register, is "turning over" or "hooking" the voice. Singers describe this sensation as if something inside the nasopharynx turned over and let the sound into the upper register. Or, it feels as if the ascending scale were shaped like a hook which proceeds out of the pharynx and turns through the nasal cavity into the masque. Both these descriptions are related to the release of middle register weight and the broadening of the oro- and nasopharynx which affects the singers' ears. I have found both metaphors useful in teaching men to negotiate the *passaggio*.

Physically Easy but Mentally Hard

Most singers agree that singing properly in the high register is no harder physically than in the middle register, but at first it is very difficult to achieve mentally. The new feelings of placement, the loss of weight in the tone, the new vowel sound, and the new technique of control are hard to correlate. The sense of covering a tone, when most of their previous training had been in developing brilliance and ring, is almost a reversal of good principles to many singers. In the high register the singer learns to rely on how the tone feels, that is, how easy it is to produce and how good his throat feels while he is singing.

Male Register Vocalises

Vocalise 1. Practice the vocalise (Illustration 6.2) in the keys of E-flat, E, F, F-sharp, and G. The vocalise combines vowel modification and covering. The mouth opens vertically as the vowel changes from "eh" to "ih." The mouth relaxes on the descending arpeggio. The lips may round on "ih" to effect a slight cover. Later this will not be necessary. The singer feels more space in the pharynx on the upper notes, which gives the sound a darker quality. Do not carry up the weight of the lower tone. Use depth instead of weight. Keep the upper vowel in front of the tongue, or perhaps in front of the face. Let the ring remain constant when the register changes. An alternate vocalise is "zeh-ay." Return to the original vowel on the descending arpeggio into the middle and low registers. When the vocalise is sung in high keys, the first note may need to migrate in order to equalize the two registers.

Zeh- ih- eh- - - - -

Illustration 6.2

Vocalise 2. This vocalise (Illustration 6.3) is related to No. 1. Since "oh" has a much lower second formant than "ah," the upper note will be above the second lift in high register. If the singer rounds the mouth only slightly, the result will be a covered "ah." At first there may be too much cover, but with some experimentation the singer will find the proper relationship of "ah" and "oh." Eventually there will be no need to think of covering or modifying the vowel, and all the sounds will be "ah." The high pitch will then be in the upper register without a break. An alternate vocalise is "ah-o͞o."

Illustration 6.3

Vocalise 3. The formants of "ah" and "uh" are practically the same, but the configuration of "uh" is such that it may be viewed as a covered "ah." The sounds are so close they can hardly be distinguished in the high register, and "uh" is usually much easier to sing. Practice this vocalise (Illustration 6.4) as in Nos. 1 and 2.

Illustration 6.4

Vocalise 4. This vocalise (Illustration 6.5) is based on the principle of the progressive umlaut and presents another way of covering the vowel "ay" to facilitate the register change. Begin the vocalise with the vowel "oh." Then alternate with the exercise beginning with "ay." Think of the umlaut on the inside. Practice without rounding the lips. Keep the vowel in front of the tongue; think of the sound resonating about eye level in front of the face.

Illustration 6.5

Vocalise 5. These vocalises (Illustration 6.6) are examples of register changes as well as vowel shifts. In the key of E-flat the highest note is in the upper register. The singer should hear the turn around the tonic note as a continuum which shifts up and back smoothly. Support the entire phrase so the high notes are not overemphasized. Try to feel the notes as well as hear them.

Illustration 6.6

Vocalise 6. This long roulade (Illustration 6.7) makes use of all the registers on a single vowel. After practicing the previous exercises, the singer should hear this as a single vowel, but there should be smooth shifts through the middle register into the upper and back again.

Illustration 6.7

Vocalise 7. Some tenors who have too much tension above high F may find vocalises based on head voice useful. The idea is to develop as much depth and brilliance as possible while maintaining a free flowing tone. Head voice releases the excess tension of an open tone. Be sure the larynx stays low while singing head voice. Eventually, the singer should be able to crescendo from a soft sound to an intense sound without a break in the voice.

Musical Examples

Example 1. The singer may have to experiment to find which procedure or combination of procedures is the best. The proper pronunciation (Illustration 6.8) is the bright (**a**) in the British "bask." The mouth is open with plenty of space in the pharynx. Keep the air flowing. The sound "turns over" or "hooks" into the upper register. Avoid darkening to "uh."

An alternate approach is to change "shall" to "shell" or a covered "shayl." This relieves most of the weight of "ah." The singer may sing a slur from B-flat to high A-flat on the syllable "yay" or "yee-ay" to find the placement for the high register. A slight "h" is also helpful before the high note to keep the air flowing and the tone bright, as in "yee-hay." Then change to "ye shayl" or "ye shell," letting the A-flat move to the high register, keeping the tone free and flowing. As the singer gains strength and can sing this approach well, he may broaden the vowel toward bright (**a**). This process may take time, as it depends on muscular development as well as technical skill.

"If with All Your Hearts" from *Elijah* by Mendelssohn

Illustration 6.8

Example 2. This example (Illustration 6.9) is more difficult than No. 1 because it requires the singer to shift registers on an ascending scale. The singer begins by changing the second syllable to "foot." Do not round the lips. Omit the "r." Keep the mouth open as if to sing "ah." Feel the weight of the vowel disappear as it "turns over" into the upper register. The sound seems to escape and feels very free. Watch that the "m" does not pull the upper lip and velum down. By experimenting the singer can find a way of producing "m" with the upper teeth on the lower lip, the position of "f." The high vowel may also be "ah" if the singer lets it shift into upper register. He should not carry up the weight of the middle register.

The singer may sing the ascending third on "ah-o͞o" to find the proper placement of the high register. Then he may sing "kah-foot," and find that it sounds very much like "com-fort." He may also try a progressive umlaut, as in "kah-föt," emphasizing the space of the "o͞o" and the brilliance of "ay." An exercise such as "kah-fay" may be helpful to relieve weight and encourage forward placement.

"Comfort Ye" from *Messiah* by Handel

Illustration 6.9

Example 3. In his religious zeal Gounod quoted the tenor passage in No. 2 in the baritone aria in *Faust*. The lyric baritone is quite similar to the tenor voice, so this example (Illustration 6.10) of register changes is only a half-tone lower than No. 2. The second syllable of "quiet" shifts to "ay" as the voice lifts over the register change. On the second high G the vowel may be "uh" to relieve pressure and help cover the bright "aw." Do not round the lips. Try singing the high G and F on "uh," then add the consonants.

Valentine's Aria ("Even Bravest Heart")
From *Faust* by Gounod

Illustration 6.10

The result will be a high register covered tone. Keep the placement forward so the "uh" will ring in front of the tongue.

Not too long ago a young baritone came to study with me whose approach to the high voice was to push the breath out as hard as possible while lifting the chin. The result was more a shout than singing. First, we began working on vowel modification exercises to prepare the way toward register change vocalises. Most of the early exercises were based on "ee," "ay," and "oh," with an occasional "oo" vocalise when appropriate. When the concept of modifying open vowels to closed was firmly established in his muscles' memories, we graduated to the register change vocalises above. The aria from *Faust* was especially useful because of the ascending scale across the *passaggio*. Even after the vowel modification regimen, he was not able to negotiate the change into the upper register smoothly. But practice with the tape recorder, which showed him that the sound was big and bright outside while it sounded small and muffled inside, and concentration on releasing the weight of the lower and middle registers helped him master the technique of changing register smoothly. Now he is a fine professional baritone with an outstanding high range.

CHANGING REGISTERS SMOOTHLY: FEMALES

High Female Register

Some female students have trouble changing into the high register above the second lift, although the problem is not as widespread as with men. The sound of the female voice does not change as much between middle and high registers, because women sing in head voice rather than chest voice above the chest register lift. But there is an acoustical shift in the female voice above the second lift which has to be dealt with. Exercises suggested earlier, such as the fire siren, will help female students learn to negotiate the *passaggio*. Also, since all vowels migrate to "ah" or "uh" in the female high register, the vowel modification vocalises in the preceding chapter are particularly important.

Low Female Register

A matter of some controversy is the use of low register in the female voice. The "break" around the bottom of the treble clef is especially annoying in the heavier voice. Some singers try to mask the problem by not allowing the voice to shift into the low, intense sound, but this produces a soft, often breathy tone similar to the falsetto in men. If there is a female falsetto register, I believe it is this sort of phonation.

There are several reasons why women should learn to negotiate the *passaggio* into the low register. First it is a more satisfying sound which offers more variety of color, dynamics, and emotions. Second, a judicious use of the low register strengthens the entire voice because of the vigorous use of the entire vocal band. However, use of the low register means the singer has to learn techniques for changing registers smoothly.

Similar to Male Voice

Earlier I mentioned my belief that the human voice is a unity, with the high male and low female voices overlapping. Thus, the female may use techniques similar to the male high register exercises. There are some differences in the male and female which are worth mentioning.

Low Velum Problem

One problem in the female voice not generally found in the male is the tendency to sing with a low velum in the low register. This is the source of the strident sound known as "belting," or "torch singing." It is a common sound among popular singers, and there is a distinct difference in their low and high registers. The registers are not unified as in the classical style of singing. A consistently low larynx will help overcome this problem, as well as the high velum exercises mentioned earlier.

Range Problem

Because the female voice is near the bottom of its range in low register, there are some differences in phonation from the male voice in the upper middle of its range. The female vocal bands are relatively more massive and more relaxed than the male. It is more difficult to keep enough tension on the bands and to maintain proper support for an equalized sound. It is much easier to let the support drop and sing a speechlike tone. The vocal tract must be about the same size and shape for the low register as for the middle and upper in order for all notes to sound as if they came from the same instrument.

Middle Register Problem

In most female voices the middle register sounds more like male head voice than male high register chest voice. The vocal bands are more supple, there is much less breath pressure, and the sound is less intense. Because of this difference, the female singer experiences different sensations shifting from low register to middle than the male shifting from middle register to high. Some females complain they cannot hear their voices as well in middle register, just as the men in high register. There is also not the same sense of "hooking" or "turning over" the voice as in the men's voices. The voice feels weaker and less controlled. The tendency in some women to push the low register up to strengthen the middle should be assiduously resisted. The lift of the breath is quite important in shifting from low to middle register. The middle register may be trained much better by bringing down the resonance of the high register through descending scales and arpeggios. As the middle register becomes more brilliant, the upper notes of the low register should be sung with less weight to equalize the two registers.

Resistance to Low Register

Occasionally a woman singer will resist shifting into the low register because of the nature of its sound. To her ears the more intense tone is raucous and brassy. It may be too masculine for her aesthetic sensibilities. Often the singer's middle and upper registers have developed well from voice training, but her low register has not developed and sounds unschooled. All these present problems to the teacher in convincing the singer that excursions into the low register are beneficial to her entire voice as well as to the overall quality of performance.

Female Low Register Vocalises

Vocalise 1. (Illustration 6.11.) Begin slowly. Be sure that breath precedes each note. Keep the larynx low and velum high. Slur the "ah" into "ee" on the arpeggio. The highest note may shift out of low register. Be sure the descending arpeggio returns to low register. Do not take the vocalise very high. The register changes should be initiated by the breath. Do not drive the voice upward. Get rid of weight on each ascending passage. Try to match the qualities of the two registers with intensity and high frequency overtones. Notice that the low "ee" does not feel as strong as "ah,"

Illustration 6.11

but it has carrying power in its resonance. Keep the tone clear, although the first "ah" may feel a little breathy. At this point too much breath is probably better than "sitting on" the voice.

Vocalise 2. (Illustration 6.12.) The descending scale feels wider at the bottom than on the first note, which feels rather vertical. The student may visualize a pyramid-shaped vocalise in which the lower notes seem to broaden but maintain their connection with the upper point of the pyramid. Try this vocalise first with the teeth closed to release pressure. The back vowels keep the hum too deep in the throat and hinder a smooth register change.

Illustration 6.12

Vocalise 3. (Illustration 6.13.) Feel the difference in the placement of the vowel when the pitch leaps an octave. On the descending scale try to keep the instrument the same shape and size. The jaw may close a little to relieve pressure, but the ring, depth, and brilliance of the line should be maintained.

Illustration 6.13

Vocalise 4. This vocalise (Illustration 6.14) is based on the principle of open and covered tones explained earlier in the male vocalises. The "ee" serves as a covered vowel; the "eh" is open. There is quite a difference in the feel and sound of the two vowels inside, but the voice does not break as the registers shift. Keep the line supported as if it were ascending into the high register. An alternate vocalise is "may-eh-eh-eh" which shows the register change around E even more clearly. Eventually the student should sing the latter vocalise without a break.

Mee - - - - meh.

Illustration 6.14

Vocalise 5. This vocalise (Illustration 6.15) is related to No. 4. Try to keep the forward placement of "ay" in the " æ ." After practicing this vocalise, an alternate may be "meh-matt" or sing the entire phrase on "matt." Feel the broadening of the vowel like a pyramid.

May - - - - matt.

Illustration 6.15

Registration Vocalises Made from Songs

Example 1. a. In this example (Illustration 6.16) the singer may open the word "lift" to "left," keeping the high placement of "ih." The word "up" may be in low or middle register, depending on the singer. In either case the vowel should be brightened to "ah" to maintain the brilliance of the low register. Be sure the open vowels are produced with a vertical feeling to help them match the middle register.

"O Thou That Tellest" from *Messiah* by Handel

Illustration 6.16

b. Be sure the low note is sung "ah," not "uh" as in the speech pronunciation. Keep the vocal tract large and the vowel bright. The "oo" of "Judah" should be bright and ringing whether in low or middle register.

c. Try humming this passage to feel the register changes. Sing the first two words with a bright (a) to facilitate the shift upward to the roulade. Sing "aw" instead of "oh" in the run. Practice slowly to feel the register changes. Lift over the changes, carrying the phrase on resonance, not force. Since the D's may be either in low or middle register, the singer must determine proper register according to the surrounding notes. Usually the D should be in middle register in an ascending scale which runs into the treble clef, but it may be in low register in descending scales. Brackets have been inserted to show the suggested registers, but the final determination should be the teacher's.

Example 2. a. This example (Illustration 6.17) is similar to No. 1a. The final syllable may be opened to "leh" for placement in the low register. Keep the broad feeling of "eh" and close the vowel

"Patiently Have I Waited"
From *Christmas Oratorio* by Saint-Saëns

Illustration 6.17

to "ih." The syllable "tient" should be sung "shent" or "shant" rather than "shunt" to keep all the vowels in line. The last syllable may be pronounced "lee," but the sound will not carry as far as the lax "lih."

b. The singer may modify "heard" to "uh" or to open umlaut "ö." "Uh" will probably carry farther in an auditorium, especially if the singer keeps a forward placement in the tone. The vowel should feel vertical and should ring. The umlaut "ö" is closer to the original "er," and is easier to equalize with the middle register than "uh," but it will not carry over an orchestra.

Example 3. (Illustration 6.18.) The singer may begin by singing the entire passage on "ah," since all the vowels are variations of "ah." The first scale moves over the first lift, so the word "heart" shifts downward even if it does not reach the low register. This shift prepares the singer's voice and the audience's ears for the next sequence which does reach the low register. The D probably should be in middle register because of the ascending scale. Hum the slur from G to C to feel the register change. Support the G as if

"Thou Art My Peace" by Franz Schubert

Illustration 6.18

it were a high note and add weight and intensity as the pitch descends to C. The low register will sound much louder than the middle at first, but this will pass. Eventually the student will be able to open the vocal tract and let the registers change rather than make them change. Keep the velum high and the breath flowing so the voice does not click or break.

Example 4. (Illustration 6.19.) Sing the last two syllables on the vowels "ee-uh" and "ee-aw." "Uh" is easier to sing with a high velum and is closer to the normal pronunciation, but will not carry as far as the brighter vowel. "Ee-ah" may also be used, but the "ah" will tend to let the velum fall. After practicing the last two syllables without consonants, the student inserts a slight "d" between them by flicking the tongue. Watch that the "m" does not pull down on the preceding vowel. When the student is able to sing both "free-dawm" and "free-dum" with equalized registers, he may decide which is better.

"Dedication" by Robert Schumann

Illustration 6.19

Example 5. This example (Illustration 6.20) shifts back and forth across the register changes and makes good use of the principle of lifts. Begin by singing the phrase on "oh" to feel the open low register and the covered middle register. Next, sing it on "ah" and "uh," using the bright vowel in the low register and the neutral vowel in the middle register. Next, sing the phrase on the vowels of the words without consonants. Think of the pyramid while singing the first three notes, broadening the base of the tone as the

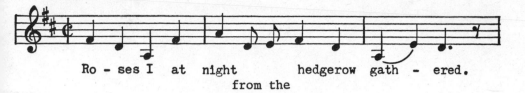

Ro - ses I at night hedgerow gath - ered.
from the

"Sapphic Ode" by Brahms

Illustration 6.20

arpeggio descends. This figure returns on the last words of the phrase. Let the breath lift the voice over the register changes between "I" and "at" and between the two notes on "gath." Do not sing a "y" between "I" and "at." Slur as if there were no diphthong, letting the tongue rise and fall quickly between the two syllables. Sing a bright (a) on "gath." Diminish and lighten the E to lift over the register change. The final syllable should be sung on "uh" to deemphasize the strong beat on an unaccented syllable.

After learning proper breathing, phonation, resonance, vowels, and register changes, the performer must make sense out of the resultant sound. In the next chapter we will discuss articulation as the fourth and final element of singing.

7

MAKING SENSE OUT OF SOUND:
How to Teach the Communication of
Ideas, Emotions and Situations

The ultimate purpose in singing is the communication of ideas, emotions, and situations. Thus, in many ways the most important element of singing is articulation. Without understandable words, singing would lose much of its power to entertain, educate, and persuade.

CONSONANTS OF PRIMARY IMPORTANCE

Consistently clear consonants are the key to understandability, whether in public speaking or in singing. Whereas the beauty of the voice is in the vowels, the beauty of language is in the consonants. The interruption of the vocal airstream transforms meaningless tones into intelligible sounds. Consonants are so important that Semitic languages are written only in consonants. The words are understood without vowels through combinations of consonants.

Consonant formants are much higher than vowel formants, so vowel sounds are enhanced by good consonants. The energy required to sound a consonant is transferred to the adjacent vowel, lending it proper placement, high frequency overtones, musical pitch, and impetus. Consonants are only a fraction as loud as vowels, especially "ah," but their high frequency energy is peculiarly adapted to human ears, so that crisp diction fairly crackles in a good acoustical setting.

SOUNDS ≠ WRITTEN LETTERS

In making sense out of sound, the singer and teacher have to solve many enigmas of language. Some letters of the alphabet represent many different sounds, and English is filled with inconsistencies of spelling and pronunciation. Often there are such regional differences that idiomatic expressions are unintelligible to a stranger. Foreigners are perpetually amazed at the intricacies of learning proper English. With just a bit of manipulation we can construct a sentence in English in which each vowel sound is different, but every word contains the same vowel letters: *Though rough wounds, shouldst thou court ought scourge?* It is no wonder there are differences of opinion in pronouncing our language.

SUNG LANGUAGE NOT THE SAME AS SPOKEN

In the classical style of singing there is a quality to every language which makes it different from everyday speech. Syllabic stresses are tied to note values, the time span of words is lengthened, and there is an elegance which raises the sound of the language above its common denominator in the same way a fine painting ennobles color and canvas above the stray doodles on a telephone pad.

The suggestions made in this chapter are based on a classical approach to singing. They are not intended to be disapproving criticism of any student's natural manner of speaking, but to polish the singer's artistry.

Further, there are a number of good books which explain at length the functions of the articulators—tongue, lips, teeth, palate, and velum—and classify each consonant accordingly. Therefore, this chapter should be seen as an adjunct to such books.

Exercises will be suggested which are designed to strengthen and activate the various articulators. Vocal problems which are related to consonant formation and articulation will also be discussed.

CONSONANT EXERCISES

Lazy Tongue

Exercise 1. Practice this vocalise (Illustration 7.1) as if there were only one long vowel sound, flicking the tongue for the "l." In this way the consonant assumes the same pitch as the adjacent vowel, that is, it is "voiced." The vowel should be uniform throughout the exercise. If the tongue is not free, the vowel will change to "uh" or even disappear. There should be no jaw movement. Only the tongue is active. Other vowel combinations may be used, such as "lah-lee."

Illustration 7.1

Exercise 2. This exercise (Illustration 7.2) is related to No. 1. The tongue should move freely and flexibly. The vowel should remain pure, as if there were one long sound interrupted by the tongue. The consonant assumes the same pitch as the vowel. The

Illustration 7.2

velum should lower for the consonant and rise for the vowel, otherwise the vowel will be too nasal. The purity of the vowel may be checked by holding the nose while singing the vocalise. The vowel should sound the same as in "lah-lah." The jaw should not move in this exercise. Alternate vocalises are "nah-nee," "nay-nay," and so forth.

Exercise 3. This exercise (Illustration 7.3) is also related to No. 1. The "d" builds up a bit more pressure in the mouth than "l" or "n," because the tongue closes more tightly against the palate. There should be no subglottic pressure in the consonant, however. Keep the vowel pure throughout the vocalise, and sing legato to

Dah,dah,dah,dah,   dah.

Illustration 7.3

avoid a double consonant, as in "dod-dod." Try to sing the "d" on the same pitch as the adjacent vowel. The jaw and chin are more apt to move in this exercise than in those above, but with practice the student will eventually be able to articulate a series of "d's" with only the tongue. Also, the jaw should remain loose. Locking the jaw to keep it from moving will impede the adjacent vowel sounds. Alternate vocalises are "dah-dee" and "day-day."

Exercise 4. This exercise (Illustration 7.4) is the unvoiced equivalent to No. 3. There is no musical pitch in the consonant, as

Tah,tah,tah,tah,   tah.

Illustration 7.4

"t" is one of the few consonants which stop the vowel sound completely. "T" builds up more oral pressure than "d," but should not involve subglottic pressure. Some students find it extremely difficult to keep the jaw and chin from moving in this exercise. However, slow practice will help the student learn proper articulatory movements, and speed will come with agility.

Exercise 5. This exercise (Illustration 7.5) combines Nos. 1-4 into a single vocalise. There is a slight difference in the placement of the tongue with each consonant. The object here is to learn to articulate with the tongue as rapidly as possible, maintaining pure vowels and clearly understandable consonants.

Tee,dee,nee,lee,   lee.

Illustration 7.5

Exercise 6. Rather than moving up and down, as in the former vocalises, here (Illustration 7.6) the tongue moves forward and back between the teeth. A common error in diction is to substitute "z" for the voiced "th" [ð] and "s" for the voiceless "th" [θ]. To keep the vowel pure the student may think of singing one long sound while rubbing the upper teeth with the blade of the tongue. An alternate exercise combines voiced and unvoiced "th," as in "though they think thin then," or "then they think thin though."

They,they,they,they,   they.

Illustration 7.6

Flaccid Lips

Exercise 1. This exercise (Illustration 7.7) pulls the lips into a small circle, as if with a drawstring. The lips should move independent of the jaw and chin. The vowel sound will change as the lips open and close, but the inside of the mouth may maintain a constant shape and size. The semivowel glide "w" has the same pitch as its adjacent vowel. The lip action should be vigorous so the "w"

Wow-wow — wow— wow— wow.

Illustration 7.7

will not sound simply like "oo." Alternate vocalises are "woo-woo" and "way-way."

Exercise 2. This exercise (Illustration 7.8) requires the inside of the mouth to change as the lips open and close. The tongue movement back and forth combined with the activity of the lips may cause the jaw and chin to move. However, practice should enable the student to articulate this exercise with a minimum of chin and jaw movement. The student should avoid spreading the lips into a smile for the "ee." The tongue alone forms the vowel, as in the vowel exercises described in an earlier chapter.

Wow-wee — wow-wee — wow.

Illustration 7.8

Exercise 3. This exercise (Illustration 7.9) is related to No. 2. The lips close completely for the "m" but without subglottic pressure. Here again the student avoids letting the mouth spread for

Mum — mum — mum — mee — mee — mee—

mum — mum — mum — mee.

Illustration 7.9

the "ee." The velum lowers and rises as in the "nah-nah" vocalise above, and the vowels remain pure rather than nasal. The "m" is sung to the same pitch as its adjacent vowel.

Exercise 4. This vocalise (Illustration 7.10) is the non-nasal equivalent to No. 3. Again there is no subglottic pressure when the lips close for the "b." The student should try to sing the "b" on the same pitch as the adjacent vowel. A more vigorous exercise is "bob-bee." It is virtually impossible to execute either of these vocalises without moving the chin. However, the hinge of the jaw may be fairly passive so the interior of the mouth can maintain its shape and size.

Bah – bee – bah – bee – bah.

Illustration 7.10

Exercise 5. This exercise (Illustration 7.11) is the unvoiced equivalent to No. 4. There is no musical pitch to the consonant, as "p" is another plosive which stops the vowel completely. The vowel sound is somewhat shorter here than in No. 4 because of the unvoiced consonant. A more vigorous exercise is "pop-pee." In both cases the chin may move, but the hinge of the jaw should remain rather quiet.

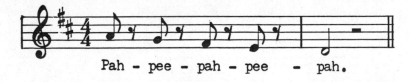

Pah – pee – pah – pee – pah.

Illustration 7.11

Exercise 6. This exercise (Illustration 7.12) combines the use of the tongue and lips. The student should avoid spreading the lips for "ee." Rapid and distinct execution will require a frontal "l" rather than retroflex. If the tongue moves backward for the "l," the adjacent vowel sounds become impure, and the exercise becomes slower because the tongue has to travel farther.

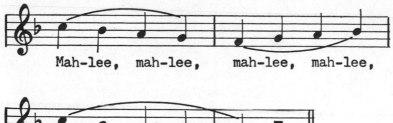

Mah–lee, mah–lee,   mah–lee, mah–lee,

mah–lee, mah–lee,   mah.

Illustration 7.12

Tense Jaw or Clenched Teeth

Exercise 1. In this exercise (Illustration 7.13) the jaw moves loosely straight up and down, or may swing back a bit. The chin should not thrust outward. The hinge of the jaw is quite active, and the chin travels the maximum possible distance. This stretches the chewing muscles and may need to be very vigorous to overcome the tendency to contract and close the jaw. Even in the most vigorous execution of the vocalise the jaw movement does not disturb the position of the larynx (if all parts of the vocal mechanism are free of tension), and there is a legato vowel sound at all times.

Yah–yah–yah–yah – yah.

Illustration 7.13

Exercise 2. This exercise (Illustration 7.14) is more utilitarian than artistic. That is, it accomplishes a purpose even if the resultant sound is not of concert quality. The better articulation of these vowels would be with the tongue alone, not moving the jaw. But if the student's jaw is clenched, this is a good vocalise to coincide with No. 1. The chin movement is not so vigorous, and the stretching aspect lasts longer because the jaw does not snap back as in No. 1.

Ee - yah,   ee - yah,   ee.

Illustration 7.14

Exercise 3. This exercise (Illustration 7.15) combines movement of the jaw with articulation of the lower lip with the teeth. The consonant is sung to the same pitch as the adjacent vowel. There should be no subglottic pressure in the consonant. Sing the "v" as if it were a glissando into the next pitch. Connect the syllables with an audible, vocalized "v."

Vah - vee,   vah - vee,   vah.

Illustration 7.15

Exercise 4. This exercise (Illustration 7.16) is the unvoiced equivalent to No. 3. The consonant has no musical pitch. There is a tighter closure of the teeth and lip, creating greater pressure in the mouth, but there should be no subglottic pressure. Some air must escape around or through the closure of lip and teeth before the vowel sounds. Therefore, the "f" seems to steal time from the previous note so the attack will not appear to be late. The vocalise should be sung as legato as No. 3. The rests here only indicate an expulsion of air which stops the vowel sound.

Fah - fee,   fah - fee,   fah.

Illustration 7.16

Exercise 5. This vocalise (Illustration 7.17) was introduced in the chapter on vowels. Here it is intended as a combination of tongue, lips, and jaw excercises. Most of the principles of good singing are found in this simple but effective vocalise. The concept of humming and forward placement are present in the consonants, the tongue moves down and up between "ah" and "ee," the tongue forms both the consonant "n" and the adjacent vowel "ee," and every syllable has a legato sostenuto sound.

Mine-y,   mine-y,   mine.

Illustration 7.17

Aspirate Consonants

Exercise 1. The consonant "h" has been used earlier in the book in staccato exercises and the like. Thus, it need not be treated further here.

Exercise 2. A combination aspirate-labial consonant is "hw." In many regions this sound has almost disappeared, giving way to "w." The student should take care to distinguish between such words as "which" and "witch," "whether" and "weather," and so forth. There should be a definite pulse from the diaphragm coordinated with the rounded lips. Both "h" and "w" sounds should be heard, almost simultaneously. The phonetic symbol for this combination consonant is [**M**].

Faulty Sibilants

Exercise 1. (Illustration 7.18). To articulate "z" the sides of the tongue hold firm against the upper molars, leaving an opening between the tongue tip and palate. The vocal bands produce a buzzing sound on the pitch of the adjacent vowel. Depending on the vowel sound, the "z" in each syllable requires a slightly different tongue and lip position. There should be hardly any sound of escaping air, and the vocalise should be completely legato.

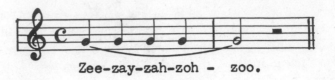

Zee-zay-zah-zoh - zoo.

Illustration 7.18

Exercise 2. This vocalise (Illustration 7.19) is the unvoiced equivalent to No. 1. There is no musical pitch to the consonant, but there is a high frequency hiss. Keep the tongue against the middle upper teeth, so the "s" remains firm and does not lisp. The student may have to alternate "z" and "s" to learn the correct tongue position for the latter. It may also be necessary to practice with the teeth together to avoid a "th" lisp. Use only the breath in the mouth for "s" to avoid loss of breath on the consonant. Here again each tongue position is slightly different, depending on the adjacent vowel.

See-say-sah-soh - soo.

Illustration 7.19

Exercise 3. The consonant "zh," phonetically spelled [ʒ], found in such words as "pleasure," "azure," "vision," and so on, is related to "z" but is farther back in the mouth and is lower pitched. There is also some lip rounding not found in "z." The lateral lisp associated with "zh" is usually the result of a lazy tongue which does not stay against the upper molars. The student may alternate "z" and "zh" to find the difference in tongue position and formant (not musical pitch). The consonant is sung to the musical pitch of the adjacent vowel, and the tongue position is slightly different for each vowel.

Exercise 4. The consonant "sh," phonetically spelled [ʃ], is the unvoiced equivalent to No. 3. It is also related to "s," but is farther back in the mouth and is lower pitched. Use only the breath in the mouth to articulate "sh" to avoid loss of breath. Keep the tongue against ths upper molars so the consonant remains firm. The student may alternate "s" and "sh" to find the difference in tongue position and formant (not musical pitch).

Exercise 5. The consonant "j," phonetically spelled [**dȝ**], found in such words as "*judge*," "*j*azz," "*g*em," and so forth, is slow to execute because of the several movements involved. The tongue first forms "d," then slides backward for "zh," then drops away, during which actions the vocal bands phonate. Adjacent "j" sounds, as in "h*uge j*udge," are awkward to articulate and require quite a bit of practice. The important detail is to keep the "j" from deteriorating, becoming mushy, or disappearing altogether. Even slower is the combination "j-d," as in "jud*ged.*" The student must plan a phrase such as "judge not, that ye be not judged" to allow enough time to articulate the slow consonants and leave enough space between the words to make them understandable.

Exercise 6. The consonant "ch," phonetically spelled [**t∫**], found in such words as "church," "fea*t*ure," and so on, is the unvoiced equivalent to No. 5. However, it is easier to articulate rapidly because there is much less tongue pressure and the vocal bands are inactive. Use only the breath in the mouth to avoid exploding "ch." Keep the sides of the tongue against the upper molars to insure the clarity of the consonant. The student should take care to distinguish between words such as "choke" and "joke," "chew" and "Jew," and so on.

Velar Consonants

Exercise 1. In the chapter on resonance there was a discussion of the action of the velum in conjunction with the consonant "k" in remedying overly nasal voices. Actually, this consonant is not really made on the velum, but is produced by action of the tongue against the hard palate. The tongue humps to touch the roof of the mouth about half way back, the tip pointing down almost to the lower teeth. The tongue then moves forcefully into position for the adjacent vowel. There is a perceptible difference in the tongue movement according to the vowel. The student may practice saying or singing "kick-kick-kick-kick-kick" or "kook-kook-kook-kook-kook" rapidly to feel the placement of the tongue.

Use only the breath in the mouth and vocal tract to articulate "k" to avoid loss of breath. More difficult vocalises are "click, click" and "kicked-clicked-kicked-clicked." The latter will be quite a bit slower because of the double stop, "kt."

Exercise 2. This exercise (Illustration 7.20) is the voiced equivalent to No. 1. The consonant is sung to the same musical pitch as the adjacent vowel. There is less glottic pressure than in "k," and the tongue moves less forcefully into the adjacent vowel. Again there is a great difference in the attitude of the tongue, depending on the adjacent vowel. More complex vocalises are "glow-glow" and "great-great," which combine "g" with another lingual consonant, making the tongue move far and fast. A very slow vocalise is "glugged-glugged," which involves massive movements of the articulators, but which may be sung absolutely legato since every part of the vocalise is voiced. The student should take care to keep the consonants and vowels forward to avoid sounding like a frog.

Gah-gay-gee-goh - goo.

Illustration 7.20

Nasal Consonants

The nasal consonants "m," "n," and "ng" have been so thoroughly discussed and used in vocalises in earlier chapters of this book they need not be treated here.

The "R" Dilemma

Hardly any symbol offers more problems than "r," because it is used to indicate so many different sounds. It may be either a pure lingual consonant, a vowel, or a vowel glide similar to "w" and "y." One use of "r" is distinctly American and is not shared by other English speaking peoples, except perhaps Anglo-Canadians. Further, there are wide differences in regional treatments of "r," from omission to overemphasis.

Exercise 1. The American "R" followed by a vowel acts like a vowel glide in that it is voiced and hardly interrupts the airstream. "R" begins with the tongue tip touching the front of the palate, much like a frontal "l," the lips slightly rounded, and the back of the tongue against the upper molars. As the vocal bands phonate a sound similar to the vowel "er" [ɝ], the tongue moves quickly into the position of the adjacent vowel. The problem for singers comes from pulling the tongue so far back into the throat the resultant sound is almost swallowed. The tongue must be relaxed in articulating the American "R," and the placement must be forward. Care must be taken not to round the lips to the extent that the "R" sounds like "w." A further problem for singers is that the American "R" is not appropriate in texts other than American or perhaps Canadian origin.

Exercise 2. The flipped and rolled "r's" are lingual consonants which are produced much like "l" or "d." Hence, the British "veddy" for "very." Western European languages require either one flip of the tongue or rolling several flips in executing "r." It is not within the scope of this book to explore the various rules for "r" in foreign languages. It might be worth mentioning, however, that although both spoken French and German have uvular-velar "r's," the classical style of singing does not permit their use. The uvular-velar "r" is sung only by folk singers or cabaret singers.

Exercise 3. An "r" preceded by a consonant, as in "praise," "great," and so on, may either be treated as a vowel glide, or it may be executed with one flip of the tongue. In the first instance the "r" should not be dwelled on in the manner of the television tiger who says his breakfast cereals are "gur-r-r-r-reat!" The tongue position depends both on the preceding consonant and the adjacent vowel. In the second instance there should be only one flip, never a rolled "r."

Exercise 4. An "r" before a consonant is not actually a consonant and should not be articulated. The "r" blends with the preceding vowel, giving it a distinctive color. Thus, "card" does not sound quite like "cod" or "harmony" like "hominy," because of the blended vowels. Or, the "r" may be a slight glide between the vowel and the succeeding consonant (hah-er-mony or hah-uh-mony) as long as the tongue is relaxed and does not distort the word.

Exercise 5. An "r" at the end of a word is usually treated as a vowel and should only be linked as a consonant when there is absolutely no danger of misunderstanding. A phrase such as "your ear" can be disastrous if the "r" is linked. In treating the "r" as a vowel glide the student sings either "you-er ear" or "you-uh ear" with a hint of glottal stroke between the words. Even an innocuous phrase such as "pour on" sounds better when the words are slightly separated. If the next word begins with a consonant, as in "far gone," the final "r" is treated according to the suggestions in No. 4. This last example should never be sung "fah-ruh gone."

Exercise 6. The "r" which is associated with the vowel "er" [ɝ], whether spelled "er," "ir," "or," or "ur," is not a consonant and should not be sounded. Nor should it be connected to a following word which begins with a vowel. Such phrases as "her eyes," "honor and arms," "father and mother," and so on, should treat "er" and "or" as vowels and should separate the words. An exception would be in adding a suffix to such a word, as in "honoring," in which the "r" is treated as a consonant. In some phonetics books the unstressed "er" is spelled [ɚ], but it is still a vowel.

Exercise 7. An "r" may be considered sometimes as part of a diphthong or triphthong. The word "card" in No. 4 might be sung "cah-uhd," thereby making the vowel a diphthong. The treatment of "your" as "you-uh" in No. 5 is another example. Words such as "hear" (hih-uh), "hair" (heh-uh), "more" (moh-uh), and "sure" (shoo-uh) are further examples of "r" as the final part of a diphthong. As with most diphthongs, the final sound must be very slight and never accented. Words such as "fire" (fah-ih-uh) and "hour" (ah-oh-uh) are examples in which the "r" may be seen as the final part of a triphthong. In each of these cases the neutral sound would be phonetically spelled [ɚ].

PROBLEMS OF ARTICULATION

Changing Syllables on High Notes

The following principles and exercises will be helpful in teaching students to negotiate polysyllabic phrases in the upper range.

Exercise 1. Keep the jaw and mouth as quiet as possible to avoid disturbing the vowels. Use only the articulators necessary to produce clear and distinct words. The farther in front a consonant is produced, the better for singing.

Exercise 2. Secure the vocal line by omitting the consonants. Sing the vowels as an uninterrupted string of sounds. Unify the vowels in the manner explained in Chapter 5.

Exercise 3. Practice singing the phrase with the proper consonants but with only one of the open vowels found in the phrase, usually "ah" or "oh." Then practice with a different vowel. Think of the series of high notes and syllables as one long, supported sound. Notice how clear the words are even with a single vowel.

Exercise 4. Sing the phrase with substitute voiced or unvoiced consonants to relieve excess tensions. Also, consonants of the same type may be substituted, such as "d" for "n" or "r" and so on. For instance, the phrase "Glory to God" from *Messiah* may be rendered "klaw-dy to God" in the upper range without disturbing the sense of the words.

Exercise 5. Combine Nos. 2, 3, and 4. Sing the phrase with unified vowels, using the consonants which produce clear diction without disturbing the vocal line. The best final results will, no doubt, be a compromise which will depend on the teacher's judgment.

Vocal Tension from Tense Consonants

The exercises suggested earlier in this chapter are designed to teach independence in the various articulators. The tongue can move without the jaw, lips, or velum moving. The lips can move without engaging the other articulators. And minimal movement of an articulator will produce a usable consonant, especially in the high range.

Exercise 1. Lingual consonants may be made by simply flicking the tongue, as demonstrated in the "lah-lah-lah" exercises. If the student has trouble articulating "t," "d," "n," "l," or "r," he may try flicking the tongue at the proper moment without trying to sing a consonant. Just moving the tongue will probably insert enough vocal change to sound like the desired consonant.

Exercise 2. Likewise, labial consonants may be made by simply moving the lips toward each other. They need not touch completely to give a useful semblance of the desired consonant. The student will find that moving the lips close together will sound like "b," "p," or "m." Moving the lower lip toward the upper teeth will sound enough like "v" or "f" to be practicable.

Note: Avoid subglottic pressure in articulating these consonants.

Release of Consonants on High Notes

Exercise 1. Keep the tone supported through the consonant. Many students relax the ribs and abdomen before articulating a final consonant, which causes the vocal tract to tighten or collapse. The consonant is difficult, if not impossible, to produce under those conditions. The student should exhale after the consonant has been released to be sure he is supporting through the consonant.

Exercise 2. Practice independent, mechanical articulation. Move the articulators as described under tense consonants.

Exercise 3. Substitute voiced or unvoiced consonants as required. Lax consonants are easier to release than tense ones.

Exercise 4. In practicing a difficult phrase the student may add a neutral vowel to the final consonant. This should be only a temporary measure, however, and should be eliminated when the student is able to release the consonant without the neutral vowel.

Loss of Air on Consonants

Exercise 1. Speak the troublesome consonants with only the air in the mouth, holding the breath quiet in the lungs. Alternate consonants rapidly to feel movement of the articulators without loss of breath.

Exercise 2. Practice rapid articulation of the consonants in the phrase on one vowel and one midrange pitch, listening to hear if any excess air escapes through the vowel.

Exercise 3. Since most breath loss occurs on voiceless consonants, the student may substitute voiced equivalents in practice sessions. Later he may return to the proper unvoiced consonant, using the same mode of articulation as in the substitute.

Note: Avoid subglottic pressure in these consonants.

Physical Problems Not Soluble in Music Class

The following physical defects present problems which may not be solved by articulation exercises. The student should consult a physician or dentist in these cases.

1. Tied tongue
2. Unusual size or shape of tongue
3. Spaces between teeth
4. Crooked or missing teeth
5. Overbite, underbite, crossbite
6. Orthodontic appliances
7. Harelip or cleft palate
8. Size and condition of tonsils
9. "Adenoids"

Stuttering

Stuttering is an emotional problem rather than a physical defect. In the cases of stuttering which I have observed the student was able to sing without stuttering, which gave the student an immense feeling of accomplishment. But speech therapists who treat stutterers are generally opposed to using singing as a therapy. The concern is that the stutterer may resort to singing as a substitute without coping with his speech problem. Perhaps as the field of music therapy grows there will be opportunities to coordinate speech exercises with singing lessons to speed up the therapeutic process.

PROBLEMS OF PRONUNCIATION

As I mentioned earlier there is an aspect of elegance in the classical style of singing which bears more on pronunciation than articulation. The following suggestions are made for the student of classical vocal music and may not be appropriate to popular or folk styles of singing.

Diphthong "ew" vs. Vowel "oo"

In a great portion of the United States words which were formerly pronounced with the diphthong "ew" have now been

changed to the vowel "oo." We hear the "nooze" on television, eat
"stoo" for dinner, pay "dooze" to a club, and are "enthooziastic"
about our football team. All of these are acceptable in everyday
speech and call no attention to themselves. However, their use in
classical singing is intrusive and should be carefully screened out.
Below is a list of some, but not all, of the words in question which
should be sung with the diphthong "ew."

1. Words with "d"

dew	duke	induce
deuce	dune	produce
due	during	reduce
dues	duty	undulate
duet	endure	

2. Words with "l"

absolutely	lucid	lunatic
dilute	lucrative	lure
illuminate	luke	lurid
lewd	luminous	lute
lubricate	lunar	

3. Words with "n"

enumerate	neutron	nude
genuine	new	nutrition
neutral	nuclear	renew

4. Words with "s"

assume	sue	superb
consume	suicide	superior
presume	suit	supreme
resume	suitor	suture
sewer	super	

5. Words with "st"

stew	Stuart	studio
steward	student	stupid

6. Words with "t"

institute	tuberculosis	tumult
obtuse	tumor	tune
tube		

7. Words with "th"

enthusiasm
Matthew

Faulty Liaisons

The student often does not hear that some of his liaisons between words make the phrase less intelligible. "Your ear" has already been mentioned, as have "you are" (you war), "I am" (I yam), and "he is" (he yiz). Such linkings should be avoided. There are other, more subtle, liaisons which should be corrected, such as "And He (Andy) shall purify" from *Messiah*. There is the Christmas carol that includes the phrase "the which His mother Mary," which generally sounds like "the witches' mother, Mary." And then there is the old hymn, "Gladly the Cross I'd Bear," that seems to concern a crosseyed bear named Gladly. While such faulty liaisons may require articulation exercises as a solution, most are corrected by separating the words and changing the emphasis.

"Ing" vs. "een"

This is not the problem of the missing "g" in a phrase such as "sittin' and rockin' " but is the substitution of "n" for "ng." The tongue is too far forward to articulate with the velum. The student should practice the velar exercises mentioned earlier to be sure he sings "go-ing" rather than "go-een," "lov-ing" rather than "lov-een," and many other examples.

The "ng" and "ngg" Confusion

Another error related to "g" is the extra consonant added to "ng" words, making "singer" rhyme with "finger." The student should practice differentiating between these two pronunciations, and he may need to consult a dictionary to find whether or not there should be an extra "g" in questionable words. English is inconsistent in that words ending in "ng" never take the extra "g," but adding a suffix may or may not add a "g" to the pronunciation, e.g., "singer," "singing," "longing," and "hanging" do not have an extra "g" while "longer," "longest," "stronger," and "strongest" do.

Superfluous Neutral Syllable

In former days singers were taught to add a short neutral vowel to the ends of words ending with consonants, much in the manner of the Italian language. Nowadays it is considered better to sing through the consonant but not add the neutral vowel "uh."

Some examples are "an apple," which is neither "anuh apple" nor "an napple," "some air," which is neither "somuh air" nor "some mair," and "have any," which is neither "havuh any" nor "have vany." The important detail here is careful articulation so that pronunciation will be clear.

The Extra "t"

There are two categories of words to which are added an extra "t." First, the words with double "t"—little, battle, and bitter— which are pronounced with only one "t." These words should be rendered "lih-tul," "bae-tul," and "bih-ter." In this manner the "t" does not stop the previous vowel.

Then there are words which are not spelled with "t," but to which a "t" is added. "Pencil" becomes "pent-sul," and "answer" becomes "ant-ser." In each of these cases the consonants should be sung through without adding "t."

Long Neutral Syllable Becomes Bright Vowel

Some words appear with regular frequency in art songs which are spoken with weak, short neutral syllables but which must be changed to bright vowels when sung to long notes. Such words as "people," "heaven," "hopeful," and "strongest" sound awkward when said with bright vowels, but are dull to the ear when sung with a neutral vowel. A compromise which accepts beauty of tone over authenticity of pronunciation is better than adhering precisely to speech oriented sounds. If the syllable is short, of course, the neutral vowel may be sung almost with the speech pronunciation.

8

STRATEGIES AND TECHNIQUES
FOR DEVELOPING
A RICH CHORAL SOUND

The previous chapter completes our look at the four elements of singing: breathing, phonation, resonance, and articulation. The suggestions and vocalises have been primarily oriented toward the individual singer and the studio teacher. In the next chapters we will apply these principles to groups of singers, both in chorus and in classes.

Expect a Lot from the Singers

High school voices can be rich without strain. With the proper vocal approach high school students are capable of singing without breathiness, nasality, stridency, or other unacceptable qualities. Of course teenage voices are not as tough as they will be in ten or twenty years, but neither are they as fragile and weak as they were five years before. With today's nutrition and hygiene standards, teenage voices are as healthy as teenage bodies. If high school students can be good athletes, they can be strong singers.

Challenge the Students

High school students respond to challenge and inspiration, and they want to be treated as adults. There are sound reasons for accepting teenagers where they are musically and vocally without demeaning their tastes and opinions. If we do, they will accept our challenge to grow artistically, musically, and vocally. They will feel a great sense of achievement in persevering toward high goals.

The Big Sound

Just as a big sound is the result of good vocal training in the individual soloist, a big choral sound is the result of good singing by each person in the chorus. Good vocal habits and training help to develop the full potential of each voice. The students know they have accomplished something worthwhile, and the director was not forced to tailor the repertory of the group to the least trained voice.

It may be legitimately asked if striving for a big choral sound can be injurious to young voices. The answer is that voices can be harmed at any age through bad vocal habits. Students who follow the principles described in earlier chapters will sing well and not damage their voices, either as soloists or in groups.

SOME IMPORTANT VOCAL CONCEPTS

All the principles and vocalises suggested earlier may be used by groups of singers. However, there are a few which merit special attention and should be mentioned here.

1. Breathe deeply and slowly. Chorus singers should learn to breathe deeply and slowly in order to prepare the vocal mechanism. There is no reason to gasp for breath. Planning within each section allows part of the group to breathe while the others are singing. In fact, I once heard a chorus demonstrate that they could sing an entire piece without pausing for breath by staggering their individual breaths. Breathing quickly is one aspect of solo singing which need not be a choral problem.

2. Attack on the breath. In the interest of precision and clarity, choruses often learn a rather harsh glottal attack which is detrimental to good vocal development. Care should be taken to teach the attack on the breath, especially in phrases which begin with a vowel sound. At first the chorus may be less precise in its attacks, but practice will clear up such problems. The director's beat pattern will indicate where the vocal sound should begin, and the chorus will learn to coordinate its breathing and attacks. Letting the breath precede phonation will insure a good beginning to each phrase.

3. Release with a breath. This was discussed earlier in the chapter on phonation. The vocal bands should open to release the sound rather than close to stop it. Again, the chorus may sound imprecise at first, but practice will solve the problem of coordination. The director's beat pattern indicates where to release, and his follow-through may exemplify either inhalation or exhalation. Choruses which release with a breath create a better "echo" at the ends of phrases and sound more like sophisticated, professional groups.

Hallelujah Chorus

A good illustration of releasing with a breath is in the "Hallelujah Chorus" from Handel's *Messiah.* I ask the chorus purposely to end the opening word with a "k," as in "hal le lu yuk." The resultant cutoff is so abrupt, the group never fails to laugh. Then we practice it by releasing with a breath. The difference is immediately apparent. Then we practice the repetitions of "hallelujah" slowly until the singers feel their throats stay open between words. Gradually we increase the speed until they can articulate the phrases correctly in tempo.

4. The ubiquitous "uh." Over the years I have found the vowel "uh" to be a better tonal base for choral singing than "oo." "Uh" may be sung in all ranges of the voice and contains more high overtones than "oo." Occasionally I have some singers modify toward "oh" if "uh" becomes shallow or strident. "Uh" gives the chorus the feeling of a full-throated sound which is rich and resonant. Blending each bright vowel with "uh" creates the homogeneity necessary for a choral line. It is also a ready device for teaching upper register modifications. High notes sung on "uh" will blend with the rest of the choral chord and with the purer vowels sung on lower notes. This keeps a section from "sticking out" on high notes.

5. Humming. Every singing tone should be based on a humming quality. A proper hum resonates in several parts of the head, not merely in the nose. The vocal tract is open and free, the tongue and jaw are relaxed, and there is a feeling of continuous, flowing sound. A chorus may hum with mouths open, producing a tone quite similar to "uh." By practicing their music with closed or open humming the singers learn another method of developing a homogeneous choral line. Each vowel and consonant is related to the basic humming quality.

6. Focus above the hard palate. The chorus should think of each sound as being focused above the hard palate. This helps to avoid tension in the vocal tract. Sometimes the feeling is in front of the eyes or forehead, as if the tone were not in the singers' heads at all, especially in the upper range. This generalized concept of focus or placement emphasizes a free, rich, ringing tone which the student may feel diffused within the head.

7. Head voice. Young singers should be encouraged to use a light adjustment in the upper range, especially the tenors. This need not be a lifeless falsetto, but may be full-bodied and supported without pushing the chin out or straining for high notes. A resonant head voice is very useful in negotiating the high notes of many tenor parts, although some practice will be necessary to learn to change smoothly from head voice to chest voice and vice versa. As their voices mature the tenors may begin to add a little more weight to the head voice so it will more closely match the chest voice. In most choruses a resonant head voice is more easily blended than a vigorous chest voice.

8. Blend the registers. Descending scales and arpeggios are the best vocalises for blending vocal registers. Therefore, most vocalises should move downward. The students should not force their voices across a register change, but should let the breath lift the voice over the pressure point. The exercises for changing registers and modifying vowels are as important to a choral group as they are to solo singers.

9. Horizontal concept of scales. There is actually no up and down in the voice, although most singers think in those terms. I explain to the students that the voice is more like a keyboard instrument, that is, horizontal in concept, and is no harder to play at one end of scale than at the other. This helps them avoid reaching up or digging down for notes. There may be more support involved in the outside notes, but there is no additional pressure in the throat.

10. Dynamics come from resonance. A well-tuned voice will carry without pushing or straining. The student should always strive for quality and let loudness develop naturally. Likewise, soft singing should be resonant and free. A soft tone need not be small and constricted. Singers should use both loud and soft dynamics in each rehearsal to train the voice completely. The *messa di voce* exercises mentioned earlier are most beneficial to developing a controlled, even range of choral dynamics.

11. Construct vocalises from choral parts. Just as vocalises may be constructed from difficult phrases of solo songs, they may also be made from hard parts of choral literature. Warmup exercises may be musically as well as vocally instructive. This method will also keep the vocalises interesting and effective.

WAYS TO IMPROVE CHORAL SINGING

The following ideas are more germane to choral singing than to solo styles because they have to do with techniques of execution rather than vocal growth.

Diction

Choruses should practice the diction vocalises found in the previous chapter to improve and strengthen their articulators. All singers need to sing with freely moving tongues, lips, and so on. However, a chorus generally must be more precise than a soloist, because imprecision is so much more apparent in choral singing. Here are a few procedures which I have found valuable.

1. Sing initial consonants ahead of the beat. Because of the demands made on choruses to sing with various styles and media, the group should be taught to sing initial consonants ahead of the beat at all times. Such training may not be necessary in a cappella singing, but when the chorus performs with orchestra or band, it will be essential. If the chorus sings initial consonants on the beat, the vowels will sound as if they are late, and the ensemble between chorus and orchestra will seem not to be together. Even soloists who perform regularly with orchestras have to learn to anticipate the beat with their consonants. As a choral director I have the group practice such anticipation until they can feel it together. Since some consonants take longer than others, the chorus has to learn just when to begin each one. After a while, however, the habit becomes ingrained and only occasionally has to be reinforced by the director.

2. Sing loud consonants. Generally speaking, choruses should sing loud consonants, no matter what the dynamic marking of the piece. Composers intend the overall effect to be soft or loud, but they also want the words to be understood. In most instances the vowels may be sung as the composer has marked the music, letting good, strong consonants carry the message of the song.

An example of this is found in the word "Amen." Because "ah" and "eh" are among the innately loudest vocal sounds, most choruses sing with the result in Illustration 8.1. Only familiarity with the word carries the message to the audience.

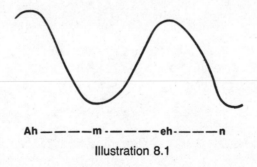

Ah ————m ·————eh·———n

Illustration 8.1

To correct this the chorus begins by singing only "m" and "n" on the requisite pitches at a loud dynamic level. Next the chorus adds the vowel sounds at a soft dynamic level. It usually takes several experimental tries to settle on how loud the consonants must be to balance the vowels. Many times the second vowel is too loud because of the support required for the "m," producing the result in Illustration 8.2.

When the vowels and consonants are finally balanced, the "m" and "n" feel much too loud to the chorus because there is so much energy required in the consonants. They have to learn to coordinate their muscles so the extra support does not lengthen the

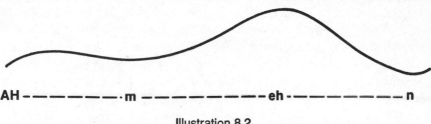

AH –––––––·m –––––––––eh·–––––––––n

Illustration 8.2

consonants and stretch the word out of shape nor exert too much intensity on the adjacent vowel. In the middle of an auditorium the various parts of the word should sound evenly energized with a continuous flow of vocal tone. A good tape recording will convince the chorus how much better the end result sounds than their first attempt.

3. Support the spaces between words. Earlier I mentioned some of the dangers of eliding words into unintentional puns and nonsense syllables. An idea I have found valuable in learning not to depend on elisions for legato singing is to support the spaces between the words. A gap between words is more apparent in choral singing if the singers relax slightly or seem to make new attacks on each syllable. A chorus will sound perfectly legato and perfectly understandable if they keep their bodies and voices functioning throughout each phrase. Intervocalic consonants will carry the words, and there will be no gap or loss of sound between them. Combination staccato-legato exercises are effective in teaching this concept.

4. Short unvoiced sibilants. The problem with the sibilants "s," "sh," and "ch" is often not the volume but the length. I tell a chorus that choral sibilants may be sixty times as loud as soloists', but they need not be sixty times as long. Really, it takes a very slight sibilant for an audience to understand the word. Some choirs have even asked only the first row to pronounce sibilants; the rest of the chorus omits them entirely. To control the length of sibilants the director may give a short, sharp movement with only one or two fingers, and the chorus will respond with a precise sibilant which takes hardly any time from its adjacent notes or rests. The chorus should take care to keep their jaws relaxed and their mouths open in articulating sibilants.

5. *Long voiced sibilants.* More time must be allowed for the sibilants "z," "zh," and "j," for the reasons given in the chapter on articulation. Because these consonants are voiced the problem of overemphasis is not as great as in their unvoiced equivalents. Care must be taken to see that each section of the chorus sings voiced sibilants on the proper pitches. Effective vocalises may be constructed from building chords on elongated voiced sibilants to teach the chorus clear, controlled execution without hissing or wandering off pitch.

EAR TRAINING

Since all the foregoing material has been directed toward teaching students to recognize good vocal quality within themselves as well as in others, this section will discuss those aspects of ear training which have to do with good pitch. It is amazing how wide a range of frequencies may be sung by a soloist with a piano and still be accepted as in tune. One reason for this is that vocal tuning is the sum of several vowel formants and musical overtones and may be almost infinitely varied. Another reason, perhaps even more important, is the piano's system of equally divided half-tones which produce somewhat out-of-tune intervals compared with a string quartet which tunes in just temperament. In order to sing perfectly in tune with an orchestra or band a chorus must learn to tune by the latter method. They must listen to each other rather than depend on a piano for good pitch. Here are some procedures which I have used to sharpen choral singers' accuity.

1. *Demonstration of intervals.* Good tuning is a learned skill and may be taught by the same methods used to distinguish between colors and shapes, e.g., demonstration, comparison, contrast, and repetition. Therefore, I begin by demonstrating the way intervals sound when they are vocally in tune. I ask one of the basses to sing with me, first in octaves then in perfect fifths. He sings the lower tonic note, perhaps C below middle C, and I sing the upper note. I explain to the group that a well tuned octave or perfect fifth is smooth to the ear, whereas being even slightly out of tune produces a "beat" or disturbance between the two notes. While the bass holds his tonic note, I sing slightly above and below the perfect interval, then resolve them until they are smooth. With a bit of practice the group is able to hear immediately whether the interval is flat, sharp, or in tune. Then the men sing in duets to

practice tuning their voices, and the rest of the group judges whether the intervals are in tune or not. Then I add more voices into quartets, sextets, octets, and so on until the entire group of men is singing octaves and fifths in tune. Of course, at every step of the way I deal with problems of vowel color, placement, and any other factors which affect tuning.

Women's Voices

The women repeat much of the same process as the men. I begin by singing the tonic note, and one of the girls sings octaves and fifths above my note. Or, I choose an alto and soprano to sing these intervals together. Then I add more women by twos, tuning pitches and vowels as we go, and let the rest of the group judge whether or not the singers are in tune.

Women and Men Together

It is then only a matter of combining the women's and men's voices. First, the altos and basses tune a tonic pitch in octaves. Then the tenors and sopranos sing the same tonic an octave higher; thus the tenors sing the same pitch as the altos. When the four sections are combined, there should be a two-octave chord without any beats. One of the most difficult parts of this exercise is tuning the tenor and alto in unison, but this may be achieved rather quickly if the tenors have a good concept of singing in head voice or with a mixture of head and chest voice.

Next, the altos and basses sing the tonic note in octaves, and the sopranos and tenors sing the fifth in octaves. When this is in tune, I ask the basses and sopranos to drop out, leaving the interval of a perfect fourth between the tenors and altos. This interval should also be smooth, although it may sound a bit flatter than most of us would like to hear. The perfect fourth is acceptable even with a subtle "wave" in the tone. The wave should never be fast enough to be heard as a beat, however.

Other Intervals and Chords

After the perfect intervals are established pretty firmly, we branch out into the major thirds, minor thirds, dominant sevenths, major sevenths, minor sevenths, augmented, and diminished intervals, in that order. These may be approached as two-, three-, or four-part chords, depending on the group. Because of the different vocal timbres and vowel sounds, many of the latter intervals are hard to judge on the basis of beats, which have a tendency to cancel out each other in a large group.

Perhaps it is worth mentioning here that while we are learning to tune vowels and intervals I rarely ever mention a vibrato problem, and I never ask a student to control a vibrato consciously. I shall explain this further when I discuss vibratos at the end of the chapter.

2. *Warmup vocalises.* Every vocalise should have several purposes, and none should be just to get the voices going. The warmup period is an exellent time to teach tuning vowel colors, vowel modification, head voice, blended registers, and pitch-interval accuity. I discovered ths importance of the warmup period some years ago while teaching in a small liberal arts college.

As with many such colleges, there were a variety of choruses in which to participate, with one elite, hand-picked group which toured the country, made recordings, and was involved with other public relations ventures. The chorus I directed consisted of about twenty personable and lively young singers who were trying to improve their singing enough to be selected for the elite group, but for one reason or another chose not to join one of the other large ensembles. We were fortunate enough to have a forty-five minute rehearsal each day, which meant I was able to meet them often, but the rehearsal had to be tightly packed in order to accomplish everything we wanted to do.

Over the course of a few years I was able to engage in some fascinating experiments in ear training. None of the group had absolute pitch, and very few had a background in music theory since none were music majors. Three early experiments are notable and could be duplicated in many high school choruses.

Vocalises

The first experiment was purely accidental. As a creature of habit I began each rehearsal with the same vocalise, a descending octave arpeggio in C major on "mah-mah-mah-mah." After a few weeks of this drill, one day quite by chance I gave the downbeat for the first vocalise before the pianist sounded the chord. With hardly a hesitation the group responded by singing the vocalise perfectly in tune in the key of C. It took all of us a moment to realize what had happened. After that, the group enjoyed being able to start a vocalise in C major without a pitch pipe or chord from the piano.

Compositions

The second experiment was born out of the limitation of re-hearsal time and the desire to make a favorable impression in the annual Christmas combined concert. The selections the group would sing were chosen well in advance, with the opening number beginning on a four-part chord in D major. For a month or so instead of beginning with our arpeggios in C we began with the first number on the concert. Before long the group was able to begin the song every day perfectly in tune without the piano. Consequently, we were able to walk onto the stage and begin our part of the concert without any preamble.

Related Keys

The third experiment was an extension of the second. When the group were sure they would be able to begin without a refer-ence pitch, I established the order of songs according to their key relationships, e.g., D major, b minor, E major, and A major. Learning to hear the relative minor of D major and the subsequent dominant-tonic relationships without outside help gave the group a deep feeling of accomplishment. In the concert we started without a pitch pipe and went directly from one song to another, finding the new keys and starting tones by key relationships. I recommend all three of these exercises in ear training as being most satisfying musical experiences.

Four-Part Vocalises

Illustrations 8.3 and 8.4 are two examples of vocalises which are effective in teaching the sounds of various chords in root and inverted positions. Before using these vocalises, the chorus should be trained in the rudimentary intervals.

The procedure for these vocalises is to have the chorus begin a cappella on a C major chord without seeing the written notes. The director points to the section whose note is to change and says, "Tenors up a half-step . . . Altos up a half-step . . . Basses up a half-step . . ." and so on. The chorus tunes each chord by ear. The note values of the vocalise are not to be taken literally. The object is to modulate by ear through a series of foreign chords to a ca-dence in C major. If the process breaks down along the way, the chorus may begin at the beginning and try again. The piano should

Illustration 8.3 Vocalise No. 1

be used as a last resort, and then to play one note rather than a whole chord. At the end of the vocalise rather than ask for note by note movement, the director may say, "Resolve the dominant to the tonic" if the group has become proficient in such terminology.

These vocalises may be transposed to any key according to the group. They are meant only as examples of the sort of ear training which is possible with a group. Both examples end in the same key as the beginning to see how closely the group can remain in tune. Of course, many others may be devised which modulate to other keys.

3. A cappella singing. The exercises suggested above rely mainly on a cappella singing with very little reference to the piano or other tuning device. There is no better medium for teaching ear training to a group than four-part unaccompanied singing. Through a cappella singing the student learns to listen to surrounding voices rather than to a piano which may be several feet away on the other side of the chorus and whose tuning may be questionable. Even pieces which are performed with keyboard or other instruments should be rehearsed unaccompanied to secure the best tone quality and tuning from the chorus.

Illustration 8.4 Vocalise No. 2

If the chorus is well tuned without instruments, there will be fewer problems of balance and ensemble. The singers who stand on the back rows will not be as bothered by not hearing the accompaniment while they are singing. Most of the time singers in the middle of a section or who are far removed from the accompaniment can only hear the instruments during rests and have to sing with reference to the other choristers. This is not to say that singers should not listen to the instruments to stay in tune; rather, the singers should not have to depend on instruments for pitch-interval accuracy.

4. Quartet seating. In the small choir described earlier, we quickly decided to rehearse and perform in quartets or in some arrangement which would allow everyone to stand next to two different parts. Hardly ever would choristers singing the same part stand next to one another. They found it much simpler to tune octaves and fifths than unisons, and it was easier for me to blend reedy and fluty voices when they stood in quartets. There have been quite a few opportunities for me to use a modified quartet arrangement in large choruses, and it has proved to be a highly desirable way to perform. In the next chapter advantages and pitfalls of quartet seating will be explored further.

SOME FURTHER CONCERNS

Besides the matters of voice training and choral problems discussed above, there are some concerns which have to do with choosing music and with the way the chorus is divided into sections.

Tessitura and Range

Obviously vocal range is a matter to be considered in choosing literature, but a more important concern is tessitura. Even if the singer has a wide range, there is a limited area of the voice which is most comfortable and in which most of the notes of a composition should fall. Voices should not be classified by range alone. Tessitura, lifts, and timbre should be the determinants. In choosing music care should be taken to see that no vocal part lies consistently above the first lift without relief, such as some of the tenor parts in Mendelssohn's *Elijah* and Beethoven's Ninth Symphony. Nor should the preponderance of notes fall in the lower third of the vocal range. The best choral writing lets the voices move above and below the first lift without staying in one area too long.

Illustration 8.5 compares ranges, tessituras, and lifts of the eight choral parts, based on my experience with good teenage singers. Of course, not every singer will have as wide a range as is indicated with each classification. These notes indicate the upper and lower limits which may be reasonably expected from such

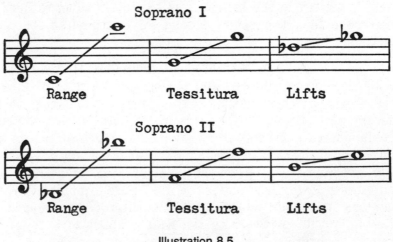

Illustration 8.5

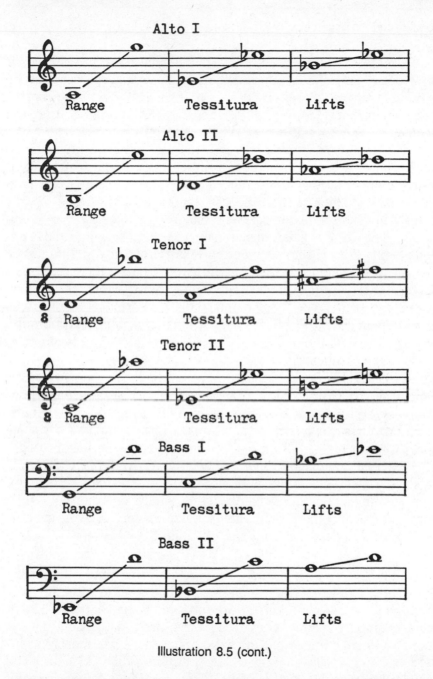

Illustration 8.5 (cont.)

choruses. The suggested tessituras for male voices lie below the second lift because of the tendency for young voices to tire quickly in the upper range.

Voicing and Arrangements

1. SATB. The most suitable arrangements for most choruses
are for four-part mixed voices. Whether in original compositions or
arrangements of other literature, SATB voicing offers the greatest
selection of choral pieces and the widest variety of styles. Also, the
voicing fits most tessituras of teenage singers.

There is quite a bit of latitude within four-part music as to
performance keys and ranges. In exposed passages I often combine the men's sections for a fuller sound. Also, the altos may help
the tenors on high notes, and the tenors help the altos on low
notes. However, I do not permit teenage girls to sing tenor exclusively. The tessitura is consistently too low for good vocal development. With encouragement and instruction any girl should be
able to acquire enough notes for the Alto II part. Of course, adult
female tenors are another matter which may be dealt with on an
individual basis. Age, health, and certain hormone medications
may permanently lower the voice without damaging it irreparably.

2. Six-part mixed. A more interesting system of choral voicing is to divide the group into three-part male and three-part
female sections. Besides the normal SATB sections there are generally several singers who may be classified "sopralto" or "bariten." The former may sing either soprano or alto in an SATB piece
and may sing either Alto I or Soprano II when the parts divide.
The "baritens" may sing tenor or bass regularly and sing Tenor II
or Bass I when the parts divide. Such a chorus may sing four-,
five-, or six-part arrangements. Thus, there are more possible
vocal colors, and the chorus members are given an even greater
amount of independence and responsibility.

3. SAB. The least suitable arrangements for mixed chorus are
those which have only one men's part. The tessitura is generally
too high for basses and baritones, and even some "baritens" have
trouble singing mainly above the bass clef. Also, there is not
enough fundamental sound in the chords, which are mostly in in-
versions, to give the choristers a feeling of solidity. Although the
tonic notes may be in the piano, the vocal lines have a steady
stream of inverted chords. Only the most desperate situation
should make the use of SAB arrangements necessary.

Such a situation was my first choral teaching position in which I was given a large catch-all group. At the first rehearsal there were ninety-one singers, eighty-seven girls and four boys. If any group had a reason to use SAB arrangements, this one did, except for my aversion to such voicing. Fortunately, the boys were one tenor, two baritones, and one bass, so I was able to seat the four of them in the center of the front row and have four-part singing. A little recruitment brought a few more boys, but we never had more than twelve to balance the large group of girls. By dividing the girls into four fairly equal sections we even performed some six-part pieces. This chorus was far from the balance I preferred, but placing the boys in the forefront and spreading the stronger girls' voices throughout their sections produced a satisfying choral sound.

4. SSAATTBB. Large, well trained groups may be divided into eight or more parts if necessary and perform far beyond the capabilities of a smaller chorus. The question with multiple part arrangements is upon what basis is the division arrived. The ultimate may have been reached by Thomas Tallis in a famous choral piece for eight five-part groups, forty independent parts. Such music offers the greatest variety of choral sound and is the most challenging in the choral medium. On the other hand, if the piece is essentially four parts doubled at the octave, that is, Soprano I and Tenor I on the melody, Alto II and Bass II on the bass line, and the inner parts similarly doubled, the result is often turgid and less interesting than more transparent SATB arrangements. Also, such writing generally sets the outer parts in consistently too high and too low tessituras.

5. SSA or SSAA. There is often something ethereal about three- and four-part women's choruses, as the sudden appearance of "Lift Thine Eyes" in Mendelssohn's *Elijah* demonstrates. The problem for teenage choruses is in finding enough cleverly arranged music to satisfy the groups' needs. Some alto parts are too low, or the tessitura is too low, for the young voices, and some of the middle parts are uninteresting. If the piece is an arrangement of an SATB composition, there may be awkward passages or hollow chords where some of the original notes are missing.

6. TTBB. There is hardly any group more fun to work with than a male chorus. The close positions of the harmonies in the male octaves yield a sound which is unmatched by any other medium. Here again, it may be difficult to find enough suitable arrangements. Many Tenor I tessituras are too high and Bass II tessituras too low for young voices.

Numbers and Ratios

Over the years I have developed the number and ratios of singers I prefer in each section of the chorus. Most choral music today is based on vertical, chordal harmonies, so the bass part is of utmost importance. Further, the altos singing in the lower parts of their voices must balance tenors in the upper range, so there should be more altos than tenors. Although the soprano part is usually the melody, their numbers need not be great to project their lines. Therefore, in a group of twenty singers I prefer four basses, three "baritens" (two baritones and one tenor), three tenors, five altos, three "sopraltos" (two altos and one soprano), and two sopranos. When the group sings an SATB arrangement, there are six basses, four tenors, seven altos, and three sopranos. The group is also capable of singing up to six parts with a good balance. For larger groups the ratios are pretty much the same as these, depending on individual vocal qualities.

THE QUESTION OF VIBRATO

One of the most perplexing problems for the choral director is the obtrusive vibrato. Because of this, I have saved this discussion for last in this chapter.

Natural Phenomenon

As has been mentioned earlier, the well developed human voice vibrates in pitch, timbre, and intensity. This vibration should be evenly distributed above and below a constant median. Vibrato indicates a free, energized vocal production. It is also more interesting than a straight tone, or string players would not work for years to perfect a vibrato similar to that which is inherent in the voice.

Early Church Music

The straight tone may be more suitable for some styles of church music, e.g., Medieval and Renaissance motets, than a fully vibrating tone. But the straight tone presents several problems which are as difficult to solve as the vibrato question. First, intonation is more critical and tuning more difficult when the chorus sings with a straight tone. Voices cannot be tuned as readily as organ pipes because of the enormous differences in vowel colors, vocal tracts, and articulators. Also, straight tones are difficult to sustain and are tiring on the singers.

Vibrato a Symptom

A vibrato problem in a chorus is a symptom, not a malady, and the cure lies in proper vocal production rather than controlling the vibrato consciously. Most vibrato problems are not in the mere presence of vibration, but are from an inconsistency of peaks. Even with well trained young voices there may be some vibrato problem from their very youthfulness and from not being fully trained, mature singers. But the solution to this is in patient training which will even out the vibrato.

Enhances Tuning and Dynamics

Rather than being a hindrance to tuning, vibrato enhances intonation in a group. In the string sections of a fine symphony orchestra one may see left wrists vibrating at every conceivable speed and distance, yet there is no obnoxious vibrato problem in the orchestral sound. The reason is that the centers of the vibratos are the same even when the intervals above and below are different. Also, perfectly tuned vibratos tend to cancel out one another by their different speeds. Similarly, voices may vibrate in dramatic or romantic music and not present unaesthetic results. Rather, there is a greater dynamic and dramatic range possible in vibrating voices than in straight tones.

Vibrato Desirable in Choruses

Since vibrato is a natural phenomenon which occurs in all well trained voices, the conscious obliteration of the vibrato requires a constriction of the vocal tract which will be detrimental to the beauty of the voice in the long run. One of the most intriguing organ stops yet devised is the *voix celeste*, a combination of slightly out-of-tune pipes designed to produce the sound of vibrating voices, a sound which may be described as truly celestial indeed.

9

EFFECTIVE PROCEDURES
FOR CHORAL REHEARSALS

In the previous chapter several solo vocal exercises were related to choral singers. To implement these vocalises I have used the following procedures in my choral rehearsals. They have proved beneficial in improving breathing, tonal quality, and diction, and in stimulating an interest in learning to sing better.

WARMUP CALISTHENICS

The best choral rehearsals in which I have been involved have begun with some sort of warmup calisthenics. Singers' bodies need to be loose to sing well, and their circulation must be speeded up for best results. After some general loosening up exercises, the group should breathe deeply to stir up the residual air in the bottom of the lungs. When singers have done this for a few minutes, they are ready to sing effectively.

VOCALISES

The vocal exercises offered earlier for soloists are excellent for groups. Choral tone quality, flexibility, and range may be improved in the same manner as a soloist's. The following procedures may help implement the most effective use of vocalises.

Change Dynamics

Young voices should not be required to sing too softly for long at a time. Soft singing is the most difficult to support and is usually the last technique achieved by trained singers. A chorus may seem to blend better when the singers vocalize softly, but their voices will not develop fully if they never sing vigorously. Good, healthy singing is like running, and becoming tired is not necessarily a symptom of improper use of the muscles. As long as the sound produced is a good singing tone, the chorus may be allowed to sing forte without damaging their voices. The problem is not how loudly the chorus sings, but how long. A wide variety of dynamic levels make the vocalises more interesting to the chorus. Besides, the groups will enjoy singing vigorously because they can feel a sense of accomplishment in their effort. Good, supported pianissimo singing is the result of learning to sing fortissimo well.

Change Pitch and Range Levels

Vocalises should change pitch and range levels often for best results. A series of legato and staccato exercises develops the muscles of the voice in the most natural ways for singing. The voice learns to shift registers easily and to sing above and below the lifts without breaking. The best songs offer such scale and arpeggio passages, and so should our warmup vocalises.

Change Vowel Sounds

Staying on one vowel sound too long in a rehearsal is like running an engine at one constant speed. The metal becomes grooved in odd shapes, and the parts wear out quickly. In the same way voices become tired more quickly singing one constant vowel than when the sounds are varied often. Choruses who vocalize on "oo" blend nicely because of the low vowel formants and the damped inharmonic overtones. But a long rehearsal on "oo" is so tiring that the voices often will not have recovered by the next day.

Difficult Passages as Vocalises

Besides the scales and arpeggios found earlier, vocalises may be designed from difficult passages in a piece of music. Thus, there will be an immediate transfer of technical instruction to musical artistry. The students will be more able to negotiate a difficult run or phrase when they have practiced it many times as a warmup vocalise. Generally it is good to have the entire chorus sing the difficult passage to avoid boredom in the sections not involved in the problem and to promote a feeling of empathy among the group.

Lower or Higher Key

A vocalise designed from a difficult musical passage may be sung in a number of higher or lower keys. In this way the voices find the proper way to negotiate it in an easy range. Eventually, the actual key of performance seems easier than at first. Voices learn a new technique slowly, so the vocalise should be easier at the start than the final performance situation.

Slower or Faster Tempo

If the difficulty of the passage stems from its speed, the vocalise may be sung slower or faster to accomodate the students. A fast phrase, such as, "His yoke is easy" from Handel's *Messiah*, must often be learned slowly so the muscles will remember the pitch and rhythm patterns. Or, a long, sustained passage, such as, "How lovely is Thy dwellingplace" from Brahms' *Requiem*, may be sung faster than usual so the overall shape of the phrase may be mastered. The slow vocalise may be accelerated as the students become more agile, and the faster vocalise may be slowed as their muscles become stronger.

Practice on One Vowel at a Time

The passage may be sung on only one vowel to minimize its difficulty. Depending on the range and choral section involved, the vowel may be "ah" or "uh" to sustain an open throat, or it may be "ay" or "ee" to cultivate a brilliant choral line. When the vocalise has been accomplished with a single vowel, others may be used to broaden the effectiveness of the exercise. Finally, the syllables of the problem phrase should be articulated within the framework of the single vowel, that is, all the syllables sung as if the vowel were "ah," "uh," "ay," or "ee."

Nonsense Syllables

Sometimes a passage is difficult because of the conflict between its normal pronunciation in speech and its modified sounds in singing. If this is the case, the problem phrase may be learned by substituting nonsense syllables for the words which maintain some of the characteristics of the actual text. Illustration 9.1 is an example of this procedure.

"Glory to God" from *Messiah* by Handel

Illustration 9.1

1. Law-lih-loo-lah. Sing the phrase with these syllables which approximate the vowels of the text. The consonant "l" is used because it appears in the first syllable and is a lingual similar to "r" and "t." Nonsense syllables such as these focus the attention of the chorus on the sounds of the vowels. Omitting consonants at the ends of the syllables teaches them to sustain the vowel through the duration of the note.

2. Klaw-lih-loo-lah. Add the first consonant to approximate the original "gl" combination. "K" is easier to articulate on a high note because it is not voiced.

3. Klaw-dih-doo-dah. Change the interior consonants to the lingual "d." There should be no subglottic pressure in "d," as there was none in the previous "l."

4. Klaw-dih-doo-gah. Change the final initial consonant to either "g" or "k," depending on the needs of the section. These combinations are similar to the original words, but the process of reaching them should avoid unnecessary tensions. The students may even sing this set of syllables before they realize how closely they approximate the actual text.

5. Klaw-dih-doo-gah-duh. This step demonstrates that there is only one stopped syllable in the phrase. The intent here is to teach the chorus to elongate the vowel and place the stopped consonant in the following rest.

6. Klaw-dih to God. The final result may require a modification of the first word. However, the lower parts should pronounce the word "glory" normally, thus obscuring the sopranos' need to modify it.

In this example (Illustration 9.2) the chorus, especially the

"Glory to God" from *Messiah* by Handel

Illustration 9.2

tenors, may tend to overemphasize the diphthong in "high," making the final result something like "hah-ee-yest." Nonsense syllables may solve this problem.

1. Hah-teh. The group sings a syllable on each note which approximates the vowels of the real word. The "t" places a definite separation between the syllables, but there is no space between them. The tenors may sing both syllables on the lower pitch to practice precision. There should be no slurring from the upper note down the octave when they sing the written pitches.

2. Hah-heh. This time the second syllable begins with a slight "h." The altos may sing "hah" on their first note followed by the tenors singing "heh" on their second note. This demonstrates the length of the vowel in each syllable. When the group sings both syllables, there is hardly any tongue movement in the shift from "hah" to "heh."

3. Hah-eh. In this step there is an imaginary "h" to initiate the second syllable. To practice precision one half of the tenors may sing "hah," perhaps in head voice to match the alto sound, then the other half sings "eh." There should be no overlapping. Then the entire section sings both syllables without slurring down the octave.

4. Hah-est. Probably the tenors should sing only two vowels in the final performance of this word. The sopranos and altos may sing a slight diphthong, but there should be no "y" in the middle of the word. Also, since the altos and tenors sing the same pitch on the first syllable, it may not be necessary for all the tenors to sing at that point. Some tenors may sing the entire word, and the others join them on the lower note.

INITIAL READING

The first time the chorus sees a piece, they should try to read it through without stopping, no matter how hard it is. This will give them an overview of the piece and will enhance their sight reading capabilities. It also helps keep the group interested in the piece, satisfying their curiosity as to length, form, difficulty, and so on. Some of the most frustrating rehearsals I have attended were those in which a new piece was introduced, but we sang only the first sixteen measures or so during the entire session. Of course, if the first reading becomes a hopeless jumble, the director may find a convenient place to start again, and continue the reading to the end.

A cursory reading of the piece, no matter how inaccurate, will help the director locate the most difficult portions. Often I have been surprised how easy some part seemed to the chorus which I had thought might be hard, and how hard an apparently easy passage was for the group.

If one section or another gets into trouble as the initial reading moves along, the director may sing along with them. I find that singers relate to another voice quicker than to the piano playing their notes. They will find their places quicker, and the reading will not be interrupted if they are joined by a voice, even in another octave.

REHEARSAL AFTER INITIAL READING

In the next rehearsal after a piece has been introduced, the director may begin by looking at the most difficult parts first. Sometimes an analysis of the musical form will help the chorus understand the difficult passages, such as sequential melodies, overlapping fugue themes, and so on. This sort of explanation involves the chorus in solving problems in the piece.

The chorus may re-read the difficult portion to isolate exactly what the problems are. These may be rehearsed in the manner the director thinks best. Of course, some problems may not be solved in a single rehearsal because they involve muscular development. After the difficult passages have been rehearsed, the chorus probably should sing the entire composition to put the hard parts in perspective. In the case of a large work, a major portion may be sung after the difficult parts have been rehearsed.

Keep the Rehearsal Moving

Choruses respond positively if the rehearsal keeps moving along without dwelling on problems. A large portion of the rehearsal should be devoted to singing materials the group has mastered to one degree or another. The director may expect a lot from a young chorus, yet he may accept a reasonable amount in each rehearsal.

Entire Piece Progresses Uniformly

If the chorus's proficiency in the entire piece is brought along at about the same pace, they will be ready to perform it without a last minute rush to finish the piece, or without the performance being the first time through without stopping. The final rehearsals will thus be equal to performances. The director may stop the music as little as he wishes and make as few corrections as he deems necessary. Also, most important of all, the students will understand the piece as a dramatic musical entity.

IDENTIFYING PROBLEM VOICES

Before discussing procedures for identifying problem voices, perhaps it would be good to tell about a fine old chorus master I knew who believed that very fine soloists could cause problems in a chorus as easily as poor singers. He often spoke of mixing lilies and roses, comparing his regular choral singers to fine lilies and a beautiful soloist to a rose. Such a combination could never work, to his way of thinking, because the rose could never hide itself among a group of lilies. I know of occasions when he asked a fine singer to leave the chorus because the voice was "too good."

While such an attitude may seem extreme, there is a corollary situation which I have encountered as a choral director: the singer is a rose who wishes to be a lily, or vice versa. Students sometimes come to a voice teacher asking to be transformed into a new vocal classification. Sopranos with low notes wish to be altos, and baritones with high notes wish to be tenors, all because those are the parts available in a prestigious or lucrative choral organization. In the long run such singers will probably cause the choral director problems of balance, intonation, and tonal quality, as well as causing themselves vocal problems which could shorten their singing careers.

Whatever the source of the problem, the following procedures have been effective in identifying the singer or singers whose voices do not blend with the others in the section.

Large Group

In a large group, after identifying the section in question, I ask half the problem group to sing a phrase. Then the half which contains the problem voice sings; then half that group, and so on until I am sure which singer I am looking for. At that time I do nothing further, but after rehearsal I meet with the individual to see what solution may be reached. Some work may be required outside the rehearsal period, especially if the student does not have a voice teacher.

Small Group

In a small group there is usually more rapport which would allow the director to treat vocal problems within the rehearsal. Since no malice is intended in pointing out new vocal techniques, the student generally appreciates learning to sing better. If necessary, of course, the director may work outside the rehearsal to correct major problems.

SEATING ARRANGEMENTS

Because the size and composition of each chorus makes its sound unique, seating charts are probably not necessary to this discussion.

Sectional Seating

The most widely used seating arrangements place the members of each section together with the better voices in the middle or front of the group. The sections may be juxtaposed to surround a small number of men with a larger number of women singers, or fairly evenly matched sections may be placed next to each other for best performance possibilities. The reasons for these sectional seating plans are good. The weaker musicians are bolstered by hearing other, stronger singers on the same notes. Seating within the section provides the best blend, and usually the chorus learns the music quicker than in some sort of mingled seating. Also, if the tenors need reinforcement on high notes or the altos on low notes, these sections may be arranged to provide for such exigencies. Further, in performance the chorus may be arranged according to height without unduly disturbing the singers.

There are some drawbacks to sectional seating, however. The individual becomes less important when surrounded by several other persons singing exactly the same part as his. The weak musicians learn to depend on their stronger colleagues without the challenge of carrying a part by themselves, thus inhibiting their musical growth.

Therefore, I believe that sectional seating arrangements should be used only if necessary. If such seating arrangments are used, the students should have the opportunity to change seats within the section. Even better is the plan of having the groups rotate so that the sections are not always seated in the same area of the room or on the choral risers.

Quartet or Mingled Seating

As mentioned earlier, I believe students benefit from mingled seating arrangements. Their interest in the group is improved because they get to hear the other parts better, they become better acquainted with their colleagues, and they can hear themselves better. The individual's ability to read music at sight is greatly enhanced, as well as his awareness of intonation and blend. Equally as important, such seating inspires self-confidence in the singer and improves his personality.

There are some drawbacks which must be faced. The non-singer may be precluded from participating in a group which depends on the individual so heavily. Each singer must display good musicianship and be able to carry his part alone. Also, performance arrangements are more difficult because of size differences among the choristers. The heights and sizes of singers are not related to the best blending of their voices.

The final performance seating chart is almost always a compromise between the very best blend and a pleasing stage picture. An advantage to mingled rehearsal seating is that the singers are not confused by a new arrangement in the performance.

10

AN INDIVIDUALIZED APPROACH
TO CLASS VOICE

Some time ago I had the privilege of singing in a series of master classes led by Mr. Gerald Moore. We singers and pianists performed for Mr. Moore in front of an audience, and he gave us a short coaching lesson. Over the years this sort of lesson has become a popular and important teaching tool on a number of university campuses. Quite a few outstanding artist-teachers spend a good deal of their time in such sessions. Most of my colleagues and I have been invited to visit other schools to teach master classes, and a logical outgrowth has been to evolve a system of teaching our own students along the lines of the master class.

Where other class voice models are based on the group as a unity, the approach I am suggesting treats each student as an individual. In the usual voice class, the students sing together, learning the same song or songs in the same languages, keys, and so on. Very little time is available for treating the vocal problems of the individual. Large classes of twenty-five to thirty make it impossible to give the sort of mini-lesson which is based on the master class approach. In the latter kind of class the optimum number of students is four to six per hour.

SUGGESTED PROCEDURES

In designing a method of group instruction which treats the student as an individual, the following procedures have been devised.

Explain the Elements of Singing

The first four class periods include brief lectures on the four elements of singing: respiration, phonation, resonance, and articulation. This establishes a common terminology among the students as well as making them aware of the components of singing. Each lecture is then followed by a group lesson in vocal techniques which emphasizes the subject of the day. After the first four lectures, the students should understand the teacher's reference to one of the elements as he comments on a particular aspect of singing in class.

Group Warm-up Exercises

After the brief lecture, the group warms up together. Usually, beginning students are shy at first, and this group warm-up period initiates them to the processes of singing. There will be less embarrassment if the first singing in class is a group activity. The students hear that they are about equal in development (as they should be in a class of this kind) and are made to feel at ease singing in a small group. The first warm-up exercises are scales and arpeggios which are applicable to voices of all kinds. Most of the easy vocalises mentioned earlier may be used at this point. The warm-up period is similar to that at the beginning of a choral rehearsal, and if the students are in a chorus, they will relate very quickly to this activity.

Students Sing Alone

The students should be asked to sing alone as soon as the first warm-up period is over. If they have participated vigorously in the warm-ups, they will be mentally and physically ready to sing. Before any apprehension can build up, the teacher matter-of-factly calls on one or the other of the students to sing alone. There may be a moment of initial nervousness, but this will pass quickly. Each student should sing in each session if there are no more than six in a one-hour class. In the voice classes which have eight to twelve students and meet twice a week, each student may sing every other class meeting.

Assign Songs According to Student's Needs

It has proved important to assign songs at the first class meeting, because the students are more interested in songs than vocalises. The reasons for and importance of vocalises come later when the students are more aware of how each element of singing is improved. The songs are assigned according to each student's vocal needs, a most important factor in the individuality of class voice instruction. Later in this chapter some suggestions will be made as to materials which teach specific vocal techniques.

Student Relates Others' Problems to His Own

Although the students are assigned different songs, there are inevitably a number of vocal problems shared by almost everyone in the group. The student hears the teacher help someone else solve the same problem as his, and he acquires a better insight into how voices work and how they are enriched. He learns to trust the teacher's judgment and is more willing to experiment with new vocal techniques.

Other Benefits

By assigning each student different songs, the teacher has the opportunity to acquaint the students with a great deal more music. The students learn various styles of performance, languages, and musical practices which they can transfer to themselves when the time comes. Also, hearing and singing a variety of songs in class increases each student's interest. Deportment does not become a problem when something interesting and exciting is happening.

Class Participation

After a few sessions in which the students have heard one another sing and the teacher has given each a short voice lesson, the class members may be brought into the teaching procedure. The instructor may ask the class if they can hear the difference some technique makes in a student's singing, pointing out that such differences will also occur in their own voices. The teacher guides the discussion, of course, so it stays on the proper track. The students learn to verbalize intelligently what they hear in a performance. All the discussion is conducted in a spirit of helpfulness, and there is no malice involved.

Peer Relationships

Class participation of this kind makes for good peer relationships and may be of great assistance in teaching. Friendly, helpful peer pressure encourages a student to try new ways of singing and reinforces each one's progress. Many times a student who is reluctant to accept a new sound or a different vocal technique is inspired by the reassurance of his classmates.

RESULTS OF CLASS VOICE

In a class such as this, students are challenged to explore their vocal possibilities and expand their horizons. They are encouraged not to classify themselves prematurely as to range and timbre, as well as to avoid any self-limiting attitudes. The student must give himself time to develop new vocal sounds and accept each emergent change in timbre as a sign of progress.

Awareness of Self

As the students hear each other in the class, attend concerts, and hear fine voices on television and radio, they begin to hear themselves in relation to others. Their understanding of singing is increased in general, as well as their knowledge of themselves as singers. This process of self-awareness plays an important part in the students' becoming mature adults.

Gain Confidence and Poise

The constant discipline of performing alone before the class is excellent in promoting confidence and poise. (My own experience as a weekly church soloist in my teens has proved invaluable through the years.) Each class session becomes a time for self-expression. With the acceptance of oneself comes the ability to accept useful criticism from the group. Each student learns better how to communicate with others diplomatically.

Teacher Educates Students' Aesthetics

One of the most important aspects of this class is the teachers' opportunity to educate their students' aesthetics as well as to train their voices. The students come to understand not only what is good singing but also what is good music. Concerts and programs suggested by the teacher become part of their growth and broaden their education. Being in a group of young singers who are engaged in learning good songs is a pervasive influence toward acquiring an educated view of the arts.

SOME MATERIALS FOR USE IN VOICE CLASS

Here are some easy to moderately difficult songs which emphasize scales, intervals, runs, or long phrases. There are a few instances of song titles in more than one category, but this has been kept to a minimum. The list is not exhaustive by any means and is only meant as examples of the kinds of songs which may be found in many anthologies.

Descending Scales

Caro mio ben—Giuseppe Giordani
Dedication (Widmung)—Robert Franz
I Love Thee (Ich liebe dich)—Ludwig van Beethoven
The Lotusbloom (Die Lotosblume)—Robert Schumann
Panis Angelicus—César Franck
Sombre Woods (Bois Epais)—Jean Baptiste Lully
Songs My Mother Taught Me—Antonin Dvořák
Verdant Meadows (Verdi prati)—George F. Handel
Vergin, tutto amor—Francesco Durante
Tu lo sai—Giuseppe Torelli
Where're You Walk—George F. Handel

Ascending Scales

I Love Thee (Ich liebe dich)—Ludwig van Beethoven
The Joys of Love (Plaisir d'amour)—Giovanni Martini
The Sea—Edward MacDowell
Still as the Night (Still wie die Nacht)—Carl Bohm
Vergin, tutto amor—Francesco Durante
Where're You Walk—George F. Handel

Narrow Intervals

Dedication (Widmung)—Robert Franz
Faith in Spring (Frühlingsglaube)—Franz Schubert
The Lotusbloom (Die Lotosblume)—Robert Schumann
O Rest in the Lord—Felix Mendelssohn
Pur dicesti, o bocca bella—Antonio Lotti

Wide Intervals

Come raggio di sol—Antonio Caldara
Elegy (Elégie)—Jules Massenet
L'Heure exquise—Reynaldo Hahn
None but the Lonely Heart—Piotr I. Chaikovski
Sapphic Ode (Sapphische Ode)—Johannes Brahms
Serenade (Ständchen)—Franz Schubert

Melismatic Runs

I attempt from love's sickness to fly—Henry Purcell
The Lass with the Delicate Air—Thomas Arne
O Sleep, Why Dost Thou Leave Me—George F. Handel
Pur dicesti, o bocca bella—Antonio Lotti
Sound the Trumpet (duet)—Henry Purcell

Long Phrases

After a Dream (Après un rêve)—Gabriel Fauré
Che fiero costume—Giovanni Legrenzi
Come raggio di sol—Antonio Caldara
The Cradles (Les Berceaux)—Gabriel Fauré
Dedication (Zueignung)—Richard Strauss
Sapphic Ode (Sapphische Ode)—Johannes Brahms
Secrecy (Verborgenheit)—Hugo Wolf
When I am laid in earth—Henry Purcell

Wide Range

All Soul's Day (Allerseelen)—Richard Strauss
Beautiful Evening (Beau Soir)—Claude Debussy
I'll Not Complain (Ich grolle nicht)—Robert Schumann
The Lotusbloom (Die Lotosblume)—Robert Schumann
Still as the Night (Still wie die Nacht)—Carl Bohm

11

HOW TO TRAIN
CHANGING VOICES

A large area of vocal training which has been relatively un-explored is that of the changing voice. It is well recognized that both male and female voices change—sometimes drastically—during the teen years, but all too often the changes are overlooked by the vocal music teacher, and the singers are left to their own devices. Many times the young singers drop out of vocal music altogether because they are not provided for in their school pro-grams.

On the other hand, some music teachers are quite careful to guide their young singers through the mutation period and thus promote healthy attitudes and approaches toward singing. They recognize the early symptoms of vocal change and help the young singers to cope with what may be a troublesome time in their lives, adolescence.

THE BOY'S VOICE

Because the mutation of the male voice is more apparent to the listener and exasperating to the singer than that of the female, it is better to begin there. There seems to be little correlation between the range and quality of a boy's voice before it changes to what it may sound like as a man's. Boys who are high sopranos or low altos may become basses or tenors. There is some evidence that the earlier a boy's voice changes the lower and heavier it will be, but there are numerous exceptions. As with many other aspects of vocal training, each singer must be accepted as an individual, and his voice must be trained according to its particular attributes.

Nature of the Change

At some time between the ages of eleven and seventeen, usually thirteen to fifteen, the boy's sex glands enlarge dramatically and begin to secrete hormones into his system which change him physically and emotionally. He grows several inches in height, gains weight at an astonishing rate, and develops an omnivorous appetite. He begins to grow hair on his face and chest, under his arms, and in his pubic area. He begins to develop an embarrassing acne which will plague him for several years no matter how he treats it. All these changes cause the boy to be ill at ease and sensitive to personal criticisms.

Concurrent with these changes is the not so subtle mutation in the boy's voice. His larynx enlarges dramatically, the vocal bands lengthen and thicken, and the pitch of the boy's voice suddenly drops several notes—perhaps as much as an octave. He may begin a sentence in one register, high or low, and shift to the other without warning. Of all the physical changes, this is the most annoying to the young man. He will happily identify with a teacher who understands and sympathizes with his dilemma.

Ways to Deal with Vocal Mutation

The major premise upon which all the following suggestions are made is that boys should continue to sing during vocal mutation. Most authorities now agree that excluding boys from vocal activities not only does not improve their chances of singing well later on, but rather hinders their musical enjoyment and aesthetic growth.

The minor premise is that boys' changing voices should be trained according to their peculiar needs. It is almost as harmful to ignore the boys whose voices are changing as to exclude them from singing.

Boys with changing voices may be separated from other singers if the teacher has time to train them either in a voice class or a special chorus. They should be told that the class or chorus is designed specifically for them, without pejorative implications, because their training is worthwhile and should not be postponed until after their voices have changed. If there is no time for a special class or chorus, the teacher will, of course, want to be aware of the boys' changing voices and treat them within a regular class period, much in the manner of the individualized approach to voice class found in an earlier chapter.

Special Vocal Procedures

The following procedures have been found to be effective in my experience with church and school choruses, as well as in private lessons for boys with changing voices:

1. Gradually lower the tessitura. As mentioned earlier, the tessitura of vocal music is much more important than its range. Boys whose voices are beginning to change should sing in a comfortable tessitura. The teacher will listen to each voice for strain and choose keys which are most conducive to the singer's progress. This is easier in a voice class where each boy sings by himself than in a chorus.

In a choral situation each boy should be auditioned frequently so the director may keep up with his vocal change. During rehearsals the director is careful to look for any visible signs of vocal strain, such as stretched necks, raised eyebrows, thrust chins, clenched jaws, and so on.

2. Limit the range. Boys whose voices are changing should not sing in extreme ranges. This not to say that upper notes should be avoided altogether. Boys who decline to sing in their upper ranges at all may lose the flexibility and roundness of tone which is associated with head voice. A good approach to low and high notes will maintain the outer limits of the voice, while a limited range will allow the strength and beauty of the voice to develop. If a boy must sing within a range of six notes for awhile to insure proper vocal development, so be it. The time will come when he can sing wider ranges, and his voice will have remained secure during its mutation.

3. Change written notes when necessary. Sometimes songs which fit a boy's tessitura have one or two notes which do not fit his range. In those cases, the problem notes may be changed to suit the voice, especially if the boy is singing a harmony part. An alternate pitch may be offered by the teacher which will fit both the song and the singer. The most obvious alternate notes are octave shifts up or down. Or, the third or fifth of a triad may be substituted for one another. In some instances whole new lines may be written so the vocal line will move in small intervals or diatonically.

4. Teach head voice techniques. While the boy's voice is changing he should rely on head voice techniques for his highest notes. The exercises suggested for changing from head voice to chest voice and back will be useful. The young man should probably not try to sing above the second lift in chest voice, even with modified vowels, as the extralaryngeal muscles are not strong enough in the mid-teens. As the young man matures, he will be able to reinforce his upper notes by blending chest voice with the head voice he has already learned, thus achieving a good upper register in chest voice.

5. Introduce bass clef when necessary. I find that boys can understand the bass clef if I explain it as an extension of the treble clef within the great staff. The boys have generally been singing below the treble clef in the alto range, so they are used to leger lines. Now those lines are seen as a part of the bass clef with middle C as the only leger line between the staves. This is easy to demonstrate on a chalk board. When the bass clef is introduced in this manner, the boys are not confused by singing one day below the staff and the next day above it.

Exercises for the Boy's Changing Voice

1. Breathing exercises. Since boys whose voices are changing are in the process of rapid physical growth, it is especially important to teach them good breathing exercises such as those found earlier. Muscular development and coordination are vital to the young singer's training. Through them the young men learn good posture, improve their physical aptitude, and increase their vital capacity.

2. *Attacks, sustained tones, and releases.* Besides breathing exercises, the vocalises concerning attacks, sustained tones, and releases are of highest importance. Most young men have not had technical vocal training before the onset of vocal mutation, so this is their first opportunity to learn to use their voices in a disciplined manner. The concepts found earlier of attack on the rebound of the breath, sustained tones, and release on the breath may be learned with all the enthusiasm and alacrity of the young. As their bodies learn to respond with better coordination, their aesthetic sensitivities become more acute, and there is a feeling of achievement in their musical studies.

3. *Descending vocalises.* As to specific vocalises, those which are based on descending scales and arpeggios are the best. They may begin fairly high in the range and descend by half-tones until the low notes fade away. Of course, the young men should not force or push down on their low notes. By beginning near the top of the range, the vocalise incorporates some of the feeling of head voice which was familiar to the boy soprano or alto. During the mutation period, it is not unusual to have the boy or young man sing in head voice (not falsetto) for the highest notes of a song. Through descending vocalises he should learn a smooth transition from head voice into chest voice. The range of the vocalises depends on the state of the boy's voice at the time.

Singing in Mixed Chorus

One of the most satisfying musical experiences for the boy whose voice is changing can be mixed chorus. The clever director may devise seating charts which place the boy between altos or sopranos on one side—whichever part he sings at the time—and basses or tenors on the other side. Thus the boy is not segregated from other young men because of his vocal range or timbre.

As the boy's voice lowers, he may be placed in different seats in the chorus. This, too, may be quite natural if the director changes his seating arrangements for all choristers often. It is not unusual for the boy alto to become a high tenor before the school year is over, a change which can be aided through close supervision by the director and assignment to the section where his voice fits best.

Sometimes a boy's voice changes so rapidly he becomes a bass almost overnight. In those cases he will sit with the other basses in the chorus. New bass voices move up and down in range and tessitura as the young men mature, so they should be careful not to sing an exclusively low part. The director will be aware of the range and tessitura of each piece, and he may write in alternate notes for the new basses where necessary.

Countertenors or Male Altos

A male choral part which has been recently rediscovered or reinstated is the countertenor or male alto. As their voices change, young men may be encouraged to retain their high notes through the use of head voice, either in the manner of Russell Oberlin, a very high tenor, or of Alfred Deller, a bass-baritone who perfected his head voice techniques. As the music of the Middle Ages, Renaissance, and Baroque eras returns to choral libraries, choruses may attain a more authentic sound through the use of countertenors and male altos. In the Rockefeller Chapel Choir of the University of Chicago I sang with two such men, and their contribution to the music of the Chapel was unique: a head voice quality of considerable size and projection which blended with altos and tenors and which was distinctly masculine. Young men may be completely assured that there is nothing effeminate about being a countertenor or male alto.

Peculiar Aspects of the Boy's Changing Voice

Over the years I have observed some peculiarities in the mutation process. I have already mentioned that it seems the younger the boy when his voice changes, the lower and heavier it will be. Another associated observation is that some of these low voices tend to rise as the young man matures. By that I mean the entire vocal range and tessitura may rise, not just that the young man will gain some higher notes. It is not unusual for a ninth-grade bass to become an eleventh-grade baritone who can no longer negotiate the notes below the bass clef. And it may be several years before the low notes return.

Some teenage baritones may become tenors as they mature, although their highest notes may not be secure until they reach their twenties or thirties. Quite a number of outstanding dramatic tenors—Lauritz Melchior, James McCracken, and Jon Vickers, to name a few—began as young baritones. At an early age, voices such as these will probably blend better in the baritone section than the tenor, but they should not be asked to sing too low. They are admirably suited to the "bariten" part I described earlier.

Another unexplained aspect of male vocal mutation has to do with the tenor whose voice changes relatively late in his teens. His range and tessitura gradually lower without a sudden drop, and his vocal quality is about the same after the change as before. He generally has very little resonance below the F below middle C until he reaches his twenties. On the other hand, whereas his chest voice closely matches his head voice so he may sing the Tenor I part easily, he may not be able to sing above E or F above middle C in chest voice. In other words, his lifts and chest voice range may be about the same as a high baritone, but his timbre is remarkably different.

These peculiarities serve to emphasize the importance of treating each changing voice individually. Each student should sing according to his tessitura and range at the moment. Where there are peculiarities such as tenors and baritones with approximately the same lifts and chest voice range, the timbre of each voice will determine which part the young men should sing in the chorus.

SONGS FOR BOYS AND YOUNG MEN

Whether intended for soloists, classes, or choruses, songs for boys and young men should be simple—melodically and rhythmically—and limited in range. It is good if the director or the accompanist can transpose readily so the boys may sing comfortably. Above all, the songs must be masculine. Romantic ballads may be introduced to young men, but they may not be accepted.

Here is a list of the types of songs which I have found best suited for young men with changing voices:

1. Folk songs, such as mountain tunes and work songs
2. Authentic Western songs

3. Patriotic songs
4. Spirituals
5. Sea chanties
6. Camp songs
7. Men's solos and choruses from Gilbert and Sullivan operas
8. Songs from Broadway musicals which fit the above criteria

THE GIRL'S VOICE

The girl's voice does not change as much as a boy's as she enters puberty, and few girls are lost to the school music program because of vocal mutation problems. But there are some things which may be said concerning the girl's changing voice.

Nature of the Change

Sometime between the ages of eleven and fourteen a girl's sex glands begin to secrete hormones which cause several rapid physical transformations, such as enlarged breasts and internal female organs, underarm and pubic hair, menstrual cycles and so on. Her emotional makeup is alternately childish and adult.

There is a relatively subtle increase in the size of the girl's larynx and vocal bands. Rather than dropping rapidly, her vocal range lowers only slightly at first. She may experience some difficulty in singing the highest notes of the Soprano I part, in which case she generally moves to Soprano II or Alto, but the change in timbre is hardly noticeable.

Thin and Breathy Tone

More than likely, the girl's voice will sound thinner and breathier than before, because her vocal bands have outgrown the surrounding muscles and are unable to close properly. This condition should clear up as the girl matures. She should continue singing and practicing good vocal techniques during mutation.

Low and Husky Tone

If the girl's voice is not thin and breathy, it may be low and husky. In the latter case the girl's range and tessitura may have dropped rapidly like a boy's, but not as far. She will have much more trouble sustaining high notes than before and should sing alto in the chorus. She should not, however, abandon her high voice altogether. Only in the rarest cases must such a girl be allowed to become a female tenor. With patience and practice her voice will respond, and she will be able to sing better later on.

Inconsistent Quality

Whether thin and breathy or low and husky, the girl's voice probably will display inconsistency of quality. She will perhaps have problems with register changes that were not apparent before the onset of mutation. The primary reason for such inconsistencies is the sudden growth of the vocal bands while the extralaryngeal muscles were growing at a normal rate. As the girl matures, this imbalance will correct itself.

Psychological Implications

Girls who are becoming young women frequently go through identity crises not unlike those of the boys becoming young men. As their self-images change, their notions of how their own voices should sound also change. In an effort to lose their little girl voices, young women may dwell too long in their low registers both in speech and in singing. Their musical heroines may be popular singers whose mature voices have settled permanently into the lower third of their ranges, and whose vocal styles equate loudness with beauty. The understanding teacher helps these girls discover their own personalities without imitating an unsuitable model.

Ways to Deal With Vocal Mutation

Since the change in a girl's voice may be subtle, she should be careful to sing with good vocal technique throughout the process. Her tone should not be allowed to become sluggish and unsupported. She should maintain a proper ratio of head voice in her entire range, not yielding to the temptation to sing blantantly or "belt" her low notes. The following exercises are recommended:

1. *Breathing exercises.* The girl's enlarged vocal bands will require more support than before, so she should continue to develop her breathing muscles. Also, as her breasts enlarge she will have to remind herself to stand up straight with her shoulders back. Her skeletal muscles will become stronger, and good posture will become easier after awhile.

2. Humming, ringing quality. The concept of a humming, ringing sound is important during this period, because of the tendency in most girls toward breathiness. Descending scales and arpeggios which mix head voice with the middle and low registers are vital to good vocal technique during mutation.

3. Light approach. The girl's voice which is supported well with a humming, ringing quality should be light. This does not mean weak or child-like, but implies a high, forward placement which is focussed above the hard palate. The voice should "spin" and be flexible. There should be no feeling that the voice is caught in the throat or is "sitting on the vocal bands." Alternate bright and dark vowels may be incorporated into vocalises to blend the brilliance and depth of the voice.

4. Practice the upper range. Young women should sing in all parts of their ranges to maintain the entire voice. Too many girls are allowed to sing exclusively in the lower two-thirds of their voices during vocal mutation, creating great difficulties in their late teens with their high registers. Vocalises such as the fire siren and songs which require a few excursions into the high range are highly recommended.

Careful Choice of Songs

Young women will accept a wider selection of songs than young men, so the major concerns in choosing materials are tessitura and range. Songs should be chosen which explore several areas of the voice, rather than concentrating in the upper or lower ranges. Girls' voices should not stay too long above the second lift, nor consistently sing closed vowels such as "oo." Dynamics should be varied as well, so the voice is exercised thoroughly. In the case of girls' choruses the parts should not overemphasize high or low notes without relief.

Frequent Auditions

Since it is hard to hear female vocal changes within a group, the girls should be auditioned frequently to establish their ranges and tessituras at the moment. Also, the teacher will be able to listen for changes in quality and offer appropriate suggestions as to vocal study. Frequent auditions also help the choral director place each girl in the proper choral section, thus satisfying the need for good choral balance and blend and the obligation to treat each singer as an individual.

BIBLIOGRAPHY

VOCAL PEDAGOGY BOOKS

Appelman, D. Ralph, *The Science of Vocal Pedagogy*. Bloomington, Ind.: Indiana University Press, 1967.

Brodnitz, Friedrich S., *Keep Your Voice Healthy*. Springfield, Ill.: C. C. Thomas, Publisher, 1973.

Brown, Ralph Morse, *The Singing Voice*. New York: Macmillan Co., 1946.

Brown, William Earl, *Vocal Wisdom: Maxims of Giovanni Battista Lamperti*. Enlarged edition. Supplement edited by Lillian Strongin. Boston: Crescendo Publishers, 1973.

Burgin, John Carroll, *Teaching Singing*. Metuchen, N. J.: Scarecrow Press, Inc., 1973.

Campbell, E. J. Moran, *The Respiratory Muscles and the Mechanics of Breathing*. Chicago: The Year Book Medical Publishers, Inc., 1958.

Cates, Millard, *Guide for Young Singers*. Ann Arbor, Mich.: University of Michigan Press, 1959.

Christy, Van A., *Expressive Singing*. (3rd ed.) Dubuque, Iowa: William C. Brown & Co., 1974.

——, *Foundations in Singing*. (3rd ed.) Dubuque, Iowa: William C. Brown & Co., 1975.

Coffin, Berton, *The Sounds of Singing*. Boulder, Colo.: Pruett Publishing Co., 1976.

DeYoung, Richard, *The Singer's Art*. Chicago: DePaul University Press, 1958.

Fields, Victor A., *Training the Singing Voice*. New York: King's Crown Press, 1947.

Fields, Victor A., and Bender, James F., *Voice and Diction*. New York: Macmillan Co., 1949.

Fisher, Hilda B., *Improving Voice and Articulation* (2nd ed.) Boston: Houghton Mifflin Co., 1975.

Foreman, Edward, ed., *The Porpora Tradition*. Milwaukee: Pro Musica Press, 1968.

Frisell, Anthony, *The Baritone Voice*. Boston: Crescendo Publishers, 1972

————, *The Soprano Voice*. Boston: Bruce Humphries, Pub., 1966.

————, *The Tenor Voice*. Boston: Bruce Humphries, Pub., 1964.

Fuchs, Viktor, *The Art of Singing and Voice Technique*. New York: London House and Maxwell, 1964.

Garcia, Manuel, II, *A Complete Treatise on the Art of Singing*. Trans. Donald V. Paschke. New York: Da Capo Press, Inc., 1972.

————, *Hints on Singing*. Reprint of 1894 pub. Canoga Park, Cal.: Summit Publishing Co., 1970.

Gardiner, Julian, *A Guide to Good Singing and Speech*. Boston: Crescendo Publishers, 1972.

Garretson, Robert L., *Conducting Choral Music* (2nd ed.) Boston: Allyn and Bacon, 1965.

Gray, Henry, *Anatomy, Descriptive and Surgical*. Edited by T. Pickering Pick and Robert Howden. Bounty Books. New York: Crown Publishers, Inc., 1977.

Greene, Margaret C. L., *The Voice and Its Disorders* (3rd ed.) Philadelphia: J. B. Lippincott Co., 1972.

Husler, Frederick, and Rodd-Marling, Yvonne, *Singing, the Physical Nature of the Vocal Organ*. New York: October House, 1965.

Jipson, Wayne R., *The High School Vocal Music Program*. West Nyack, N. Y.: Parker Publishing Company, 1972.

Judson, Lyman, and Weaver, A. T., *Voice Science* (2nd ed.) New York: Appleton-Century-Crofts, 1965.

Large, John W., ed., *Vocal Registers in Singing*. Paris: Mouton et Cie., 1973.

Lawson, James Terry., *Full-Throated Ease*. Vancouver: Western Music Co., 1955.

Lehmann, Lilli, *How to Sing*, Trans. Richard Aldrich. Northbrook, Ill.: Whitehall Press, 1972.

Mancini, Giambattista, *Practical Reflections on Figured Singing*, Trans. and ed. Edward Foreman. Champaign, Ill.: Pro Musica Press, 1967.

Marshall, Madeleine, *The Singer's Manual of English Diction*. New York: G. Schirmer, Inc., 1953.

Miller, Richard, *English, French, German, and Italian Techniques of Singing: A Study in National Tonal Preferences and How They Relate to Functional Efficiency*. Metuchen, N. J.: Scarecrow Press, Inc., 1977.

Moore, Gerald, *Singer and Accompanist*. New York: Macmillan Co., 1954.

Negus, V. E., *The Comparative Anatomy and Physiology of the Larynx*. New York: Hafner Press, 1962.

Peterson, Paul W., *Natural Singing and Expressive Conducting*, Revised edition. Winston-Salem: John F. Blair, Pub., 1966

Pfautsch, Lloyd, *English Diction for the Singer*. New York: Lawson-Gould Music Pub., 1971.

Rice, William, *Basic Principles of Singing*. Nashville: Abingdon Press, 1961.

Rose, Arnold, *The Singer and the Voice*. New York: St. Martin's Press, Inc., 1971.

Rosewall, Richard, *Handbook of Singing*. Evanston, Ill.: Summy-Birchard Co., 1961.

Rushmore, Robert, *The Singing Voice*. New York: Dodd, Mead and Co., 1971.

Saunders, William H., *The Larynx. Clinical Symposia*, edited by J. Harold Walton. Summit, N. J.: CIBA Pharmaceutical Co., 1964.

Schiøtz, Aksel, *The Singer and His Art*. New York: Harper and Row, 1970.

Stanton, Royal, *Steps to Singing for Voice Class*. Belmont, Cal.: Wadsworth Publishing Company, Inc., 1971.

Sunderman, Lloyd Frederick, *Artistic Singing: Its Tone Production and Basic Understandings*. Metuchen, N. J.: Scarecrow Press, Inc., 1970.

Swanson, Frederick J., *The Male Singing Voice Ages Eight to Eighteen*. Cedar Rapids, Iowa: Laurance Press, 1977.

Trusler, Ivan, and Ehret, Walter, *Functional Lessons in Singing* (2nd ed.) Englewood Cliffs, N. J.: Prentice-Hall, Inc., 1972.

Uris, Dorothy, *To Sing in English*. New York: Boosey and Hawkes, Inc., 1971.

Vennard, William, *Developing Voices*. New York: Carl Fischer, Inc., 1973.

————, *Singing: The Mechanism and the Technic*, Revised edition. New York: Carl Fischer Inc., 1967.

Whitlock, Weldon, *Profiles in Vocal Pedagogy*. Ann Arbor, Mich.: Clifton Press, 1975.

————, *Bel Canto for the Twentieth Century*. Champaign, Ill.: Pro Musica Press, 1968.

Zemlin, Willard R., *Speech and Hearing Science: Anatomy and Physiology*. Englewood Cliffs, N.J.: Prentice-Hall, Inc., 1968.

OTHER BOOKS

Blaine, Tom R., *Goodbye Allergies*. Secaucus, N. J.: Citadel Press, Inc., 1965.

Gallwey, W. Timothy, *Inner Tennis: Playing the Game*. New York: Random House, Inc., 1976.

VOCAL PEDAGOGY ARTICLES

Abusamra, Ward, "Small Group vs. Individual Instruction in the Performance Studio," *The NATS Bulletin*, 34 (May, 1978).

"Anatomy of Voice," *Choral and Organ Guide*, 21 (October, 1968).

Antahades, Mary Ella, "Singing Reaches Out: Creative Use of Class Voice and 'Packaging'," *The NATS Bulletin*, 30 (December, 1973).

Baer, Hermanus, "Establishing a Correct Basic Technique for Singing," *The NATS Bulletin*, 28 (May/June, 1972).

Beachy, Morris J., "Are Choral and Vocal Studio Rehearsal Techniques Compatible?" *Choral Journal*, 10 (September/October, 1969).

Belisle, John M., "Some Factors Influencing Diction in Singing," *The NATS Bulletin*, 24 (December, 1967).

Bjørklund, Adolph, "Analyses of Soprano Voices," *Journal of the Acoustical Society of America*, 33 (May, 1961).

Borchers, Orville J., "Practical Implications of Scientific Research for the Teaching of Voice," Music Teachers National Association, *Volume of Proceedings for 1947*. Pittsburgh, 1947.

————, "The Phenomenon of Vocal Tone Quality," *The NATS Bulletin*, 8 (November/December, 1951).

Bouhuys, Arend; Proctor, Donald F.; and Mead, Jere, "Kinetic Aspects of Singing," *Journal of Applied Physiology*, 21 (March, 1966).

Brodnitz, Friedrich S., "Hormones and the Human Voice," *The NATS Bulletin*, 28 (December, 1971).

————, "The Singing Teacher and the Laryngologist," *The NATS Bulletin*, 13 (February, 1957).

Brown, Oren, "Causes of Voice Strain in Singing," *The NATS Bulletin*, 15 (December, 1958).

————, "Principles of Voice Therapy as Applied to Teaching," *The NATS Bulletin*, 9 (May/June, 1953).

————, "Voice Examination of the Professional," *The NATS Bulletin*, 34 (May, 1978).

Bunch, Meribeth A., "A Survey of the Research on Covered and Open Voice Qualities," *The NATS Bulletin*, 33 (February, 1977).

————, and Sonninen, Aatto, "Some Further Observations on Covered and Open Voice Qualities," *The NATS Bulletin*, 34 (October, 1977).

Coffin, Berton, "Articulation for Opera, Oratorio, and Recital." *The NATS Bulletin*, 32 (February/March, 1976).

————, "On Hearing, Feeling, and Using the Instrumental Resonance of the Singing Voice," *The NATS Bulletin*, 31 (December, 1974).

————, "The Relationship of Phonation and Resonation," *The NATS Bulletin*, 31 (February/March, 1975).

————, "The Relationship of the Breath, Phonation, and Resonance in Singing," *The NATS Bulletin*, 32 (December, 1975).

————, "The Singer's Diction," *The NATS Bulletin*, 20 (February, 1964).

Cooper, Morton, "Vocal Suicide in Singers," *The NATS Bulletin*, 26 (February/March, 1970).

Cornwall, Burton, "A Natural Approach to Voice," *Music Journal*, 29 (January, 1971).

Delattre, Pierre, "Vowel Color and Voice Quality," *The NATS Bulletin*, 15 (October, 1958).

Donalson, Robert P., "The Practice and Pedagogy of Vocal Legato," *The NATS Bulletin*, 29 (May/June, 1973).

Doscher, Barbara M., "The Beginning Voice Class," *The NATS Bulletin*, 32 (October, 1975).

Draper, Dallas, "The Solo Voice as Applied to Choral Singing," *Choral Journal*, 12 (May, 1972).

Duschak, Alice G., "Musical Style as a Stimulant to Vocal Technique," *The NATS Bulletin*, 26 (December, 1969).

Dwyer, Edward J., "Concepts of Breathing for Singing," *The NATS Bulletin*, 24 (October, 1967).

————, "Problems Arising from Concurrent Instrumental and Vocal Study," *The NATS Bulletin*, 29 (May/June, 1973).

Eberhart, Constance, "Diction," *The NATS Bulletin*, 18 (May, 1962).

Edmondson, Frank, "Intonation in Vocal Performance of Intervals," *The NATS Bulletin*, 29 (October, 1972).

Fields, Victor A., "Art versus Science in Singing," *The NATS Bulletin*, 29 (October, 1972).

————, "A Basic Approach in the Teaching of Singing: How Mind Governs Voice," *The NATS Bulletin*, 29 (December, 1972).

————, "A Basic Approach in the Teaching of Singing: Pre-Requisites in Freeing the Voice," *The NATS Bulletin*, 29 (February/March, 1973).

————, "Review of the Literature on Vocal Registers," *The NATS Bulletin*, 26 (February/March, 1970).

Flechtner, Adalene Smith, "Low Vowel Formant in Soprano Voices," *The NATS Bulletin*, 26 (December, 1969).

Garlinghouse, Burton, "Dialogue on Vocal Pedagogy," *The NATS Bulletin*, 26 (February/March, 1970).

Gilliland, Dale, "Fundamental Precepts for Voice Educators," *The NATS Bulletin*, 21 (February, 1965).

Graham, George, "Understandability," *The NATS Bulletin*, 21 (October, 1974).

Hisey, Philip D., "Scientific versus Empirical Methods of Teaching Voice," *The NATS Bulletin*, 27 (December, 1970).

————, "Head Quality vs. Nasality: A Review of Some Pertinent Literature," *The NATS Bulletin*, 28 (December, 1971).

Howie, John, and Delattre, Pierre. "An Experimental Study of the Effect of Pitch on the Intelligibility of Vowels," *The NATS Bulletin*, 18 (May, 1962).

Husson, Raoul, "How the Acoustics of a Hall Affect the Singer and the Speaker," *The NATS Bulletin*, 18 (February, 1962).

————, "The Pharyngo-Buccal Cavity and Its Phonatory Physiology," *The NATS Bulletin*, 16 (February, 1960).

————, "Special Physiology in Singing with Power," *The NATS Bulletin*, 14 (October, 1957).

Jones, J. Loren, "What Happens in Singing," *Choral Journal*, 15 (March, 1975).

————, "What Happens in Singing—Phonation," *Choral Journal*, 15 (May, 1975).

————, "What Happens in Singing Number 3—Resonance." *Choral Journal*, 15 (October, 1975).

Jorgenson, Dwayne, "The Mirror Image in Singing," *The NATS Bulletin*, 33 (October, 1975).

Kinsey, Barbara, "Voice Class—Structure and Purpose," *The NATS Bulletin*, 30 (December, 1973).

Large, John W., "Acoustic-Perceptual Evaluation of Register Equalization," *The NATS Bulletin*, 31 (October, 1974).

————, "An Acoustical Study of Isoparametric Tones in the Female Chest and Middle Registers in Singing," *The NATS Bulletin*, 25 (December, 1968).

————, "A Method for the Selection of Samples for Acoustical and Perceptual Studies of Voice Registers," *The NATS Bulletin*, 25 (February, 1969).

————, "Observations on the Vital Capacity of Singers," *The NATS Bulletin*, 27 (February/March, 1971).

————, "Towards an Integrated Physiologic-Acoustic Theory of Vocal Registers," *The NATS Bulletin*, 28 (February/March, 1972).

————, and Murry, Thomas. "Studies of Extended Vocal Techniques: Safety." *The NATS Bulletin*, 34 (May, 1978).

————; Iwata, S.; and Leden, Hans von, "The Primary Female Register Transition in Singing: Aerodynamic Study," *Folia Phoniatrica*, 22 (1970).

Lester, John L., "Breathing Related to Phonation," *The NATS Bulletin*, 14 (December, 1957).

McGinnis, C. S.; Elnick, M.; and Kraichman, M., "A Study of the Vowel Formants of Well-known Male Operatic Singers," *Journal of the Acoustical Society of America*, 23 (July, 1951).

Madsen, Clifford K., "Toward a Scientific Approach," *The NATS Bulletin*, 22 (December, 1965).

————, "The Effect of Scale Direction on Pitch Acuity," *Journal of Research in Music Education*, 14 (Winter, 1966).

Martin, Leonard B., "The Preparation of a Song," *The NATS Bulletin*, 24 (December, 1967).

Mason, R. M., and Zemlin, W. R., "The Phenomenon of Vocal Vibrato," *The NATS Bulletin*, 22 (February, 1966).

Nelson, Howard D., and Tiffany, William R., "The Intelligibility of Song: Research Results with a New Intelligibility Test," *The NATS Bulletin*, 25 (December, 1968).

Paul, Ouida Fay, "Working with Singing Problems of Adults," *Choral Journal*, 7 (May/June, 1967).

Proctor, Donald F., "The Physiologic Basis of Voice Training," *Annals of the New York Academy of Sciences*, 155 (November, 1968).

Rubin, H. J., "The Neurochronaxic Theory of Voice Production—A Refutation," *Archives of Otolaryngology*, 71 (1960).

————; LeCover, C.; and Vennard, William, "Vocal Intensity, Subglottic Pressure and Air Flow Relationships in Singers," *Folia Phoniatrica*, 19 (1967).

Ruth, Wilhelm, "The Cause of Individual Differences in the Sensation of Head Resonance in Singing," *The NATS Bulletin*, 23 (October, 1966).

————, "The Registers of the Singing Voice," *The NATS Bulletin*, 19 (May, 1963).

Sällström, Gunvor M., and Sällström, Jan F., "On Training the Singing Voice," *The NATS Bulletin*, 34 (December, 1977).

————, "Singing Exercises that Develop and Liberate the Child's Voice," *The NATS Bulletin*, 29 (February/March, 1973).

Schneider, Dorothy, "Procedures in the Voice Class," *The NATS Bulletin*, 29 (February/March, 1973).

Scott, Anthony, "Acoustical Peculiarities of Head Tone and Falsetto," *The NATS Bulletin*, 30 (May, 1974).

Simmons, Otis D., "Neurophysiology and Muscular Function of the Vocal Mechanism: Implications for Singers and Teachers of Singing," *The NATS Bulletin*, 22 (October, 1965).

————, "A Conceptual Approach to Singing," *The NATS Bulletin*, 26 (October, 1969).

Smith, Ethel Closson, "An Electromyographic Investigation of the Relationship between Abdominal Muscular Effort and the Rate of Vocal Vibrato," *The NATS Bulletin*, 26 (May/June, 1970).

Smith, Michael, "The Effect of Straight-Tone Feedback on the Vibrato." *The NATS Bulletin*, 28 (May/June, 1972).

Stocker, Leonard, "The Singer as Actor," *The NATS Bulletin*, 21 (December, 1964).

Sundberg, Johan, "The Acoustics of the Singing Voice," *Scientific American*, March, 1977.

Swing, Dolf, "Teaching the Professional Broadway Voice," *The NATS Bulletin*, 29 (February/March, 1973).

"Symposium on Formants in Singing," *The NATS Bulletin*, 28 (October, 1971).

Taff, Merle E., "An Acoustic Study of Vowel Modification and Register Transition in the Male Singing Voice," *The NATS Bulletin*, 22 (December, 1965).

Triplett, W. M., "An Investigation Concerning Vowel Sounds of High Pitches," *The NATS Bulletin*, 23 (March, 1967).

Truby, H. M., "Contribution of the Pharyngeal Cavity to Vowel Resonance and in General," *Journal of the Acoustical Society of America*, 34 (December, 1962).

van den Berg, Janwillem, "On the Air Resistance and the Bernoulli Effect of the Human Larynx," *Journal of the Acoustical Society of America*, 29 (May, 1957).

————, "On the Myoelastic-aerodynamic Theory of Voice Production," *The NATS Bulletin*, 14 (May, 1958).

Vennard, William, "Chest, Head, and Falsetto," *The NATS Bulletin*, 27 (December, 1970).

————, and Hirano, Minoru, "Varieties of Voice Production," *The NATS Bulletin*, 27 (February/March, 1971).

————, ————, and Fritzell, Björn, "The Extrinsic Laryngeal Muscles," *The NATS Bulletin*, 27 (May/June, 1971).

————; ————; and Ohala, John, "Laryngeal Synergy in Singing," *The NATS Bulletin*, 27 (October, 1970).

————, and Irwin, James W., "Speech and Song Compared in Sonagrams," *The NATS Bulletin*, 23 (December, 1966).

————, and Isshiki, Nobuhiko, "Coup de Glotte," *The NATS Bulletin*, 20 (February, 1964).

Waengler, Hans-heinrich, "Some Remarks and Observations on the Function of the Soft Palate," *The NATS Bulletin*, 25 (October, 1968).

Wall, Joan, and Weatherspoon, Ricky, "Lessons Are Not Enough," *The NATS Bulletin*, 32 (May, 1976).

Weiss, Deso A., "Discussion of the Neurochronaxic Theory (Husson)," *Archives of Otolaryngology*, 70 (1959).

Whitlock, Weldon, "Modern Vocal Pedagogy," *The NATS Bulletin*, 26 (December, 1969).

Williamson, John F., "Training of the Individual Voice through Choral Singing," *Choral Journal*, 14 (April, 1974).

Wooldridge, Warren B., "Is There Nasal Resonance?" *The NATS Bulletin*, 13 (October, 1956).

Zemlin, W. R.; Mason, Robert M.; and Holstead, Lisa, "Notes on the Mechanics of Vocal Vibrato," *The NATS Bulletin*, 28 (December, 1971).

RELATED ARTICLES

Bekesy, Georg V., "Pitch Sensation and Its Relation to the Periodicity of the Stimulus, Hearing and Skin Vibrations," *Journal of the Acoustical Society of America*, 33 (March, 1961).

London, S. J., "Vox Humana: Theme and Variations," *The NATS Bulletin*, Part I, 21 (February, 1965), Part II, 21 (May, 1965), and Part III, 21 (October, 1965).

Sundberg, J. E. F., and Lindqvist, J., "Musical Octaves and Pitch," *Journal of the Acoustical Society of America*, 54 (1973).

Verschuure, J., and Meeteren, A. A. van, "The Effect of Intensity on Pitch," *Acustica*, 32 (1975).

Ward, W. D., and Martin, D. W., "Psychophysical Comparison of Just Tuning and Equal Temperament in Sequences of Individual Tones," *Journal of the Acoustical Society of America*, 33 (May, 1961).

INDEX